SCHOLASTICISM

To Veron,
with ongoing
affection,
rie

SUNY Series, Toward a Comparative Philosophy of Religions
Paul J. Griffiths and Laurie L. Patton, editors

SCHOLASTICISM

Cross-Cultural and
Comparative Perspectives

Edited by

José Ignacio Cabezón

State University of New York Press

Published by
State University of New York Press, Albany

Printed in the United States of America

For information, address State University of New York Press, State University Plaza, Albany, N.Y., 12246

Production by Marilyn P. Semerad
Marketing by Nancy Farrell

Library of Congress Cataloging-in-Publication Data

Scholasticism : cross-cultural and comparative perspectives / edited by José Ignacio Cabezón.
p. cm. — (SUNY series, toward a comparative philosophy of religions)
Includes bibliographical references and index.
ISBN 0-7914-3777-9 (hc : alk. paper). — ISBN 0-7914-3778-7 (pbk. : alk. paper)
1. Scholasticism. 2. Philosophy, Comparative. 3. Religion and philosophy. I. Cabezón, José Ignacio, 1956– . II. Series.
B839.S36 1998
291.2'01—dc21 97-35199
CIP

10 9 8 7 6 5 4 3 2 1

Contents

Foreword

Laurie L. Patton

Scholasticism: Comparative and Cross-Cultural Perspectives can be described best as a kind of garland of scholarly jewels. Its essays gather together a number of different authors with similar commitments. Several of the contributors to the volume (Cabezón, Griffiths, Clooney) are also authors of works previously published in this book series, Toward a Comparative Philosophy of Religions, all of which examined some comparative aspect of scholastic practice. What is more important, however, this book achieves something that a single monograph cannot do: it puts into conversation some of the diverse intellectual commitments of the series as a whole. What is distinctive about this volume in relation to the series, then, is that it takes the various suggestions about comparative scholasticism made in earlier, single-authored studies to embodying the scholastic project itself: disputation and connection across differences.

From its inception the SUNY series—*Toward a Comparative Philosophy of Religions*—has been committed to nurturing the possibility of bilocated comparison: the engagement of the vernacular and the abstract in a single scholarly perspective. The category of scholasticism combines and reflects this dual commitment in a myriad of ways. While I will leave it to José Cabezón's elegant introduction to outline these ways in greater detail, suffice it to say here that each cultural case explored in these chapters—Tibetan Buddhism, Indian Hinduism, Chinese Confucianism, Judaism, Islam, medieval Christianity—shows a

---

Laurie L. Patton is co-editor of the SUNY Series, *Toward a Comparative Philosophy of Religions*

two-fold dynamic: first, several of the chapters emphasize the cultural complexity informing the kinds of philosophical abstractions found in scholasticism. Second, several other chapters demonstrate that philosophical abstractions are necessary to make the practices of cultural exchange and contestation possible. In other words, these chapters do not simply assert that both the culturally specific and the philosophically conceptual can and should be combined, or juxtaposed, in the process of comparison. They do more than this in showing the *relevance* of one to the other in that process. This particular virtue is, of course, one of the essential properties of garlands: the inclusion of multiple elements on the string that are not simply added on, one to the other, but whose very multiplicity is essential to the definition of the whole. A garland is an adornment that comprises the juxtaposition of differences held in proximate tension.

Yet the skull necklace of Shiva in Indian mythology, or the albatross of Coleridge's Ancient Mariner also teach us that garlands can be dangerous, weighty things. The delightful danger of this work is that the volume's approach to scholasticism is itself deeply scholastic in nature. It attempts to retrieve a descriptive category which, like casuistry in ethics, has signified dusty pedantry and irrelevant distinction making. In this, the volume risks the charge that all scholiasts risk: that of elitist intellectualism. Yet just when one might think one is crossing that line, the essays pull the reader back in surprising and, I think, very significant ways. The essays in the volume, and Cabezón's introduction and conclusion even more explicitly, deftly make the problematic connotations of the term an intellectual virtue: scholasticism shows, even in its broadest comparative sense, a love of disputation and a belief that it is possible to get the answer right. The volume challenges the reader to dispute, to respond, to change the category itself in order to get the answer right. More specifically, the history of scholasticism demonstrates that the provisional nature of comparative categories is itself based on scholastic practices of testing and refutation. Comparative procedures along these lines are not something invented only by conscience-stricken religionists in the late twentieth century who realize that they must take better care in mapping their concepts across cultures. They have been practiced, and can indeed be modeled on, the scholiasts of many different cultural traditions and periods.

Perhaps what is most important, this volume has boldly constructive implications for the relationship between the fields of theology and history of religions. In *Scholasticism: Comparative and Cross-Cultural Perspectives*, these two areas of inquiry are not simply locked in mutual avoidance or mutual, and occasionally damning, critique. Instead, the normative implications of any given scholastic tradition are constantly put in dialogue with the vicissitudes of their historical and institutional formations, and vice-versa. Comparative scholasticism prevents one field from being dissolved into the other, and, at the same time, refuses to accept the recent apartheid between the two.

This book is an example of historians of religions and theologians engaging in an enterprise of intellectual risk taking and recovering what is most thought provoking about indigenous traditions of disputation, and as such it leans into a future of a new way of being religious and intellectually serious in the world. Beyond the specific ways that the usual perspectives in religious studies are shaken up by this book, ultimately, its constructive nature derives from the fact that it has, quite simply, given us something new to think about: a possible comparative category whose beads can be strung in any number of combinations. It is up to readers to find the present jewels and writers to find the future ones to attach to the garland.

Introduction

José Ignacio Cabezón

In a little known essay, Wallace Stevens (1951) suggests that "the desire for resemblance" is an innate part of human nature—one that, he implies, emerges from the order, the pattern of resemblances, that exists in the world. Hell for Stevens is precisely an imagined world where similarity to the known is absent. "What a ghastly situation it would be if the world of the dead was actually different from the world of the living . . . [where] nothing resembled anything we have ever known" (1951:77). But if dissimilarity is a fountain of pain, resemblance is as much a source of pleasure. It is the contemplation of likeness that brings us joy, and poetry, he implies, is the most suitable vehicle for bringing about this pleasure—the pleasure that comes from the satisfaction of the desire for resemblance (1951:77).

Stevens's is a generalized narcissism. One step removed from the pursuit of pleasure through perpetually gazing at our own countenance, we seek gratification instead from seeing the world through our own, familiar experiences, even if our expectation to find resemblance is so strong that "we find nothing else" *but* resemblances, remaining forever blind to difference. Nor does Stevens find this problematic. Narcissism *might* be a problem if we could be otherwise than preoccupied with the contemplation of likeness, but we cannot: "Narcissism itself is merely an evidence of the operation of the principle that we expect to find pleasure in resemblances" (1951:80).[1]

This introduction has benefited from the editorial comments of Dan Arnold and from the substanive reading given to it by my colleague Sheila Davaney. Thanks also to Eric Massanari for help with proofreading and indexing.

The student of comparative religious thought, smitten too by a desire for resemblance, also seeks a means for its fulfillment. Though of a different sort, our vehicle—more abstract, systematic and, alas, far less elegant—is nevertheless as much an attempt to satiate this desire as is the poet's art. But what of the charge of narcissism? Are comparativists, like Stevens's bards, fated forever to see the world in their own likeness? The question is not a trivial one. Most of the categories we work with as comparativists—pilgrimage, scripture, even philosophy and religion themselves—have their origin in Western culture, and on the surface possess meanings that are given to them by their respective semantic ranges in Western languages.[2] In the history of the comparative study of religious thought it is not that uncommon to find the scholar succumbing to the temptation to read the cultural other in terms of static categories imported in toto from the culturally familiar.[3]

That narcissism of this kind has existed—and continues to exist—hardly can be denied, but surely this need not be the fate of our discipline. The antidote is to be found in the nuanced treatment of the conceptual categories that we use, one that pays attention both to the similarities *and to the differences*.[4] Equally important is the realization that such categories, as the byproducts of human imagination, are malleable and subject to change in the encounter with what is culturally other. The starting point of analysis usually may be the familiar, but a familiar category becomes modified when it confronts the heterocultural, leading not to complete *un*familiarity (Stevens's hell), but to a new kind of intimacy that comes about from taking into account the broader, cross-cultural context. This process leads to a kind of de- and then re-construction of the original category, culminating not in meaninglessness, but in new meaning(s) embodied in the now modified and necessarily more complex category. This process is in principle unending. Imputing finality to a comparative analysis reifies the category under investigation, making it seem as though any further consideration of data is superfluous. But surely this is never so. All categories are by nature open, tentative, and therefore subject to further analysis and modification.

This volume represents one moment in the reconstruction of the category of scholasticism—achieved by applying it as an interpretive tool to a variety of cultural settings. But why scholasticism in particular?

As several of the contributors to this volume point out, scholasticism as a practice generally has been looked down upon by philosophers and intellectuals since the Renaissance, and the adjective *scholastic* has been used in a derogatory fashion at least since the time of Erasmus (1466?–1536). Scholasticism thus has served for modernists the role of "object to be transcended," in much the same way as modernism has for postmodernists. The modernist derogation of scholasticism continues to find expression in the work of a variety of contemporary philosophers.[5] Hence, Russell (1945) calls the scholastics "disputatious" (435), and their system "an intellectual strait jacket" (500). And Gramsci (1971:200) ascribes to scholasticism "the regressive tendency to treat so-called theoretical questions as if they had a value in themselves, independently of any specific practice." Whether as ideology, world view, or practice, scholasticism thus has been treated derisively by Western intellectuals. Still, this has not prevented its perpetuation even in the West (in the form of movements such as the neo-scholasticism espoused by Jacques Maritain and Étienne Gilson, for example). Even the early Heidegger believed that the scholastic method in its true form represented a fresh perspective on the problems of philosophy, one that, concerned more with the *actual doing* of metaphysics than with methodological speculation *about how to do it*, could be of value in dispelling what he considered the oblivion of being (see Caputo 1982:18 passim). Responses to scholasticism as a practice therefore have been various, but when considered as a whole it is clear that these reactions for the last five hundred years have been predominantly skeptical, if not out and out disapproving.

Apart from judgments about its validity as a world view, however, there can be little doubt that *as an analytical category*, "scholasticism" has been widely accepted. Even its detractors, of course, find the category valuable, if only for polemical purposes. Hence, the question of its assessment as a mode of philosophical praxis aside, in modern times there have been serious attempts to treat scholasticism as a historical philosophical category worthy of consideration. Any comprehensive intellectual history of Europe, for example, cannot but take stock of scholasticism. What is more, already in the early twentieth century there were attempts to treat scholasticism as a cross-cultural, comparative category. For example, P. Masson-Oursel (1911, 1916, 1920) makes a strong case for the importance of treating scholasticism as a pivotal phase in the history of thought *across* cultures. Whatever their view concerning the phenomenon of scholasticism as a philosophical practice—and they are varied—the chapters in this volume are unanimous in offering positive (re)appraisals of it as a category of cross-cultural and comparative analysis. Each of them will show in its own way why scholasticism is an important interpretive category worthy of consideration and further theorization.

Before turning to the chapters themselves, it might be useful to take a step back in order to see what has brought us to the present point. In an earlier book in this same series (Cabezón 1994), I argued for the usefulness of the notion of scholasticism as a way of understanding Indo-Tibetan Buddhist thought. Being interested—like Griffiths (1994)—in the intellectual-linguistic dimension of Buddhist life as epitomized by the study of doctrine, I found in the category of scholasticism a useful handle on the Indo-Tibetan Buddhist world view, one that allowed me to picture it as a holistic and unified intellectual tradition engaged in a systematic scholarly enterprise.[6] I developed in that study a picture of Buddhist scholasticism that was the result of the dialogical interaction between the Indo-Tibetan Buddist textual tradition, on the one hand, and, on the other, the sources of European scholasticism and the work of certain Euro-American theorists, chief among them P. Masson-Oursel (1911, 1916, 1920)—arguably the father of the discipline of comparative philosophy and, as I have mentioned, the first Western thinker to evolve a mature notion of scholasticism as a comparative category. But my aim in that study was not simply to suggest that scholasticism was a useful category for understanding a certain branch of Buddhist thought. I believed then—and the essays in this volume bear this out—that scholasticism also could be useful to the study of other religio-philosophical systems. Thus, through a process of abstraction and generalization, my goal also was to free "scholasticism" from its parochial associations, as an appellation for a medieval European intellectual movement, and to suggest instead a notion of scholasticism that, now more broadly construed, could serve as a preliminary locus for the comparative and cross-cultural analysis of a variety of other traditions. Though perhaps not essential to every tradition we might wish to call "scholastic," I felt that some of the characteristics that I found in my study of Indo-Tibetan Buddhism could be central to many others. And though aware that the traits of the scholasticism I proposed were peculiar to my particular analysis, I believed that they could—if only by virtue of their absence—at least serve as the starting point for a broader conversation that made the category of scholasticism available as an interpretive option to scholars of other traditions. We shall turn shortly to consideration of some theoretical issues concerning the construction of an analytical category like scholasticism, but given that several of the essays in this volume are responding to the list of characteristics in my earlier study—albeit, occasionally as foils—it might be useful to summarize them now.

1. A strong sense of tradition: self-identification with a specific tradition and lineage and commitment to its preservation. Scholastics have a strong sense of their own religious roots. Seeing themselves as the successors to a long and unbroken line of previous thinkers, their powerful sense of religious history (whether mythic or not) allows for their distinct feeling of location vis à vis the great historical figures of their particular lineage. This tradition centeredness also creates a sense of allegiance and iden-

tity that seeks to perpetuate itself through defensive polemical strategies aimed at the critique of rivals.

2. A concern with language: with sacred language (scripture) and its exegesis and with language generally as medium of expression. Scholasticism is generally confident, rather than skeptical, of the communicative ability of language and is committed to the importance of conceptual thought and categories. This is not to say that linguistic analysis is for scholastics an end in itself. As the early Heidegger was wont to point out, scholasticism and the religious (especially mystical) life go hand in hand (Caputo 1982:44). Of course, the religious life that is the post- (if not extra-) linguistic expression of scholastic speculation manifests itself differently in different religious traditions. In some, it consists of a series of transformative mystical experiences, in others, of proper behaviors (social, ritual, and so forth).

3. Proliferativity: the tendency to textual and analytical inclusivity rather than exclusivity. Scholastics, I maintian, opt for broader (even if inconsistent) canons and for minute and detailed forms of analysis that leave no question unanswered, no philosophical avenue unexplored. Rather to include, even if this requires reconciling inconsistent texts or positions, than to exclude, thereby risking the loss of what might be soteriologically essential.

4. Completeness and compactness: the belief that the tradition overlooks nothing and contains nothing that is unessential. Related to the proliferative tendency of the scholastic mindset is the generally held scholastic tenet that the tradition is complete: that nothing essential to the project of salvation has been neglected. Moreover, to insure that the tradition is taken seriously *in its entirety*, scholastics often maintain that their traditions are what I call "compact": that no doctrine, text, or custom is extraneous.

5. The epistemological accessibility of the world: the belief that the universe is basically intelligible. Scholastics share with modernist science the fundamental axiom that the world is knowable. Some maintain that, at the very least, everything that is of soteriological importance is accessible, while others go farther and claim that every phenomenon, every fact, is knowable. This latter position especially is related in a direct way both to the proliferative character of scholasticism and to the claim of completeness.

6. Systematicity: order in exposition. Scholastics strive to reproduce in their writings the basic orderliness they believe to be

found in the world. Their philosophical literature often evinces a complex structure that divides and subdivides the subject matter under discussion to insure (a) a logical flow to the "narrative," seen as essential to pedagogy, (b) consistency between former and latter points, and (c) completeness (that nothing has been omitted).

7. Rationalism: the commitment to reasoned argument and non-contradiction. Although not *sufficient*, that is, not an end in itself, rationality is nonetheless considered soteriologically *necessary*. Scholastics consider reasoning to be integral to the religious path. The systematic elucidation of doctrine, the "elimination" of inconsistency, and the rational defense of tenets are perhaps the most central attributes of scholasticism. At the same time scholastics see the rational/conceptual understanding of doctrine to be transcended either in mystical experience, in action, or both. Hence, scholasticism as a method strives for a reconciliation of the rational and experiential/active dimensions of human religiosity.

8. Self-reflexivity: the tendency to objectify and to critically analyze first-order practices. Hence, scholastics not only engage in the first-order task of exegesis or commentary, but also in the second-order task of hermeneutics, the self-critical reflection on the rules, principles, and problems related to the act of exegesis. They are concerned not only with systematicity and rational argumentation, but with developing criteria for what constitutes a rational argument, that is, with logic as a second-order discourse.

Now the characteristics of scholasticism just outlined are, as I have mentioned, the result of my reflecting upon texts and movements within the Indo-Tibetan Buddhist tradition. If scholasticism as an abstract category came to be applied successfully—that is, in such a way that it yielded new and interesting questions—to other religious and philosophical traditions, these characteristics would of necessity, I thought, undergo modification, raising in turn new questions of the present analysis. Hence, as far as the present project is concerned, the foregoing list is meant as a heuristic, as a starting point of inquiry. Scholasticism emerges as a cross-cultural, comparative category by the cultural decontextualization that takes place as different traditions are brought into conversation with each other dialogically. This is what this volume seeks to do. But how does one choose which traditions—let us call them "candidates for scholasticism"—to bring into the conversation in the first place? The theorist would seem to be caught in what I will call "the comparativist's dilemma": she cannot choose which exemplars to compare until some decontextualized, general category has been established, while the establishment of such a category presumes a process of comparison that requires choices to be made regarding the comparanda.

One solution to this dilemma has been offered by Robert Baird (1971). Focusing not on scholasticism but on the category of religion, Baird has argued that, as a methodological principle, it is incumbent upon the historian of religion first to offer a stipulative, functional definition of religion. Such a definition will determine unambiguously what will count as a religion, thereby marking out the limits of a study. The functional definition offered, he says, is semiarbitrary: "arbitrary" in so far as "there is no inherent reason why any word cannot be used for any thing" (7), but "semi-" because not all categories are equally useful "in enabling the scholar to do what he has chosen to do" (126).

There is much that I find valuable in Baird's treatment of this issue. Although he does not identify it as such, his essentially *pragmatic* stance on what makes a definition valuable is, I believe, on target, as is his emphasis on the stipulative nature of categories. However, Baird's insistence that categories need to be delimited in order to be useful is problematic.[7] Baird presumably would solve the comparativist's dilemma by contending that a stipulative, functional definition of scholasticism must precede any study of the subject. The category "scholasticism" is first delimited, and the exemplars that fall within such limits then are studied. Unfortunately, the rules for interesting scholarship cannot be prescribed so neatly. How are we to choose the limits of the category? The traits that I have outlined above are based on a process of comparative decontextualization that takes into account only two traditions. Why should *these* be privileged in delimiting a category that may be equally—and perhaps even more—applicable in elucidating the dynamics of other traditions? True, *scholasticism* is a term whose original semantic range extends over things European, but this is of little consequence to the comparativist, whose goal is to encourage its cultural decontextualization for analytical ends. What is more, is it not the case that considering the candidacy of a movement that is only marginally scholastic can yield valuable insights (if only by way of providing a contrast to more prototypically scholastic traditions)? By virtue of its rigidity, Baird's method would preclude such potentially valuable forms of analysis.

In the process of decontextualizing a concept like 'scholasticism' cross-culturally, no single definition, no one set of features born from reflection upon the practices of one or two historical traditions, can be considered normative—the standard against which all other traditions are judged to be scholastic or not. As Ernest Gellner (1989:169), paraphrasing Wittgenstein, states, "All data in our possession are always, inevitably, finite. We can never be sure that data which come our way in the future will still fit into the generalisation set up on the basis of past data."

Rather than delimiting the category "scholasticism" from the start, I believe that a different strategy is called for: one that *from the outset* opts for leaving the category open and malleable, that encourages the new data that "may come our way," and that urges vigilance against inflexibility. Now it is true that we must start somewhere, and so I have offered my reflections upon the Indo-Tibetan scholastic tradition vis-à-vis that of medieval European, heuristically, as a point of departure; but these are meant as *nothing more than* a heuristic point of departure. Rather than forming the basis for a definition, they should be viewed instead as an invitation to modification.[8]

Though I see no value in—or need for—an a priori definition of scholasticism preceding comparative work on the subject, I do recognize that as a result of such work there may emerge a series of traits that will be considered more characteristic of scholasticism than others. They will become so not by virtue of being part of the innate character of scholasticism—its essence—but because the traditions that have most benefited from being considered under the rubric of this category have these as *their* traits. Not every encounter of a religious or philosophical tradition with scholasticism as an analytical category will be equally profitable. Those that are will leave a much more durable imprint on the category in the wake of such an encounter. In this way, over time, and as the a posteriori result of the unpredictable nature of scholarship, the texture of scholasticism as a category will emerge: a texture given to the category by the fact that certain traits will be more prominent than others, and this as a result of the fact that certain traditions will be considered more prototypically scholastic than others. If scholasticism is a useful category—if it yields new questions and insights, if it spawns new research programs—then, like other such categories (religion, myth, symbol, scripture, ritual), it will survive and evolve in this way over time. Although the chapters in this volume go a long way toward providing scholasticism as a decontextualized category with the kind of texture just mentioned, it would be foolhardy to consider an a priori delimitation of the category either necessary or useful at the outset.

Let us now turn to the chapters in this volume. My characterization of the various contributions is here at most impressionistic and is intended only as a way of whetting the reader's appetite. A more detailed treatment of the essays and their relationship to the broader project is to be found in the Conclusion.

The Latin West is of course one of the principal sources for the history of the study of scholasticism. It was the flourishing of scholasticism in that particular context that led to the identification of scholasticism as a category in the first place; and hence it is fitting that the volume begin by considering medieval Latin scholasticism as its first exemplar. What Louis Roy finds as he investigates this tradition, however, is not a simple, pristine, uncontaminated intellectual movement, but one that bears the traces of many culturally heterogeneous ideas. Daniel Madigan's contribution focuses on Islam, and, like Roy, he finds there to be a great deal of complexity to the phenomenon of scholasticism *even within* a single religious tradition. By considering several movements within Muslim history as possible candidates for the term *scholasticism*, Madigan shows us how complex the question of identifying an intellectual tradition as scholastic really is. In his contribution, Robert Goss demonstrates how common scholastic presuppositions made possible the polemical dialogue between an eighteenth-century Jesuit missionary and his Tibetan Buddhist interlocutors. Michael Swartz's contribution is concerned with Rabbinic Judaism. Through his analysis we glean how many of the characteristics of scholasticism outlined above (and still others not mentioned there) can be exemplified in very different ways and to varying degrees in a different religio-philosophical context. Like Swartz, Livia Kohn, who writes on Taoism, emphasizes the social context of scholasticism. Kohn, like several other contributors, also stresses the importance of investigating the historical moments at which different scholastic traditions come into contact. In my own essay I explore the relationship of Tibetan Buddhist scholastic ideology and material culture by suggesting that a thesis defended by the medievalist Erwin Panofsky regarding Gothic architecture might be applicable (albeit with some modification) in a very different cultural milieu. John Henderson, whose work centers on Neo-Confucianism, begins his essay with some remarks on the historical evolution of scholasticisms generally, and then goes on to explore how this is played out in a Chinese context. In his contribution Francis Clooney uses three examples from the Hindu tradition to demonstrate some of the problems involved in using scholasticism as a comparative category. And finally, Paul Griffiths offers us an example of the way that scholasticism can be used as an instrument of cultural criticism by suggesting that an ideal-typical form of scholasticism is a way of responding to the deficits implicit both in modernist and in postmodernist modes of intellectual practice.

In the Conclusion I examine in greater detail the ways in which the various essays transform the category of scholasticism by engaging and challenging the different characteristics of scholasticism as I have laid them out above. In that chapter, I explore, in effect, how the cross-cultural analysis of the category that forms the bulk of this book effectuates its further decontextualization, and how this in turn leads to new questions, the subject-matter of possible future research.

In a recent book, *A Study of Concepts,* Christopher Peacocke (1992:177–97) argues that what he, as a philosopher, and what cognitive psychologists have to say about concepts cannot be independent of one another. Peacocke believes that psychological theories are relevant to the philosophical study of concepts (and vice versa). How relevant is cognitive psychology to *our* task as scholars of comparative religious thought—as wielders of comparative, conceptual categories? I would like to suggest, by way of conclusion, that it is quite pertinent. Recall that I began with the simple question, Why scholasticism? As comparativists we are used to justifying our categories in a variety of ways: practically (in terms of their usefulness), historically (in terms of precedence), pedagogically (by virtue of their utility in the classroom). I would now like to propose that there may be a cognitive-psychological[9] answer to the question, Why scholasticism? Psychologists provide us not so much with a justification of the concept as they do (or might do) with an explanation of why it is that we tend to construct categories such as scholasticism in the first place.

Eleanor Rosch (1978) has argued "that human categorization should not be considered the arbitrary product of historical accident or of whimsy but rather the result of psychological principles of categorization" (27). Rosch and her colleagues conducted a series of experiments and found that the human mind tends to categorize the external world into classes of objects of differing levels of abstraction or inclusiveness. They found, moreover, that of these different levels of abstraction one—an intermediate level of abstraction—tended to be more "basic" than the rest. These basic level categories had the property of being "the most inclusive level of classification at which objects have numbers of attributes in common" (Rosch 1978:32). Superordinate categories are categories more abstract than those at the basic level, and subordinate ones are less so. Hence, if "chair" is a basic level category, "furniture" represents its superordinate counterpart, and "kitchen chair" its subordinate. When subjects were asked to list all of the attributes they could think of that were shared by all of the members of a particular category, the researchers found that comparatively few such attributes could be named for the superordinate class (furniture), many more for the basic class (chair), and not *that many more* for the subordinate class (kitchen chair). Put another way, basic-level categories are the most general categories which evince for subjects the greatest richness of detail. They are also the most general categorical levels at which an object belonging to the category is identified. Hence, when shown a picture of an object with four legs that could be used to sit on, the natural response was to call that thing a chair (not furniture or a kitchen chair). The human mind, Rosch concludes, tends naturally to categorize the world at the basic level.

The obvious question then is this: do we, as taxonomists of religion, tend naturally to categorize our—albeit more abstract—world into basic-level objects? If so, do these correspond to the categories that have today (or will in the future evolve to) become the backbone of the field: scripture, pilgrimage, *and scholasticism*? Scholasticism then might become a natural categorical construct for comparativists because it is a class of the most abstract level at which our minds can work with the greatest number of attributes. Hence, to the question, Why scholasticism? the answer might be, Because it is in some sense basic.

With some exceptions,[10] cognitive psychologists and anthropologists have focused their research on "real-world" objects such as colors, plants, and furniture. And of course, it is not at all clear that their findings with regard to this relatively circumscribed area can be generalized to the kind of hyper-abstract categories used by scholars. However, there is no a priori reason why this should not be the case. What, cognitively speaking, should make a category such as scholasticism natural or useful for scholars is *in principle* an askable and interesting question. Even if the cognitive sciences are able to offer no substantive answers to questions of this sort, however, this by no means implies that the data of the cognitive sciences cannot or should not be used heuristically to stimulate discussion, for example, among comparativists, concerning the evolution, nature, and function of comparative categories.

As might be expected, even in regard to simple, real-world phenomena, there is considerable controversy as to *why* the mind tends more naturally to categorize objects at the basic level, and as to the *implications* of the existence of such natural categories. Lakoff (1987) suggests that our tendency so to categorize the world has to do, not with anything intrinsic to the categories themselves (the objectivist view), but with *our* nature as embodied beings. We do so because "at this [basic] level, people function most efficiently and successfully with discontinuities in the natural environment . . . so that our bodies can interact optimally with them" (269–70). Integrating the work of Mark Johnson and Gilles Fauconnier, Lakoff suggests that complex cognitive models about abstract things are based on image schemas that have their origin in our embodied experiences. It is obviously beyond the scope of this introduction to go into any detail concerning Lakoff's views on the formation, nature, and function of categories. Suffice it to say that his is one attempt to extrapolate from the cognitive scientific data concerning categorization, one that I see as having major implications for a cognitive theory of cross-cultural comparison.

The preceding discussion obviously represents an oversimplification of the cognitive scientific research data. My hope in raising some of these issues here is to be provocative rather than conclusive. I leave it to other scholars to determine whether I have achieved even that more modest goal. Whether the conceptual category "scholasticism" is in some sense basic or not, whether it is analyzable in terms of Lakoffian kinesthetic image schemas, what such an analysis might look like, and what its implications might be for comparative theory generally are questions that can only be pursued elsewhere.

However the cognitive sciences do or do not impact on our construction of a category like scholasticism, at the very least the essays in this volume are a testament to the fact that a variety of traditions benefit from being considered through the lens of such a category. As a whole, the essays also confirm the importance of a nuanced treatment of categories: one that, giving equal weight to both similarities and differences, is far removed from Stevens's narcissistic paradise of likeness only. They also, it seems to me, cause us to pause and reflect on the likelihood of a postulate set forth by Durkheim almost a century ago, namely, that "comparison is the only practical means we have for the understanding of things" (1898, reprinted 1974:1).

Notes

1. That Stevens's theory is motivated in part by a philosophical attraction to realism is evident from his work. What is perhaps less apparent is the way in which his views are the expression of his white, suburban, middle-class social situation and ideology. See Morse (1970) and Gioia (1992: 113–14, 141–53).

2. As Ames (1989: 265) points out, "When a concept is assigned an English equivalent, much of the depth of the original concept tends to be lost: its word image, its allusive effectiveness, its morphological implications. At the same time, especially with philosophical vocabulary, inappropriate associations are evoked by the translated term to the extent that it is burdened by its own cultural history." When this is so of translation—where there is presumably some level of semblance to a term in the source language—how much more so must it be of conceptual categories derived originally from the culturally same, where such semblance is not at all guaranteed. See also Daya Krishna 1989 and Smart 1989.

3. For an critique of the tendency to impute an etic category in toto to other cultures, to the detriment of the analysis, see Mary Douglas's charge against Malinowski in her foreword to Marcel Mauss's *The Gift* (1990: vii–viii). For a more general, theoretical treatment of this problem, see Larson 1989.

4. This point of course has been emphasized repeatedly in the theoretical literature on cross-cultural comparison. See, for example, J. Z. Smith (1982:21 passim) and John B. Carman and Steven P. Hopkins (1991:302).

5. An interesting exception is Alfred North Whitehead, who presents a more balanced picture (1933: 117).

6. As an aside, it is worth reiterating that my emphasis on the intellectual dimension of Buddhism as expressed in its preoccupation with doctrine is not meant to exclude other forms of analysis: anthropological, literary critical, sociological, art-historical, and so on. This is a point that I have explicitly made in the conclusion to my *Buddhism and Language* (1994: 197–198), one that seems to have escaped Eckel (1994: 1094) in his characterization of my approach. But even if Eckel had read my last chapter more carefully, it is probably the case that even my more modest claim—that the philosophical and systematic study of doctrine was / is central to Buddhist intellectuals and therefore must be so to us in our study of those intellectuals—would be problematic for him. Eckel's basic position, at least as expressed in his *To See the Buddha* (1992), is that (a) the identity of Bhavaviveka as a philosopher is somehow secondary to—perhaps even having its source in—his identity as a religious figure, which comes "to a climax with a devotional vision of the Buddha" (7) achieved through grace (94, 146), and that (b) his more philosophical language as expressed in formal argument is secondary to his use of metaphorical and other literary devices, which, far from mere embellishments (22), somehow reveal "the deeper structures of Bhavaviveka's thought" (21, 141), make it cohere in ways that formal philosophical argument cannot (144), and are what truly make the tradition "his own" (114). Indeed, Eckel goes to the extent of making Bhavaviveka's philosophical vision "gratuitous" (146–47). Much could be said in response to such a view. Suffice it to summarize my reply as follows: though I grant Eckel the importance of nonphilosophical forms of analysis when it comes to understanding the identity of Bhavaviveka, I deny his claim that these can take precedence over—that they carry greater explanatory weight than—philosophical ones.

7. Ludwig Wittgenstein, of course, has written, if not extensively, at least influentially, on this topic. And Lofti Zadeh's fuzzy set theory represents a formalization of this intuition in the realm of mathematical logic; see Lakoff (1987: 14, 21–22).

8. This, incidentally, is similar to the view espoused by anthropologist A. R. Radcliffe-Brown, a view which Eggan (1975: 205) characterizes thus: "In place of the comparative method he (R-B) proposes the 'experimental method,' in which preliminary conclusions are formulated and then tested by the same or other social anthropologists on different societies, thus gradually developing broader and more adequate hypotheses." However, I see no reason for considering such a method comparative. Nor, apparently, does the later Radcliffe-Brown (1958). This same approach also seems to be taken by Bronislaw Malinowski in his few comparative forays, in regard to which Lowie (1937: 240–41) states: "His generalizations purport merely to provoke parallel in-

quiries in other regions; he has indeed expressly demanded 'a fuller testing in the various anthropological provinces.' "

9. In actuality, the field I am drawing from, called "categorization theory," is interdisciplinary, being comprised of the work of psychologists, linguists, and anthropologists (see Rosch and Lloyd, 1978), but I will chiefly be invoking the work of the psychologists in what follows.

10. See Lakoff's (1987: 45–46) discussion of the work of Lawrence Barsalou on ad-hoc categories, "categories that are not conventional or fixed, but rather are made up on the fly for some immediate purpose." Although closer to the analytical categories used by academics than those normally considered by cognitive psychologists, Barsalou's examples ("what to get for a birthday present") are still considerably more mundane and concrete than categories such as "scholasticism."

References

Ames, Roger T.
1989 "Confucius and the Ontology of Knowing." In *Interpreting Across Boundaries: New Essays in Comparative Philosophy*, 265–79. Ed. Gerald James Larson and Eliot Deutsch. Delhi: Motilal Banarsidass, reprint of the 1988 Princeton ed.

Baird, Robert D.
1971 *Category Formation and the History of Religions*. The Hague and Paris: Mouton.

Cabezón, José Ignacio.
1994 *Buddhism and Language: A Study of Indo-Tibetan Scholasticism*. Albany: State University of New York Press.

Caputo, John D.
1982 *Heidegger and Aquinas: An Essay on Overcoming Metaphysics*. NY: Fordham University Press.

Carman, John B., and Steven P. Hopkins.
1991 *Tracing Common Themes: Comparative Courses in the Study of Religion*. Atlanta: Scholars Press.

Daya Krishna.
1989 "Comparative Philosophy: What It Is and What It Ought to Be." In *Interpreting across Boundaries: New Essays in Comparative Philosophy*, 71–83. Ed. Gerald James Larson and Eliot Deutsch. Delhi: Motilal Banarsidass, reprint of the 1988 Princeton ed.

Durkheim, Émile.

1974 "Individual and Collective Representation." In *Sociology and Philosophy*, 1–34. D. F. Pocock, trans. NY: The Free Press.

Eckel, Malcolm David.

1994 "The Ghost at the Table: On the Study of Buddhism and the Study of Religion." *Journal of the American Academy of Religion* 62.4:1085–1110.

1992 *To See the Buddha: A Philosopher's Quest for the Meaning of Emptiness*. Princeton: Princeton University Press.

Eggan, Fred.

1975 "Social Anthropology and the Method of Controlled Comparison." In *Fred Eggan, Essays in Social Anthropology and Ethnology*, 191–217. The University of Chicago Studies in Anthropology, Series in Social, Cultural and Linguistic Anthropology, No. 1. Chicago: Department of Anthropology, University of Chicago.

Gellner, Ernest.

1989 "Concepts and Community." In *Relativism and the Social Sciences*, 167–86. Cambridge: Cambridge University Press, reprint of the 1985 ed.

Gioia, Dana.

1992 *Can Poetry Matter: Essays on Poetry and American Culture*. St. Paul: Graywolf Press.

Gramsci, Antonio.

1971 *Selections from the Prison Notebooks of Antonio Gramsci*. Quintin Hoarse and Geoffrey Nowell Smith, eds. NY: International.

Griffiths, Paul J.

1994 *On Being Buddha: The Classical Doctrine of Buddhahood*. Albany: State University of New York Press.

Lakoff, George.

1987 *Women, Fire and Dangerous Things: What Categories Reveal about the Mind*. Chicago and London: The University of Chicago Press.

Larson, Gerald James.

1989 "Introduction: The Age-Old Distinction between the Same and the Other." In *Interpreting across Boundaries: New Essays in Comparative Philosophy*, 3–18. Ed. Gerald James Larson and Eliot Deutsch. Delhi: Motilal Banarsidass, reprint of the 1988 Princeton ed.

Lowie, Robert H.
1937 *The History of Ethnological Theory*. New York: Holt, Rinehart and Winston.

Masson-Oursel, P.
1920 "La Scholastique." *Revue Philosophique de la France et de l'Étranger* 90:123–41.

1916 "La Sophistique." *Revue de Métaphysique et de Morale* 23:343–62.

1911 "Object et Méthode de la Philosophie Comparée." *Revue de Métaphysique et de Morale* 19:541–48.

Mauss, Marcel.
1990 *The Gift: The Form and Reason for Exchange in Archaic Societies*. W. D. Halls, trans., with foreword by Mary Douglas. New York and London: W. W. Norton.

Morse, Samuel French.
1970 *Wallace Stevens: Poetry as Life*. New York: Pegasus.

Peacocke, Christopher.
1992 *A Study of Concepts*. Cambridge, MA: M. I. T. Press.

Radcliffe-Brown, A. R.
1958 "The Comparative Method in Social Anthropology." In *Method in Social Anthropology*, 108–29. Chicago: University of Chicago Press.

Rosch, Eleanor.
1978 "Principles of Categorization." In *Cognition and Categorization*, 27–48. Ed. Eleanor Rosch and Barabara B. Lloyd. Hillsdale, NJ: Lawrence Erlbaum Associates.

Rosch, Eleanor and Barbara B. Lloyd.
1978 *Cognition and Categorization*. Hillsdale, NJ: Lawrence Erlbaum Associates.

Russell, Bertrand.
1945 *A History of Western Philosophy*. NY: Simon and Schuster.

Smart, Ninian.
1989 "The Analogy of Meaning and the Task of Com parative Philosophy." In *Interpreting across Boundaries: New Essays in Comparative Philosophy*, 174–83. Ed. Gerald James Larson and Eliot

Deutsch. Delhi: Motilal Banarsidass, reprint of the 1988 Princeton ed.

Smith, Jonathan Z.
1982 *Imagining Religion: From Babylon to Jonestown*. Chicago: University of Chicago Press.

Stevens, Wallace.
1951 "Three Academic Pieces, I." In *The Necessary Angel: Essays on Reality and the Imagination*. New York: Vintage Books.

Whitehead, Alfred North.
1933 *Adventure in Ideas*. NY: Free Press.

Chapter **1**

Medieval Latin Scholasticism: Some Comparative Features

Louis Roy, O.P.

During the twelfth century C.E., in French cathedral schools, the cleric in charge of the education of priests was called a *scholasticus* (Piltz:49–51). *Schola* used to designate a group, be it military, monastic, or academic (the teacher and his students). The derivation of the Latin word from the Greek one, *schole,* which means leisure, suggests the resurgence, in the medieval West, of the Socratic desire to know truth for its own sake. However, the Christian and, more precisely, biblical-liturgical ambience that gave birth to Latin scholasticism marks it off from the Greek cultural context and also from other non-Latin environments in which different forms of scholasticism flourished. But for all its distinctness, Western scholasticism is not a unique phenomenon, as Henderson shows in his description of commentarial assumptions and strategies (Henderson, introduction and chaps. 4–5).

This chapter will try to characterize this particular brand of scholasticism as being comparative in the sense that, far from drawing solely from its own inner resources, it discussed and appropriated a huge amount of foreign ideas. The first part will present the cultural setting in which medieval Latin scholasticism came about. The second part will discuss how a quest for intellectual consistency and an exposure to competing world views led to its emergence. The third part will introduce a case in point, namely, one of Albert the Great's commentaries on Dionysius.

Major Cultural Factors

Among the major unifying factors that shaped medieval Latin scholasticism, one ought to include the following four: the Bible, the liturgy, the role of symbols, and the pedagogical customs inherited from the ancients.

In the first place, we must stress the fact that the great cultural matrix of the medieval West was the Bible. Not the Bible in a book form privately perused at home, as in the Renaissance and modern times, after the invention of the printing press; nor the Bible as an object of historical-critical study, as in Germany and the West since the end of the eighteenth century; but the Bible as publicly proclaimed, sacred Scripture.[1] In his most recent work, Wilfred Cantwell Smith has shown that, across very different cultures in the history of humankind, certain bodies of sacred texts have functioned as scripture. They have been approached scripturally, that is, heard, read, and received as transcendent messages, as revelations that transform human lives. Those sacred texts have enabled believers, as Smith puts it, to relate scripturally to the world.

The Bible molded the medievals' outlook on the world, their spontaneous response to events, their social relations, their intellectual life. The medievals saw "reality" through the eyes of the biblical writers, of the early Christian commentators, and of the Greek and Roman thinkers after they had been expurgated of what was deemed incompatible with Christianity. Because they thought that both their biblical ancestors and the Graeco-Roman sages were engaged in the quest for wisdom, the medievals quietly assumed that there could be solely one basically coherent world. For all its inscrutability, creative divine wisdom was manifested in a well-ordered universe, a hierarchical whole, at once the physical macro- and the human micro-cosm. The Dionysian representation of the world, to which we shall return in the third part of this chapter, was full of theophanies, descending influences, and analogies between several levels of reality. Beginning with Cassiodorus and Isidore of Seville in the sixth century, until its consolidation with Abelard, Hugh of St. Victor and Lombard in the twelth century, that unitary vision spontaneously displayed an encyclopedic propensity which was to culminate in the thirteenth-century summas (see Pieper 1964:41–44, 95–99). This sense of overall harmony, which consisted of the multiple correspondences that could be deciphered in the universe, not only permeated learning but expressed itself in the complexity of the cathedral.

In the second place, it is important to highlight the connection between the way the medievals prayed and the way they thought. Both ways stemmed from an intimate acquaintance with their sacred texts. Their relationship to the Bible is characterized by the solemnity and reverence typical of the liturgical setting. The pages of the big manuscripts used in choir displayed highly ornate upper-case letters, in color, as well as illuminations. Those liturgical books were handled with great respect, in a ritual context that included the burning of candles and incense, Gregorian music, gestures such as standing up to hear the Gospel, bowing, and kissing the page that had been proclaimed.

Excerpts from the Scriptures were read aloud or chanted in a prayerful atmosphere and addressed to a nondiscursive mode of attentiveness. Before and after the biblical passages were heard, receptiveness was enhanced by the singing of antiphons and responses. Thus, the approach was oral / aural, both in public and in private, since even the individuals who extended the collective reception of the word of God into personal meditation would read to themselves in a low voice (Leclercq: 1982, chap. 5). In the choirs and cloisters, monks and clerics practiced their *lectio divina;* at the same time, in churches and cathedrals, statues and stained-glass windows provided all the faithful, including the unlettered, with what I would call a *"visio divina."*

The cultured people of that time had access to biblical interpretations given either in patristic homilies, usually chanted, or in sermons delivered by the bishop, the abbot, or a designated cleric. A holistic representation of history was shaped by those commentaries, which privileged the book of Genesis (creation, fall, promise, covenant, providence), the psalms (Israel's prayer), the Canticle of Canticles (love between God and humankind), the Gospels (Incarnation, passion, and resurrection), and St. Paul's epistles (law, sin, and redemption).

In the third place, out of this biblical-liturgical mold flowed a mentality that was first and foremost symbolical. "In the whole range of its culture, the medieval period was an era of the symbol as much as, indeed more than, an era of dialectic" (Chenu 1968:103; see also 99–145). In an allegorical construing of the Bible and of the world, not only words but things themselves became signs. For example, human situations, ideas, feelings, virtues, degrees of moral and religious existence would be successively evoked or even personified by a huge variety of beings: materials of contrasted texture (straw, wood, stone, gems); the four seasons; the four elements (air, earth, water, and fire); a city (Jerusalem, Babylon, Rome); animals; social relationships; light and darkness; colors; numbers; musical tones. For the many, nature was present in the stained glass and sculptures of the churches and cathedrals; for the few, it was present in the illustrations seen in Bibles, liturgical books, commentaries, and even historical, philosophical, and scientific writings.

Patterned by the yearlong calendar, with its seasons and feasts, the conjunction between heaven and earth was represented and differentiated into a complex network of figurative and dynamic correspondences.

For instance, knowledge of the physical world was not separated from self-knowledge; science always went along with wisdom. Thus, for Hugh of St. Victor, author of the learning rationale *Didaskalicon*, all the varieties of knowledge could help to restore the image of God in the person who sincerely pursued wisdom. The symbolic thrust of the medievals was such that the whole of the human person—imaginative, intellectual, affective—was constantly addressed by everything heard or read. All the voices they listened to—the sacred texts, the liturgy, the diaphanic cosmos—mediated the unique voice of God. Therefore, in their very thinking, rational activity was balanced by a religious and emotional receptivity that we rarely find in modern philosophy.

In the fourth place, we must notice that, by themselves, these three cultural forces—the Bible, the liturgy, and the symbolic sense—could not have produced scholasticism. The Socratic propensity to ask logically linked questions became the catalyst which triggered the series of intellectual reactions that made up scholasticism.[2] But again, this logical bend is in no way unique to the West. What played a key role in the Latin world was the decision made by a few sixth-century men—Boethius, Cassiodorus, Isidore—to bring together, comment on, and hand on documents of Graeco-Roman learning to the coming generations. Such an option fostered an attitude of openness to non-Latin ways of envisioning the world. Thus, despite resistances from a large segment of Christendom, repeatedly throughout the Middle Ages bold individuals had the audacity to read and translate thinkers from different cultures. Owing to this curiosity regarding any expression of truth, the medievals assimilated the *Greek* philosophical-scientific mind. This process of appropriation lasted from the sixth to the fifteenth century—a long stretch of time in which periods of intense engagement alternated with slumbering interludes. The interest in *Jewish and Arabic* thought arose later, around 1200. It was limited to Jewish and Arabic philosophers to whose thinking style the Latin medievals responded because it was at once Greek and monotheistic. Thus the challenge posed by the Aristotelian "secularism" was attenuated by the fact that the Christians had been preceded by the Jews and the Muslims, from whom they learned how to take it up philosophically.

The Rise of a New Way of Thinking

In the West, this new way of thinking, called "scholasticism," arose in the twelfth century. What were the stepping stones that made its development possible? Two of these stepping stones were put in place at the very outset of the Middle Ages: grammar and logic. These disciplines were adopted from the Greeks and Romans in the sixth century. They never ceased playing a part in the medievals' access to the Bible. Understanding Scripture required the solving of hermeneutical issues that a good mastery of poetry, rhetoric, and other literary genres (with their several senses, particularly the allegorical) could help unraveling (see Evans, 1984, esp. chap. 10).

Premedieval Christian thinkers had made some use of grammar and logic to interpret the Bible correctly. This practice was amplified in the Middle Ages. The expansion of scholarship demanded a more frequent recourse to grammar—in order to improve the quality of the liturgical idiom—and to logic, later to be also called "dialectic"[3]—in order to enhance precision in catechetics and theology. All began with the juxtaposition of passages culled from ancient authors, both non-Christian and Christian. In Carolingian Europe (around 800), in the great endeavor to recover ancient teaching, a threefold phenomenon took place. First, the monks circulated selected texts from classical poets and learned authors of the late Roman Empire. Second, they compiled Roman and early medieval laws and decretals. Third, from the works of various patristic commentators on the Bible, they extracted excerpts which they wove together (Gibson 1993: 12–13). Each of these three basic kinds of literature could be accompanied with marginal comments called the "gloss." Those comments were meant to be clarificatory rephrasings, according to grammatical and logical rules.

Thus, in the Middle Ages, the biblical text was usually flanked on both sides with marginal glosses, made up of patristic reflections and placed according to an ingenious art of composition that prefigured printing. By the middle of the twelfth century, however, thanks to the labor of the Laon school in France, there appeared another type of gloss, this time interlinear, made up of contemporary reflections. On the whole, the so-called *glossa ordinaria,* which eventually accompanied all the books of the Latin Bible, remained a static and conservative work of reference, because it was meant to serve as a mere introduction to the Bible.

The twelfth century also saw the emergence of the sentence literature. We owe to the patient work of the Laon school, in France, the first collections of "sentences," that is, of statements from the Bible, early Christian writers and contemporary scholars, to whom were subsequently added reflections from Greek, Roman, Arabic, and Jewish thinkers. All such assertions—the texts, not the authors themselves (Chenu 1976:355)—were treated as "authorities," that is, as worthy of respectful consideration. The best known of those compilers is Peter Lombard, who also commented on the sentences he had put together.

What is important to observe is the extraordinary challenge that this ever-growing body of diverse assertions inevitably raised. "The labour of compilation led in itself to more independent work. It showed up the inconsistencies and gaps in the patristic tradition. Scholars could hardly avoid comparing and then discussing, and filling in by their own compositions" (Smalley 1984:38). By being placed alongside divergent or contrary affirmations, each singular doctrine could be doubted or at least relativized. In response to this uneasy situation, the best minds felt compelled to highlight the contrasts between discordant opinions and to come up with satisfactory solutions. For them, the resolution of a problem could be obtained by marshalling the unequal "authorities," introducing definitions, distinctions, classifications, applying worldly concepts analogously, advancing a reason or a cause, and eventually situating the issue within an explicit theory of knowledge or a full-blown metaphysics. Although this process of contrasting incompatible assertions began with John the Scot in the ninth century, it was interrupted in the next two centuries, only to resume with Anselm at the end of the eleventh, and to push forward with renewed vigor in the twelfth thanks to the wealth of "authorities" added to the debates.

Thus the problem-solving mentality, which is characteristic of scholasticism, asserted itself. It entailed a revolutionary treatment of the Bible: no longer the purely symbolic approach which consists in expounding the various levels of meaning, but a more and more systematic endeavor to tackle interpretive problems. Instead of merely handing on the tradition by compiling texts with their glosses, more and more twelfth-century scholars began to write personal, more flexible, and innovative commentaries, later to be followed by disputed questions and summas. The problems they grappled with had to do with the shifts of meaning entailed by the encounter of very different cultural contexts. For example, what to make of an Old Testament writing in an interpretive setting framed by the New Testament? Or, how to construe a Christian doctrine in an intellectual cast of mind heavily influenced by Neoplatonism and Aristotelianism?

Prior to this strictly scholastic period, three geniuses had approached the Bible with that new attitude. First, the ninth-century John the Scot (Eriugena), who knew Greek, wrestled with conflicting statements expressed by writers such as St. John the Evangelist, Augustine, and Dionysius (Smalley 1984:38–44). Second, in the eleventh century, Anselm of Canterbury departed from his contemporaries' style in that he did not offer a continuous reading of biblical texts, but selected a few excerpts as a springboard in order to launch into discussions based on Boethius' logical rules (Evans 1984:17–26). And third, a few years later, the powerful dialectician Abelard enunciated hermeneutical rules in the Preface to his *Sic et Non* and proceeded to list antithetical opinions to be discussed, with several remaining unresolved (Minnis and Scott 1988:67–69, 87–100).

However, there is an important difference between what these three great figures had accomplished and the new phenomenon that we observe mostly in the second half of the twelfth century. It is the fact that the discussion of statements made by various authorities began to take into consideration a host of recently discovered texts. One can say without exaggeration that at that time Western scholasticism became genuinely comparative. It had long grappled with books originally written in Hebrew (the Bible) and in Greek (by the church fathers). As early as in the eighth century, a few monks could read those languages. But the novelty of the twelfth-century renaissance was the large-scale enterprise of translating (or retranslating) non-Latin texts: hitherto unknown or poorly translated works by authors such as Aristotle, the Church Fathers, Byzantine thinkers such as Dionysius, Maximus Confessor and John of Damascus, the Jewish scholar Maimonides, and several Arabic figures among whom were Avicenna and Averroes. Thanks to this enormous effort of translation, a good number of foreign voices were allowed to speak for themselves and the circle of participants in the intellectual conversation was considerably widened.

Out of the commentaries on the Bible and on the sentences, Latin scholasticism came forth. The linchpin was the *question*. The running exposition of the sacred text was interrupted by questions suggested by the text in connection with current and varying positions on the topic. Thus theological discussions were inserted into the simple line-by-line explanation of the text. They reflected the practice of the *lecture*, in which rather brief discussions would alternate with the exposition of biblical passages. The next stage in the development of scholasticism was the extraction and the circulation of longer discussions apart from their original exegetical framework. And this later custom is concomitant with the establishment, around 1200, of the *disputed question* (also called "disputation"), held in the afternoon, which complemented the morning lecture on the Bible (Smalley 1984:208–11).

The negative side of those intellectual changes is the fact that medieval debates sometimes displayed an excess of logical virtuosity, at the expense of a pious attentiveness to the divine Word. Medieval theology progressively detached itself from its original context of biblical commentary. What was one single endeavor—thinking through and communicating the meaning of divine revelation—became a threefold enterprise. The great thirteenth-century theologians—Albert, Bonaventure, Thomas, to name but a few—all performed the three tasks of commenting on biblical writings, discussing questions, and preaching to the university body. But at the beginning of the fourteenth, theologians such as Scotus and Ockham did not put a high premium on writing biblical commentaries (if they wrote any, none of them is extant); they remained content with lecturing on the "sentences."

To sum up: Latin scholasticism was shaped in a biblical, liturgical, and symbolic matrix. The factor that allowed it to emerge out of that matrix, without ceasing to be nourished by it, is the following: the logical inquisitiveness inherited from the Greeks, coupled with the exposure to a great amount of conflicting religious and philosophical assertions. For all the routine attacks against Jews and Muslims, carried out in popular literature, among scholars of that time a new listening disposition toward non-Christian sources struggled to resist the temptation of proving them wrong too expeditiously. In Thomas Aquinas, for instance, one observes a genuine effort to get a glimpse of the truth from any "objection," because there is always a sense in which the objector is right (insofar as the objection conveys a resistance to some caricature of truth). The aforementioned factor prompted an ardent quest for intellectual consistency by the most brilliant minds of that epoch, namely, those who were convinced that faith and reason could be reconciled, in an attitude of discriminating openness to all expressions of truth, be they biblical, Greek, Roman, patristic, Byzantine, post-Christian Jewish, or Arabic.

A Case in Point: Albert the Great

The German Albert the Great (c.1200–1280) was both an encyclopedic and an original scholar, who excelled in theology, philosophy, and the natural sciences.[4] I have chosen him as an illustration of Latin scholasticism for the following reasons. First, by writing commentaries on the Bible and Dionysius, he has left us abundant evidence that his thinking was greatly influenced by the word of God, liturgy, and the symbolic *Weltanschauung* issuing both from the biblical revelation and from the Neoplatonism that Dionysius had christianized.

Second, he ranks as a model of ecumenical commitment in that he was the first Catholic thinker to make a case for including Aristotle among the "authorities." He had to fight against the influential conservative party of those who thought that Christians could learn nothing useful from Aristotle. Fortunately, he managed to convince a strong minority and, indeed, many among his own brethren, the Friars Preachers, an order which Thomas Aquinas would soon join and in which he would become the greatest disciple of Albert.

Third, for all the dissimilarities between Albert's style and twentieth-century scholarship, he can be said to exemplify the comparative method in his commentaries on the Greek Aristotle, the Muslim author of the Book of Causes, and the Byzantine Dionysius. He paraphrased or commented on many of Aristotle's works. He paraphrased the Book of Causes, which he thought had been written by the twelfth-century Jew Ibn Daoud; the book actually had been written two or three centuries earlier in an Arabic cultural milieu heavily influenced by Neoplatonism (Brand 1984:4–6). He also commented on all the works of the anonymous Christian author sometimes called "Pseudo-Dionysius" because he introduces himself as Dionysius the Areopagite, whom Acts of the Apostles 17:34 mentions; in fact, he probably lived and wrote in Syria around 500. This article will restrict itself to Albert's engagement with the latter, mainly because, for readers who do not know Latin, an English translation of his commentary on *The Mystical Theology* is available.[5] It is to be remarked, however, that in this commentary (composed in Cologne around 1250) Albert also discusses ideas expressed by non-Christian authors such as Aristotle, Averroes, Avicenna, the author of the Book of Causes, Cicero, Isaac Israeli, Maimonides, Plato, Ptolemaeus, to mention but the most frequently alluded or referred to (see in the critical edition, index "Auctores ab Alberto ipso allegati").

Albert's and other thirteenth-century thinkers' interest in the Book of Causes and in Dionysius made available to their contemporaries an alternative version of Neoplatonism, different from the one represented by Augustine. Despite episodic attempts at propounding Dionysius' thought (such as those made by Eriugena and Hugh of Saint Victor), not until Albert's epoch did several scholars—Thomas Gallus, Robert Gosseteste, Albert the Great, and Thomas Aquinas—produce commentaries on the whole Dionysian corpus which were very influential (see Minnis and Scott 1988, chap. 5).

Our presentation of Albert's commentary on *The Mystical Theology* will unfold in two parts. First, his commentarial procedures will be described. Second, a comparison will be made between his intellectual style and Dionysius'. At the outset, however, let us briefly note that, as a commentator, Albert is concerned with the adequacy of the translation he uses. Whenever the Latin translation he has adopted—Sarracenus'—proves questionable, he has recourse to an alternative translation—Eriugena's (148, 169, 179, 187).

Albert's exegetical method is worth examining. His commentary on Dionysius' *Mystical Theology* begins with a general introduction to the book. After quoting the translator's short prologue, he inserts a quotation from Isaiah: "Truly God of Israel, the Savior, you are a hidden God." Then he writes: "From these words we can deduce four things about this teaching which is entitled *Mystical Theology*: its nature (*modus*), its content, its audience and its objective" (134). Noteworthy is the fact that the nature (revealed truth), content (the knowledge of a hidden reality), audience (mature believers), and objective (everlasting salvation) are deduced not directly from an analysis of Dionysius' text, but from four words of the biblical quotation: "truly," "hidden God," "Israel," and "Savior" (134–36). According to this standard thirteenth-century practice, one finds in a particular excerpt from Scripture the key to the work—scriptural or nonscriptural—one is going to comment on. This custom is based on the assumption that there must be a fundamental consistency between Scripture and any other Christian writing. Albert thinks that even the non-Christian Aristotle, quoted as "the philosopher," fits into his coherent world view.

This preamble is followed by a disputation which discusses the question of why the book is called "mystical." The disputation comprises three sections: the listing of eight objections, the commentator's global response to these points, and his reply to several of the points in particular (136–41).

After settling the dispute, Albert presents the structure of Dionysius' book in great detail (141):

1. Method of teaching
    - 1.1 Situation of the person
        - 1.1.1 Knowledge of God
            - 1.1.1.1 Teacher
            - 1.1.1.2 Student
        - 1.1.2 Union with God
    - 2.1 Method of the discussion
2. Actual teaching.

Finally, Albert remarks that a prayer, itself concluded by a very brief recapitulation, introduces Dionysius' writing. The presence of a prayer in a theological work gives rise to a second disputation, which mentions two objections against and one opinion in favor of the assertion that theology must begin with prayer. After which, Albert takes a stand, based on an "authority" (Gregory the Great) and on a reason (*ratio*). For him, theology is not divorced from prayer. As we saw, he thinks that the objective of teaching is everlasting salvation. He also remains close to the liturgical context of Dionysius, who states that understanding how we alternately use the divine names and negate their imperfections is for the sake of praising God in the best possible manner (167–69, 198). And the reason he adduces enables him to situate prayer and theology with respect to each other: the former consists in listening to the inner teacher, while the latter presents the external teaching. Both inner light and outer words are indispensable for our (always very modest) grasp of divine realities (141–43).

After this substantive introduction, Albert proceeds to comment on the five chapters of *The Mystical Theology*. In each chapter, he breaks down Dionysius' text into units generally consisting of one long paragraph. He enunciates difficulties of interpretation in order to clarify Dionysius' position. For instance, at the beginning of chapter 1, Albert writes: "Several questions arise about details of the text which need clarifying" (143). Distinctions and semantic precisions then allow him to defend Dionysius against the possible charges of self-contradiction (first and third difficulty) or useless repetition (second difficulty). This strategy to counter objections recurs elsewhere in his commentary, as well as the insertion of disputed questions. The commentary also includes plainer passages, which simply state and unpack the meaning of the text, phrase by phrase, with many *idest* ("that is") (for example, 145–46). Furthermore, as he moves forward, Albert usually declares how the section under consideration is divided and subdivided (for example, 147).

Having just explained how Albert proceeds as a commentator, let us now ask: Does he merely reflect Dionysius' text, or does he add something significant in terms of content? We observe in his commentaries on Dionysius exactly what has been stated concerning his treatment of Aristotle: "Nearly always, if one is puzzled at a peculiar or obscure thought, Albert's commentary is reliable and helpful. Indeed, Albert generally tries to systematize the often fragmentary thoughts of Aristotle both intensively and extensively" (Craemer-Ruegenberg 1980:49). This systematic penchant is noticeable all along in his Dionysian commentaries as well. Its explication is intensive insofar as it highlights what Dionysius has left implicit, and it is extensive by drawing from other writings of Dionysius and from many authors.

Dionysius' thinking is binary. Most of the time, as he approaches mystical experience, he sees and presents two sides of it. For example, mystical knowledge is for him a matter both of affirming and of negating. *The Mystical Theology* expresses these two aspects by employing a wealth of adjectives which evoke the complexity of accessing the infinite mystery. The beauty and fascination of Dionysius' style have much to do with the reader responding to, and being intrigued by his great metaphors. The author multiplies and balances them in such a way that neither side of the coin will be disregarded. Finally, the pair affirming/negating is only the first member of a second, more encompassing pair, namely, knowing/unknowing (190). The twofold knowing process of affirming / negating is itself transcended, so that unknowing goes beyond any human knowledge, to culminate in a reverent silence which is, in Jones' words, "the cessation of all discourse" (in Pseudo-Dionysius 1980:5; see also 20 n. 20).

In the encounter between the sixth-century Dionysius and the thirteenth-century Albert, what is intellectually interesting is the fact that, while by and large he agrees with his predecessor, Albert transposes Dionysius' views, indebted to the Neoplatonist Proclus, into a conceptual framework of his own, which is basically a Neoplatonist Aristotelianism enriched by medieval Arabic thinkers (see De Libera). Albert's Aristotelian-Arabic epistemology enables him to explicate and analyze Dionysius' thought (see Wéber 1993:27–30). In the course of this recasting of Dionysius' vision, much of the imaginative and rhetorical forcefulness of the original writing is lost. However, another kind of beauty is gained: the luminosity of clear definitions systematically correlated in an overall metaphysical synthesis. For example, to return to the tension knowing / unknowing, Albert goes beyond Dionysius by showing more precisely how in their intertwinement affirming and negating need each other, what we know and what we do not know (both on earth and in heaven, although in different ways), and on what grounds Dionysius' assertions are based (153–54, 191–98).[6]

For lack of space, we can only mention here a few of the other pairs that Albert skillfully integrates: God's direct and indirect illuminating action (more direct according to Albert than according to both non-Christian and Dionysian Neoplatonism); the relationship between the cognitive and the affective in mystical experience (against the contemporary medieval voluntarism); the two dimensions natural / supernatural, a theoretical distinction which supplants Dionysius' more metaphorical notion of the 'supracelestial' (see Tugwell:39–129; Wéber:7–58).

In conclusion, Albert's commentary on *The Mystical Theology* can serve as an illustration of Latin scholasticism. On the one hand, it does not purport to replace the original religious experience of hearing the word of God in a liturgical setting, of interpreting it in a symbolic context, of appreciating the literary suggestiveness of Dionysius' writing, and of being challenged by its profundity. On the other hand, Albert's desire to know raises questions the answers to which require the epistemological and metaphysical conceptuality he has himself painstakingly worked out in dialogue with Christian doctrine, Aristotle, Neoplatonism, and Jewish and Arabic philosophy.

Albert's scholarly life is an interesting case of comparative scholasticism. In the Catholic medieval world, monastic theology and scholastic theology were at loggerheads on the issue of whether one ought to dialogue with non-Christian thinkers. Albert is one of the first to have come down resolutely on the side of openness. His work proves comparative in its engagement with Aristotle, Dionysius, and medieval Jewish and Islamic figures. For him, however, to be comparative does not mean exploring the Greek, post-Christian Jewish, and Islamic thought-patterns for their own sake. Albert, Thomas Aquinas, and the Jewish and Islamic thinkers of that age had a common interest in Aristotle which made them consider one another's more or less Aristotelian views and discuss them. For instance, Albert and the other Latin scholastics of his time pondered very seriously questions asked by the Arabs—questions such as what is the status of the agent intellect, or whether the world is eternal. They even took Averroes' bold speculations more to heart than the Muslims themselves did.

Of course, Albert's intellectual concern is not to be equated with the historical consciousness that the West has developed in the last two hundred years. Nevertheless, his work is comparative by displaying a life-long quest for understanding and assessing (that is, adopting, modifying, or discarding) the positions enunciated in philosophical literature of non-Christian origin. In this restricted sense, it can be asserted that Albert and several other Latin scholastics were indeed comparative.

Notes

1. According to Châtillon (1984:164–65), the feminine singular *biblia* (the Bible) rarely appears in the Middle Ages. Instead, what we come across are various renderings of the Greek neuter plural *ta biblia: sacri libri, sacri codices* (sacred books), *divini libri* (divine books), *divina dicta* (divine elocutions). In the singular form, we also find *sacra scriptura* (sacred scripture), *sacra pagina* (sacred page), *verbum Dei* (the word of God).

2. Its relentless insistence on comparing the relevant sources and asking questions is the characteristic that distinguishes medieval Latin scholasticism from the thesis approach typical of modern Western scholasticism. See Lonergan 1975:46–47, 57; 1972:277–81; and 296–97. On the thesis approach of the relatively recent manualist tradition in Roman Catholic theology, see Quesnell. For a different appraisal, limited to medieval and modern scholastic *philosophy*, see de Wulf.

3. In Aristotle, dialectic, which attains the probable, is situated half-way between logic (strict demonstration) and rhetoric (conjecture). In Latin scholasticism, *logica* and *dialectica* most of the time are used interchaneably.

4. In English, the best account of Albert's life is by the medieval scholar Tugwell (1988:3–39).

5. In Tugwell, who also offers an English translation of the Latin version of Dionysius that Albert used. From now on, all numbers in parentheses will refer to Tugwell's translation. For two recent translations of Dionysius, see Pseudo-Dionysius in the References. All the commentaries by Albert on Dionysius have been published in the critical edition.

6. See Catania (1980) for a full treatment, based on Albert's commentary of *The Divine Names*.

References

Alberti Magni.

1978 *Super Dionysii Mysticam Theologiam et Epistulas*. Ed. Paul Simon. In *Opera Omnia*, vol. 37, pt. 2. Cologne and Aschendorff.

Brand, Dennis J.

1984 "Translator's Introduction." In *The Book of Causes*. Milwaukee: Marquette University Press.

Catania, Francis J.

1980 " 'Knowable' and 'Nameable' in Albert the Great's Commentary on the Divine Names." In *Albert the Great: Commemorative Essays*, 97–128. Ed. Francis J. Kovach and Robert W. Shahan. Norman: University of Oklahoma Press.

Châtillon, Jean.

1984 "La Bible dans les Écoles du XIIe siècle." In *Le Moyen Age et la Bible*, 163–97. Ed. Pierre Riché and Guy Lobrichon. Paris: Beauchesne.

Chenu, M.-D.

1976 *La théologie au douzième siècle*. Paris: Vrin (3e éd.)

1968 *Nature, Man, and Society in the Twelfth Century: Essays on New Theological Perspectives in the Latin West*. Trans. Jerome Taylor and Lester K. Little. Chicago and London: University of California Press.

Craemer-Ruegenberg, Ingrid.

1980 "The Priority of Soul as Form and Its Proximity to the First Mover: Some Aspects of Albert's Psychology in the First Two Books of His Commentary on Aristotle's *De Anima*." In *Albert the Great: Commemorative Essays*, 49–62. Ed. Francis J. Kovach and Robert W. Shahan. Norman: University of Oklahoma Press.

Evans, G. R.
1984 *The Language and Logic of the Bible: The Earlier Middle Ages.* Cambridge: Cambridge University Press.

Gibson, Margaret T.
1993 *The Bible in the Latin West.* Notre Dame: University of Notre Dame Press.

Henderson, John B.
1991 *Scripture, Canon, and Commentary: A Comparison of Confucian and Western Exegesis.* Princeton: Princeton University Press.

Leclercq, Jean.
1982 *The Love of Learning and the Desire for God: A Study of Monastic Culture.* New York: Fordham University Press.

Libera, A. de.
1990 *Albert le Grand et la philosophie.* Paris: Vrin.

Lonergan, B. J. F.
1974 *A Second Collection.* Philadelphia: Westminster Press.

1992 *Method in Theology.* Toronto: University of Toronto Press (original ed.: 1972).

Minnis, A. J. and Scott, A. B.
1988 *Medieval Literary Theory and Criticism c.1100–c.1375: The Commentary-Tradition.* Oxford: Clarendon Press.

Pieper, Josef.
1964 *Scholasticism: Personalities and Problems of Medieval Philosophy.* New York: McGraw-Hill.

Piltz, Anders.
1978 *The World of Medieval Learning.* Trans. David Jones. Oxford: Blackwell.

Pseudo-Dionysius.
1987 *The Complete Works.* Trans. Colm Luibheid. New York / Mahwah: Paulist Press.

1980 *The Divine Names and Mystical Theology.* Trans. John D. Jones. Milwaukee: Marquette University Press.

Quesnell, Quentin.
1988 "A Note on Scholasticism." In *The Desires of the Human Heart: An Introduction to the Theology of Bernard Lonergan,* 144–49. Ed. Vernon Gregson. New York / Mahwah: Paulist Press.

Smalley, Beryl.

1984 *The Study of the Bible in the Middle Ages*. Oxford: Blackwell.

Smith, Wilfred C.

1993 *What Is Scripture? A Comparative Approach*. Minneapolis: Fortress Press.

Tugwell, Simon.

1988 *Albert and Thomas: Selected Writings*. New York / Mahwah: Paulist Press.

Wéber, Edouard-Henri.

1993 "Introduction" In *Commentaire de la "Théologie Mystique" de Denys le Pseudo-Aréopagite suivi de celui 1993 des Epîtres I–V*. Paris: Cerf.

Wulf, M. de.

1956 *An Introduction to Scholastic Philosophy, Medieval and Modern*. Trans. P. Coffey. New York: Dover. A reprint of *Scholasticism Old and New*, 1907.

Chapter **2**

The Search for Islam's True Scholasticism

Daniel A. Madigan, S.J.

ما شيء ابغض اليّ من الكلام واهله

There is nothing more loathsome to me than speculative theology and its practitioners.

—Imâm al-Shâfiʿî

Islamic Intellectual History and the West

It is perhaps an indication of our approach to Islam that books about it are shelved in the Eastern philosophies section of many bookstores. Very few think to display them under Western religions, for, even though we might allow Islam a measure of proximity by qualifying it as *Near* Eastern, it remains firmly fixed in the minds of most Westerners as foreign and "oriental." Yet its origins, its history, and, increasingly, its present are inextricably entwined with its "Near Eastern" siblings, Judaism and Christianity. Apart from a sketchy memory of the shameful episode of the Crusades there is little general awareness of just to what extent they are intertwined. Of course, the role of the Arabs in keeping alive the tradition of Greek philosophy at a time when Europe was unable to do so is legendary; Avicenna (Ibn Sîna) and Averroes (Ibn

Rushd) are perhaps more famous by their European than by their Arabic names. And these *falâsifa* (sing. *faylasûf*—those who deal with Greek philosophy) played a much more active role in the development of the Western intellectual tradition than merely that of "archivist": even in the earliest period, they reshaped and interpreted the tradition as they translated it (Arnaldez 1965: 769–75). The familiarity of those names in connection with European scholasticism might suggest that it is this branch of Muslim intellectual endeavor that qualifies as Islam's scholasticism. In many respects, however, this group was occupied with matters that were marginal to the central concerns of the Muslim community, and this kind of intellectual endeavor is not to be considered the Islamic equivalent of scholasticism. However, there were other movements of thought among the Muslims that proved both central to Islam and profoundly significant for the West.

The intellectual life of Islam can be divided into four fields: *falsafa* ("Greek" philosophy), *kalâm* (speculative theology), *fiqh* (law or, more precisely, juridical theology) and *adab* (humanities). These fields are not sealed off from one another by any means, and the first three especially took their shape in reaction or response to one another: at times they might have seemed more like armed camps than fields. This is particularly true of *kalâm* and *fiqh*, which engaged in a long struggle from which the latter would emerge with the stronger hold over the mind and heart of Islam. Our investigation of scholasticism will concentrate mostly on the philosophical theology of *kalâm*, though we shall see that *fiqh* has at least as strong a claim to the title—some would say the only real claim.

We should be alert to this issue from the beginning, even though it cannot be resolved straight away. Western observers have not been slow to apply the term *scholastic* to the practitioners of *kalâm*—the *mutakallimûn* or *ahl al-kalâm* (Niewöhner 1974: 7–34).[1] The way we translate these names will depend on whether we see them as terms of approval or opprobrium. A noncommittal translation would be "The Discussers" or "The People Who Concern Themselves with [God's] Speech." On the lips of al-Shâfiʿî (d. 820), the pivotal figure in the development of Islamic jurisprudence, who despised this group and their methods, it probably meant something more like "The Chattering Classes," since their talk (*kalâm*) was fruitless. However, the actual origin of the term is lost to us. Although it seems likely that the title refers to their dialectical style of argumentation, it is also conceivable that it refers to one of the major questions to which they addressed themselves: the ontological status of God's speech (*kalâm Allâh*)—an issue that had far-reaching consequences for the doctrine of divine unity.[2] George Makdisi (1990a: 2) has insisted that *scholastic* is a misnomer for this group, since their type of rationalist, philosophical theology was banned from the curricula of Islamic scholasticism's eponymous schools. He prefers to apply the term to the practitioners of *fiqh*—the *fuqahâ'* (sing. *faqîh*), the juridical theologians of the guilds of law and their colleges. This, as we shall see, is more than mere etymological pedantry: the schools had their own characteristic approach to rationality, to Scripture, and to the significance of consensus in establishing authority, an approach that clearly distinguished them from the philosophical theologians of the second Islamic century. So let us for the moment put aside the question of whether the *mutakallimûn* (or *ahl al-kalâm*, or simply *kalâm*) should be considered "scholastics" within the terms of this comparative project. When we come to it, the answer to that question and a consideration of Makdisi's claim on behalf of the jurists may prove helpful in focussing our definition.

There is a substantial body of evidence, most of it mustered by Makdisi (1990a, 1990b, 1989, 1981, 1974), to support the claim that the phenomenon of medieval scholasticism developed its characteristic style and context within Islam before it took root in the Christian West. If we accept even the possibility of this, then any synchronous comparison must bear in mind this likelihood of historical dependency. We would be deceiving ourselves, therefore, if we were merely to place Christian and Islamic scholasticism side by side and use the similarities between them to bolster the argument that the concept of "scholasticism" is a valuable analytical tool across cultures and religions. It is more fruitful, perhaps, to treat them diachronically and to examine how a methodology that proved itself so valuable to the medieval Christian West had first emerged and taken shape in the quite different context of Islam's early centuries.

In this chapter I have opted to sketch a brief history of rationalist theology in Islam: its origins; the very brief political hegemony it enjoyed among the Muslims; the repeated reversals it suffered at the hands of the Traditionist movement that had grown up in reaction to it—the *ahl al-ḥadîth* or *muḥaddithûn*, those who collect and study traditions (*ḥadîth*) of the Prophet; and its often unnoticed survival in the emergence of the great schools of Islamic law (*fiqh*). This narrative will take us from the seventh to the twelfth centuries, from the career of al-Ḥasan al-Baṣrî (d. 728) to that of al-Ghazzâlî (d. 1111). I will then look at this period using the categories, descriptors, and distinctions introduced in this volume and elsewhere by José Cabezón, Paul Griffiths, and Francis X. Clooney—both testing their usefulness in understanding Islam's particular kind of scholasticism and seeing how the shape that scholasticism took within Islam might confirm, question, or amplify these authors' insights.

The Origins of Islamic Theology

Theology certainly does not occupy the same important place in Islam that it does in Christianity. As a nomocracy, Islam is much more concerned with jurisprudence, and it is in the field of law, rather than in theology or philosophy, that its greatest intellectual capital has been invested. Yet theological issues are bound to arise in any religion, and the Muslim community in the first century found itself perplexed and divided by several such questions. An unambiguous answer could not always be found in the Qur'ân and the Prophetic *ḥadîth*—indeed it is generally accepted by Western scholars that many of these traditions reflect later interpretations by a particular school of the scripture's true intention. Even orthodox Muslim scholarship always has recognized that traditions claiming to go back to the Prophet need to be carefully sifted for authenticity.[3] In the absence of a clear judgment from canonical sources, reason naturally played a role in the development of a response.

The two issues that most exercised the community were the status of the grave sinner, and the related issue of predestination. It might have surprised the early Muslims to see these questions referred to as theological problems, for in fact they grew out of practical questions of community and politics. The issues underlying the doctrinal conflicts of the foundational period of Islam were always the following: Who constitute the community of the Muslims? and Who may be the legitimate leader of that community? Does grave sin constitute unbelief and therefore place the sinner outside the community? What precisely constitutes the faith that qualifies one as a Muslim? Can a leader claim that all his actions have been predetermined by God and so claim immunity from criticism and impeachment?

The questions were originally raised, and the more morally rigorous responses given, by a group (or, more precisely, a number of groups) known as the Kharijites (*khawârij*, 'those who have seceded').[4] The more lenient approach—deferring to the final, as yet unknowable, judgment of God—was taken by the Murji'ites (*murji'a*, 'those who postpone the question'). Ultimately, the unity of the community and the viability of its politics proved more important than the moral purity that the Kharijites sought to uphold, and so the community settled on a position close to that of the Murji'ites. Yet the issues, once broached, would not be laid to rest even after the political crises that prompted them had been weathered.

There is an undeniably strong predestinarian strain within both the Qur'ân and the Traditions (*ḥadîth*), although in the former it is somewhat balanced by a number of verses that speak up for human responsibility. Most scholars attribute such predestinarian views to a pre-Islamic, atheistic fatalism among the Arabs, which, though challenged by Qur'anic teaching, survived and re-asserted itself in the Traditions (Watt 1948: 20–30). The thinkers who challenged this strand of thought were referred to as the "Qadarites" (*qadariyya*) because they dwelt on the subject of *qadar* (lit. 'measuring', 'determination', 'power'). The name fits awkwardly since they actually *opposed* the notion of *qadar*—that is, the idea that God is the sole determiner of all things, including human actions. Against this they asserted human responsibility, though they are often depicted inaccurately as proponents of human freedom or free will. The extreme predestinarian view, on the other hand, was espoused by the so-called Jabarites (*jabriyya*), who effectively made no distinction between humanity and inanimate nature, in as much as all human action is subordinated to the compulsion (*jabr*) of God.

At the root of the Qadarite's antipredestinarian position lay two important conceptions: that human beings should be considered accountable for their actions, both now and in the hereafter, and that it would be contrary to common sense if God were to command the good and yet predestine people to commit evil or predestine some to heaven and yet overlook their evil actions that merit punishment.

It was during the continuing discussions of the issues of predestination and faith that a crucial shift gradually began to take place: from theology as a search for practical religio-political solutions to what seems to have been a theology more for its own sake; a theology always looking for an opponent, even an imaginary one; a theology that was largely an intellectual pursuit. It was this shift that was to prove the undoing of theology as a discipline within Islam, and the ultimate rejection by mainstream Islam of the *kalâm* theology that is usually counted by Westerners as scholasticism.

Primary sources for the study of theological reflection in early Islam are scanty; most are of uncertain date and disputed authorship. So we rely to a large extent on the elaborate taxonomies of later heresiographers and intellectual historians for descriptions of the doctrine of earlier thinkers—not always reliable guides.[5] However, we have available on this subject one of the least disputed of early texts, a letter on *qadar* by the eminent al-Ḥasan al-Baṣrî (d. 110/728) addressed to the Umayyad Caliph ʿAbd al-Malik.[6] Al-Ḥasan's methodology is clear: he approaches the issue quite rationally and cites only Qur'anic texts (not even one *ḥadîth*) to prove his point. Though the letter is systematic and reasoned, it would be inaccurate to call this rationalist theology. It relies almost completely on the authority of scripture, which it interprets with what we might call reasonableness rather than rationalism:

> For the Book of God is light in the face of darkness and life in the face of death. God did not leave those who worship Him any other proof apart from the Book and the prophets, "so that he who was to die might perish after a clear sign and he who was to live might live in the light of a clear sign." (Q 8:42) So reflect, O Commander of the Faithful, on the word of the Most High: "Whoever of you desires to progress or lag behind . . ." (Q 74:34) The meaning is that God has created in them some ability [*qudra*, from the same root as *qadar*] by which they progress or lag behind, with the result that whoever does good deserves heaven and whoever does evil deserves the fire. If what the deceivers [i.e., the predestinarians] hold were the case, then people would not have any ability to make progress or to lag behind. Therefore, there would be nothing to praise in what the person who progresses has done, nor anything to blame in the one who falls behind, since, according to what they claim, it neither comes from them nor belongs to them, but it is rather something that is done to them.[7]

Al-Ḥasan is without doubt a theologian, but he does not qualify for the title *mutakallim*. That is normally reserved for those who "discuss" their opponents into a corner by asking questions and reducing their position to meaningless alternatives. The dialectical structure of the so called *kalâm*, the style characteristic of classical Muʿtazilite theology, is not to be found in al-Ḥasan's treatise (dated ca. 700) nor in another theological letter to the same caliph by ʿAbd Allah b. Ibâḍ, defending the Kharijite position. However, there are a few sources from around the same time in which we do find the characteristic *kalâm* style. For example, van Ess (1975: 91–98) has argued for the authenticity of a treatise against the Qadarites by Ḥasan b. Muḥammad b. al-Ḥanafiyya (d. ca. 718).[8] Although it is known only partially through quotation by one polemicizing against it, it is clear that the style has much in common with later *kalâm* works. In this excerpt (91) he seeks to use the creation of hell as a proof of God's having predestined some to evil:

> Tell us [Ḥasan b. Muḥammad b. al-Ḥanafiyya addresses his Qadarite opponents], whether God (only) wanted the Good with them (i.e. with mankind) and then later established it (i.e. Hell) for them, or whether he wanted the Evil with them (right from the beginning)!—If they say: "He wanted the Good with them," they should be answered: "How is that, as He created it (Hell) knowing that they would not have any profit from it and that it would only do harm to them?" If they, however, assume that He created it for them in order to do harm to them, their doctrine is refuted.

It is the clearly polemical setting of such writing that has suggested to several scholars that the source of the style is to be found in the dialectical techniques of Christian polemics.[9] Yet not all agree on which polemical setting might have provided the real model; most scholars have ignored intra-Christian polemics in favor of suggesting that the source was Christian/Jewish polemic. (Cook 1980: 33–34) Michael Cook (1980: 40–43) has questioned the sources proposed by van Ess and published excerpts from a Syriac document of the late seventh century (a guide for Monotheletes disputing with Dyotheletes) in which the style of argumentation very closely parallels the later work of Ḥasan. He argues for a Syriac (hence intra-Christian) origin both for the genre of *kalâm* and also for the term *mutakallim*.[10]

Such an origin should not surprise us. It is often forgotten that the Muslim community of this period included many converts from Christianity, who naturally brought with them their characteristic habits of thought and styles of argumentation and put them to use in developing an apologetic and in contributing to the building of a coherent theological edifice for their new religion. It is also significant that the Christian apologists of the first ʿAbbâsid century (mideighth to midninth century) were actual participants in formal scholarly conversations with Muslim intellectuals as well as in written exchanges (Griffith 1992: 116–18 and passim). So the dealings of the *kalâm* theologians *ad extra* reinforced the methodology that they were using in their own internal disputes with other Muslim groups.

The Muʿtazilites and the Development of Speculative Theology

This style of theology comes to its full flowering in the work of the Muʿtazilites (*muʿtazila*, 'those who have separated themselves'—originally, it is claimed, from the pupils of al-Ḥasan al-Baṣrî). It is this particular group that is most often seen as the exponents of scholasticism in Islam.[11] However much this group may have come to be identified with speculative intellectualism, it too originated in a political position adopted vis à vis the caliphates of ʿAlî and ʿUthmân.[12] Its emergence as a theological movement is attributed to a student of al-Ḥasan al-Baṣrî, Wâṣil b. ʿAtâ' (d. 131/748), who taught that the grave sinner is neither an unbeliever (as the Kharijites maintained) nor a believer (as the Murji'ites held) but rather occupied a position between the two (*al-manzila bayn al-manzilatayn*). As opponents of the Umayyad dynasty, they became closely associated with the ʿAbbâsid movement; indeed one could call them the court theologians of the ʿAbbâsid dynasty, which succeeded the Umayyads. Such was their political power that they were able to have instituted an inquisition, lasting from 833 to 848, against those who disagreed with their doctrine that the Qur'ân is created). The Umayyads were strong supporters of the notion of predestination (*jabr*) since it could be used to shore up their political claims. However, a belief in human responsibility was more useful to those who challenged the legitimacy of the regime, and it is reported that Maʿbad al-Juhanî, sometimes called the "father" of the antipredestinarian Qadarites, was killed on the orders of the Umayyad Caliph ʿAbd al-Malik in 699. The Muʿtazilites seem to have united a number of Qadarite groups.

Muʿtazilite Doctrine

We know little of the actual teaching of Wâṣil and his immediate follower ʿAmr b. ʿUbayd (d. 145/762). The true founder of the dogmatic system of the Muʿtazilites was Abû-l-Hudhayl Muḥammad b. al-Hudhayl al-ʿAllâf (d. 840).[13]

The Muʿtazilites liked to be called (*ahl al-ʿadl wa-l-tawḥîd*)—"those concerned with justice and unity" for it is these two issues that are raised most clearly by the discussions of the Qadarites. Enquiry into the matter of predestination can scarcely avoid calling into question the justice of God. Once one begins to examine any attribute of God, the question of the status of all God's attributes and their relationship to the divine essence is unavoidable. The answer of the Traditionists to the question of *qadar* was that all things that happen, human actions included, are the products of the divine decree that had fixed them even before the world was created. As we have seen, the primary objection to this position was ethical and political rather than intellectual. Yet it came to focus more on the ethical nature of God than of humanity. God would be acting contrary to justice if he were to condemn people to hell for having acted in ways they had been predestined to act. It would make a nonsense of the eternal divine decree if it were at odds with itself: commanding people to seek the good and yet at the same time decreeing their evil actions. Al-Shahrastânî (1923: 30) describes their position succinctly:

> The Muʿtazilites are agreed that man is possessed of ability (*qâdir*) and is the creator (*khâliq*) of his own acts, both good and evil; that it is on the basis of what he does that he merits reward or punishment in the next world. In this way the Lord, may He be exalted, is deemed safe from any accusation of evil or wrong or any act of unbelief or transgression. For if He had created the wrong, He would be wrong, in the same way that if He had created justice, he would be just.

Because of the importance to the Muʿtazilites of the doctrine of divine justice, they had a much more severe view of retribution and a firmer rejection of intercession than that found in what is now considered orthodox Islam. (Wensinck 1932: 61) To the Traditionists, a much more troubling consequence of the Muʿtazilite view was that it set up the human person as a creator (*khâliq*) apart from God. It also gave rise to an interest in theodicy, where the rationalism of the Muʿtazilites came fully into play. Reason is trusted as the guide to what is right in itself: "The *ahl al-ʿadl* (defenders of divine justice)," al-Shahrastâni tells us, "maintained that everything that is good is known from reason and is seen to be obligatory in the light of reason" (1923: 29). God commands it because it is right; *that* it is right is known from reason not from the divine command.

Three other doctrines flow from this; although they are subsidiary to the doctrine of divine justice, they are nonetheless constitutive of the Muʿtazilite position: (1) the doctrine of the promise and the threat (*aṣl al-waʿd wa-l-waʿîd*); (2) the doctrine of the intermediate position of the grave sinner (*aṣl al-manzila bayn al-manzilatayn*); and (3) the doctrine of the obligation to call people to do what is right and to forbid them from doing what is wrong (*aṣl al-amr bi-l-maʿrûf wa-l-nahy ʿan al-munkar*).[14]

The second of the major doctrines of the Muʿtazilites was *tawḥîd*—the strict profession of monotheism. This, of course, is a fundamental dogma of Islam, and the Muʿtazilites did not invent it. What distinguishes them is the interpretations they give of the doctrine and the way in which they apply it to other areas of theology. In this the group probably had two opponents in view: the Traditionists with their anthropomorphic views of God and belief in the eternity of the Qur'ân; and the extreme Shîʿites, who had assimilated and so imported into Islam a substantial amount of Manichean dualism (Nyberg 1953: 424). Of the two groups of opponents, it was the Traditionists who ultimately proved the more formidable.

The Muʿtazilites sought to avoid all anthropomorphism in their theology and refused to read literally those they found in the Qur'ân, preferring an allegorical interpretation: God's hand (e.g. Q 3:26) is understood as his bounty, and his face (e.g. Q 2:115) as his favor. Their description of the godhead is primarily negative, partly because of the logic of their system, but also in order to counter the positive statements that their opponents made about God on the basis of the Qur'ân and Traditions. In order to avoid compromising the divine unity, they refused to allow any real existence to the divine attributes. They thought the position of the Traditionists, that God *has* knowledge, power, life, hearing, and so on, to be tantamount to *shirk* (polytheism) and asserted that the attributes were not entities added to or possessed by the divine being, but rather that they were identical with that being.

It is worth quoting at some length a few accounts of their theology, in order to appreciate the development that had taken place since the earlier theologians quoted above. Al-Ashʿarî (d. ca. 324/935), for many years one of their number, describes their position this way (1979: 1: 235–36):

> The Muʿtazilites are agreed that God is one, and that there is nothing like Him; He is hearing and seeing; He is not a body, nor an object, nor a volume, nor a form; neither flesh nor blood, nor a person; neither a substance nor an accident; possessing neither color nor taste; no smell nor feel; possessing no heat or coldness, moisture or dryness; having no length, breadth or depth, no union or separation; He does not move nor remain at rest; He is not divided. Neither does He possess parts or divisions, limbs or members; He has no direction, possessing no right or left hand, before or behind, above or below. No place can surround Him, nor time pass Him by. It is not possible to be in contact with Him, nor separate from Him, nor is it possible for Him to occupy places. He cannot be described by anything that can be applied to creatures, since such descriptions indicate their createdness. . . . He cannot be described by measure nor by movement in a direction, nor does He have boundaries. He is neither begetter nor begotten. No powers can succeed in encompassing Him; no senses attain to Him, nor veil cover Him. Humanity can find no analogy for Him, nor does He resemble creation in any way. Neither accident nor detriment can touch Him. Nothing of what occurs to any mind or is pictured by any imagination resembles Him. He has not ceased to be eternal, pre-eminent, pre-existent, present before created things. He has not ceased to be knowing, deciding, living, nor will He cease to be so. Eyes do not see Him, sight does not reach Him, fantasy cannot conceive of Him, nor can He be heard with the ears. He is a thing, but not like other things; He is knowing, powerful, alive, but not in the same way as other knowledgeable or powerful or living beings. He alone is eternal; there is none eternal besides Him, nor any God except Him; there is none who shares in His sovereignty, nor any to whom is delegated His authority. There was no one put in charge of instituting what was instituted nor creating what was created. He did not create the creation after a pre-existing pattern, not was the creation of any one thing easier or more difficult for him than the creation of any other thing. . . . No pleasure or delight can affect Him, nor harm or pain touch Him. He has no limit, which would result in His being finite. The idea of ceasing cannot be applied to Him, nor is He subject to any inability or lack. His holiness precludes his touching a woman or choosing to have a consort and offspring.

Al-Ashʿarî has, perhaps, done the Muʿtazilites a service in thus presenting their position in a compact credal form. He has spared us the rather aggravating dialectical argumentation that was the stock-in-trade of the *mutakallimûn* and which surely must have played a role in this kind of rationalist theology's falling from favor. We get a feel for the lengths to which their argumentation took them in another description from al-Ashʿarî:

> One section of the Muʿtazilites declare it forbidden to say that the Creator has not ceased creating, or that he has not ceased not-creating. Likewise it is forbidden to say that He has not ceased sustaining, or that He has not ceased not-sustaining. They treat the other qualities in the same way. . . .
>
> A second section assert that the Creator has not ceased not-creating and not-sustaining. If they are asked: Did He not cease to be not-just, they say: He has not ceased to be not-just and not-wrong; He has not ceased to be not-being good and not-being bad; He has not ceased to be not-honest and not-lying. . . .
>
> A third section assert that the Creator has not ceased not-creating and not-sustaining. But they do not say: He has not ceased to be not-just, not-good, not-bounteous, not-honest, not-wise. They reject any such utterance, whether relative or absolute, because they assert it to be ambiguous. This is the position of some of the Muʿtazilites of Baghdâd and of some of those of Baṣra.[15]

Controversy over the Creation of the Qur'ân

The most prominent point at issue between the Muʿtazilites and the Traditionists, the status of the Qur'ân, grew out of this concentration on the divine attributes and their relationship to the unity of God. The issue was not the Qur'ân's role as an authoritative source for law and theology; both were agreed on that. The question was its status as God's speech. The Muʿtazilite denial of the eternity of the Qur'ân, or their thesis that it was created, was a logical consequence of their denial of eternal qualities. Neither party made a distinction between God's speaking, God's attribute of speech, and the Qur'ân. For the Muʿtazilites God's speaking to Moses (Q 7:143ff.; 28:30ff.) was a single act. Neither his attribute of speech nor the Qur'ân had any deeper significance than that. However, the Traditionists considered all three to be eternal qualities. This of course raised the question of the relationship between the eternally uncreated Qur'ân and the copies in which it is written, or the sounds made when it is recited. A Traditionist credal statement, dating probably from the first half of the ninth century, expresses the faith of this party about the Qur'ân:[16]

> Art. 9: We confess that the Kuran is the speech of Allah, uncreated, His inspiration and revelation, not He, yet not other than He, but His real quality (*sifa*), written in the copies, recited by the tongues, preserved in the breasts, yet not residing there. The ink, the paper, the writing are created, for they are the work of men. The speech of Allah on the other hand is uncreated, for the writing and the letters and the words and the verses are manifestations of the Kuran for the sake of human needs. The speech of Allah on the other hand is self-existing, and its meaning is understood by means of these things. Whoso sayeth that the speech of Allah is created, he is an infidel regarding Allah, the Exalted, whom men serve, who is eternally the same, His speech being recited or written and retained in the heart, yet never dissociated from Him.

In denying that the Qur'ân was created, the Traditionists were seen to be compromising God's status as creator of all things and also to be flirting with something dangerously close to the Christian doctrine of the uncreated Logos. It was around just these issues that the Muʿtazilites were able to have Caliph al-Ma'mûn institute the *Miḥna* or Inquisition of 833 through 848.[17]

However, this use (or abuse) of state power in support of a rather narrow theological position was in many ways to prove the undoing of the *mutakallimûn* as the dominant force in Islamic thought. Their most prominent opponent among the Traditionists—he is even mentioned derisively by name in the caliph's letter instituting the Inquisition—was Aḥmad b. Ḥanbal (d. 241/855). His courageous resistance in the face of the state theology and his risking death by remaining adamant dealt a severe blow to Muʿtazilite prestige. According to van Ess (1975: 87), at the time of the *miḥna* theology came increasingly to be seen as "a dangerous game of autocratic intellectuals." Confronted with the tortuous dryness of the *kalâm* style, the lack of practical application to most of their thought, and the arrogance of their politics, one is left wondering what religious point and purpose such speculation ultimately serves. It is hardly surprising that orthodoxy came ultimately to be identified with the more straightforward way of the Traditionists.

The style of these Traditionists is well illustrated by a treatise written by Ibn Ḥanbal (1393:40) refuting the positions of the Manichaeans (*zanâdiqa*) and the Jahmites (a group who held similar opinions to the Muʿtazilites on the subject of anthropomorphisms, but who were nonetheless firm predestinarians). This excerpt demonstrates their predominant reliance on scriptural proofs, while also showing that they had learned well enough the dialectical style favored by their opponents and were not averse to using it to their own advantage. It should be noted, however, that the dialectic here usually proceeds on the basis of scriptural rather than rational grounds:

> If you wish to know that the Jahmî does not profess God's knowledge, say to him: "God says, '. . . They can grasp nothing of his knowledge (*'ilm*)' [Q 2:255]. And again, 'But God Himself bears witness to what he has sent down to you: He sent it down with His knowledge' [Q 4:166]. And again, 'But if they do not respond to you, then know that it has indeed been sent down to you with the knowledge of God . . .' [Q 11:14]. And again, '. . . No fruit comes forth from its coverings, neither does any female conceive, nor is she delivered without His knowledge'[Q 41:47]." Then let someone say to the Jahmî, "Do you or do you not profess this knowledge of God that He has made you aware of by signs and proofs?" If he says, "God does not possess knowledge," he has denied the faith. If he says, "God's knowledge is something caused (*muḥdath*)," he has denied the faith by asserting that there was a time when God did not know until he created knowledge—only then did he know. And if he says, "God possesses knowledge and it is uncreated and uncaused," he has completely abandoned his position and adopted the doctrine of the *ahl al-Sunna* [the Traditionists].

One of Ibn Ḥanbal's most memorable, if not most successful, theological tactics was *balkafa*—that is, using the term *bilâ kayfa* (without [asking] how). The Qur'ân and Sunna were to be accepted without asking questions: if God says He has a face, He has a face, without any questioning of how this could be. This tactic could not meet the objections of the opponents nor satisfactorily deal with even the legitimate desire of the Traditionists to probe the matter further. It represented merely a refusal to play the *kalâm* game, an attempt to cut through the constrictive net of the *mutakallim*'s questioning.

Although many scholars (e.g. Seale 1964: 20–21; Wensinck 1932: 78) have identified the logic of the *mutakallimûn* as Aristotelian, van Ess (1970:27–42) has shown how much in common it has with Stoic logic, in spite of the strong representation of Aristotelian ideas and some Platonic elements. Louis Gardet (1965: 1146) has pointed out that the more Aristotelian style is characteristic of later *kalâm* when it is arguing with the *falâsifa* (philosophers) but that the two-term oppositional logic of the early, more theological *kalâm* is characteristically Semitic.[18] The final emptiness of the characteristic styles of *kalâm* argument, van Ess suggests, may be the reason that "some of the profoundest spokesmen of Islam turned away from *kalâm* with contempt and disgust; they heard only idle talk, *kalâm*, not theology" (1970: 42). Although it has never really died out,[19] rationalist theology lost its hegemony to juridical theology as the principal concern of Muslim thinkers. With the failure of the

Inquisition, rationalism in theology began to lose its political support; yet it managed still to keep its adversary Traditionism engaged in an intellectual dialogue, for its questions were not so easily silenced. In some respects, as we shall see, it survived by infiltrating those very schools of law that were set up as a bulwark against it.

The Moderation of Traditionism and the Development of Juridical Theology

The *Risâla* of al-Shâfiʿî (d. 820) formed the systematic basis of the new juridical theology. It provided the Traditionists with a clear methodology based on the dual "scriptural" sources of Qur'ân and Sunna (the "way" of the Prophet as discerned from Traditions about his sayings, actions, and tacit approbations). Though in the *Risâla* he does not directly indicate his antipathy toward the *mutakallimûn*, it is clear from his statements in the introduction that al-Shâfiʿî intended it as an antirationalist treatise. God is only to be characterized by the attributes and epithets he gives to himself in the Qur'ân, Shâfiʿî maintains, not by anything one might draw from rational speculations. Furthermore, revelation not only provides us with all we need know about God, but guidance for every possible situation a person will ever face is provided by the Qur'ân and the Traditions (Makdisi 1990a: 13). In Islamic jurisprudence, there is no room for natural law argument; law is command and prohibition and is based directly on God's revealed law. The role of the jurist is to make clear all that one needs to know of one's obligations to God (*al-ʿibâdât*) and to one's fellow human beings (*al-muʿâmalât*). As al-Shâfiʿî conceived the task of the scholar, it is to study God's law, not God Himself. It is to study God's commands and prohibitions, not whether God is, or what God is (Makdisi 1990a: 14).

As Traditionism grew in strength, there were, understandably enough, attempts at compromise. In this connection two important figures should be mentioned. The first is Abû al-Ḥasan ʿAlî al-Ashʿarî (d. ca. 935), who defected from the Muʿtazilite camp and declared himself completely faithful to the position of Ibn Ḥanbal. Although the list of his writings is very extensive, very little of his output is available to us, and it is difficult to piece together a coherent view of the development of his thought. His name is taken by a school of thought that sought to find a middle way between the fideism of the Traditionists and the excessive rationalism of the Muʿtazilites. He is usually credited with having developed the notion of *tanzîh* (lit. removing imperfections; removing the human element from expressions about God). This enabled him to affirm the reality of God's face, hands, sitting, and so on, at the same time as maintaining that they are not like the imperfect and limited examples of hands, faces, and so on, that creatures have. In this way he sought to avoid, on the one hand, the rationalist trap of *taʿtîl* (depriving God of something rightfully his) and, on the other, the Traditionist traps of *tajsîm* (in effect believing that God has a body) and *tashbîh* (anthropomorphism). One can see in this excerpt from the Fiqh Akbar II, a somewhat later, almost certainly Ashʿarî creed, how Ibn Ḥanbal's *bilâ kayfa* ("without [asking] how") is retained even while philosophical language is being employed (Wensinck 1932: 190):

> God has hand, face and soul, for He refers to these in the Qur'ân; and what he says in the Qur'ân regarding face, hand and soul, this belongs to His qualities, without how. It must not be said that his hand is His power or His bounty, for this would lead to the annihilation of the quality. This is the view of the Qadarites and the Muʿtazilites. No, His hand is his quality, without how. Likewise His wrath and His good pleasure are two of his qualities, without how.

A second theological tactic of al-Ashʿarî and his school is the notion of *kasb* (acquisition). This is an attempt to deal with the issue of predestination and human responsibility. God is acknowledged as the sole creator of human actions, but human beings are responsible because they "appropriate" to themselves those actions that have been created for them. Having thus acquired or appropriated them, they are justly rewarded or punished for them.

It was Ashʿarism's ability to compromise while continuing to cling to a rationalist methodology that allowed its survival even during the ascendancy of Shâfiʿî's juridical theology. Perhaps the greatest figure to emerge from its ranks, arguably the most important thinker in the history of Islamic theology, was al-Ghazzâlî (d. 1111). He is too important a figure to deal with within the limits of this chapter, so we confine ourselves to a few observations. Ghazzâlî's mastery of all the disciplines that were struggling to gain ascendancy in Islam, as well as a period of disillusionment in which he turned to explore the esoteric side of religion, enabled him to stand back from the struggle and enunciate a clearer vision of the respective roles played in Islam by reason, experience, and authority. He could see the limitations of rationalism yet did not fear it as the Ḥanbalites did. He could see the attraction of a simple faith, yet knew also the need for explanation and guidance in order to deal with disputes. He could recognize the difference between, on the one hand, the kind of advice and gentle argument needed to deal with doubts, and, on the other, the contrived intricacies of *kalâm*. Ultimately, he places great store by religious experience as the touchstone of interpretation:

> The true middle path between a complete allegorism and rigid Ḥanbalism is narrow and obscure. It is found only by those who enjoy divine help and who reach the heart of things by divine light, not by hearsay. Then, when the mysteries of things are revealed to them so that they see them as they are, they return to Scripture and Tradition and their wording; whatever accords with what they have witnessed by the light of certainty, they affirm and whatever does not accord with it, they interpret allegorically.[20]

It is Wensinck's opinion (1932: 248) that Ghazzâlî's crisis, and the new synthesis at which he arrived, can be understood only in the context of the increasing intellectualization of Islamic theology that continued even after the decline of the extreme Muʿtazilite ascendancy.

Scholasticism or Scholasticisms?

It is George Makdisi's contention (1990a: 1) that the juridical theology created by al-Shâfiʿî and practiced from the latter part of the ninth century is the only truly scholastic theology in Islam. Before going on to a brief description of that form of theology and to a consideration of Makdisi's claim, it may be worth asking how the *mutakallimûn* we have been examining, who so often are called scholastics by the West, relate to the description that has been developed by José Cabezón to form the starting point of this comparative project.

Put briefly, his working definition of scholasticism is that its discourse is marked by (1) a strong sense of the accessibility of the real to systematic human rationality; (2) a commitment to the preservation of the tradition and its definition and defense against other traditions; (3) an inclusive attitude (he calls this its "proliferative" character) in regard to the texts to be dealt with, the arguments and questions to be entertained, and the phenomena to be tackled by the system; and (4) a self-reflective quality that turns the tools of scholastic enquiry onto the practice of that enquiry itself (Cabezón 1994: 11–25).

On the face of it, the title *scholastic* is well-enough deserved by the Muʿtazilites and others of the more developed *mutakallimûn*. They were unmistakably committed to the idea that their rationality could deal with any issue they needed to confront. Although we have dealt above almost exclusively with their theology, the Muʿtazilites also were interested in other branches of philosophy, anthropology, and physics, all discussed under the headings of *tawḥîd* and *ʿadl*, since they bore on the issue of God's relationship to creation and on the issue of human responsibility (Nyberg 1953: 425–26). Even though they were pitted against those who wished to make scripture (understood as Qur'ân and Traditions) the sole locus of authority, the Muʿtazilites themselves were staunch defenders of the authority of the Qur'ân, though rather more limited and selective in their use of Traditions from the Prophet. The difference was in the way the two groups chose to read these scriptural sources: the Muʿtazilites in the light of reason, with a confidence that the scriptures could not possibly contradict it; their opponents with an attitude of *balkafa,* asserting the form of words and asking no questions. The Muʿtazilites were prepared to approach scriptural sources with a nonliteralist hermeneutic where necessary, since they were seeking to preserve and defend the Islamic tradition's central tenet of monotheism (*tawḥîd*), which they considered was threatened by scriptural literalism. As the decree of the Inquisition and some parts of their writings showed, they were keenly aware of the danger of Christian and Manichean ideas diluting the Islamic tradition.

If there is one area where the *mutakallimûn* would stretch Cabezón's categorization of scholastics, it is their style of argumentation and what that reveals about their commitment to rationality and system. Even though from quite an early period they sometimes analyzed the structure of their logical arguments, the results, as van Ess has pointed out, were less than impressive. The aim of the method was not careful deduction from undisputed premises, but rather their refutation of the opponent. The method relied on the *argumentum ad hominem,* not in the often-used sense that it was a personal attack unrelated to the subject, but rather in the sense that it was an argument tailored to the particular adversary with his unique mixture of views and his own weakness in argument. The adversary in question was often, in fact, made of straw and was given no real opportunity to control his own side of the argument and so challenge the *mutakallim*'s version of his answers (van Ess 1976: 26–27). Cabezón's scholastics, on the other hand, are always open to the demands of the rational process, wherever it may lead: "They are ever willing to answer an opponents 'why?'" (1994: 21). Van Ess (1970: 25) points out that for the Muʿtazilites "many of the arguments were made for momentary success; they proved that one was right, but not always that one had the complete truth. They were critical, but not constructive, valid, but not formally valid."[21] He presents (1976: 23–24) a rather unflattering picture of the *mutakallimûn* plying their trade in the mosques:

> Muslim theologians sometimes caused a stir in the mosques because they were making too much noise. The Basran poet Muḥammad b. Yasîr al-Riyâshî, a contemporary of Abû Nuwâs (d. ca. 825), attributed this to the fact that each wanted to have the last word over the others; each one shouted to be heard above the others in order to bring home his *ad hominem* argument. This is cer-

> tainly not a sympathetic portrayal, yet it brings out saliently something quite characteristic: Theology is in Islam, moreso perhaps than in other religions, a combative science, dialectical in argumentation and dialogical in style. One can already see this expressed in its name: while a Christian speaks of "theo-logy" and thereby places the theme of this science, namely God, in the foreground, in Islam one usually uses the term ʿilm al-kalâm, "science of discussion," i.e. the knowledge of how one should discuss something with an opponent in order to refute him.

What most gives us pause when it comes to including the early *mutakallimûn* in the category of scholastics is that they so circumscribed and controlled the rational process with their chosen methodology. This may be somewhat less the case as time goes on, and the systematic nature of the work of al-Ashʿarî has been hotly defended against critics of the *kalâm* by Richard Frank (1968: 295–309).[22] Yet even if one were able to discern a coherent and elaborate system lying behind the argumentation, it is the argument that seems to have remained primary. This was the burden of al-Ghazzâli's critique of the *mutakallimûn*: they were "largely unable to distinguish between skill in disputation and true knowledge and insight" (Frank 1994a:15). Furthermore, their disputation had the effect of making them more partisan. They were more concerned for the doctrines of their own schools than for the truth that might be reached by genuine intellectual enquiry.

To use Frank Clooney's terminology from elsewhere in this volume, *kalâm* began with a "performative" rather than an "intellectualist" agenda. The initial focus on faith and membership of the community, then on the ethical implications of a belief in the justice of God, were clearly performative. Yet somehow in the course of its development the only performance that came to matter was in the dialectic of argumentation. Speculative theology lost its performative focus without at the same time attaining to the broad openness of rational enquiry that would characterize an "intellectualist" scholasticism. There is probably only one figure in Islamic intellectual history who achieved the kind of intellectual rigor in theology—al-Ghazzâlî. However, he was not merely concerned for his intellectual system, but combined the rigor of his thought with a concern for the piety and faith of the enquirer that would characterize what Clooney calls performative scholasticism.

Paul Griffiths' insight into reading as the root metaphor of scholasticism, explored later in this volume, provides a useful paradigm for understanding the struggles between the *kalâm* theologians and the Traditionists. We could say that the Traditionist's main objection to *kalâm* theology is that it went beyond the paradigmatic "reading" of true scholasticism and by its interpretations had effectively begun rewriting the sacred text. This was the charge of *ta'ṭîl*, that the *ahl al-kalâm* were depriving God of what was rightfully his by interpreting Qur'anic terms such as God's face and hands as meaning God's presence and power or bounty. In return the *mutakallimûn* might well have answered that reading scripture without being able to ask 'how?' (*bilâ kayfa*) is in effect really no reading at all.

It seems that the *mutakallimûn* challenge the definition of 'scholastic' within the current project. One should then ask, perhaps, whether the definition, as formulated by Cabezón and amplified by the insights of Clooney and Griffiths, needs to be amended in order to admit a group so often identified as Islam's scholastics. The reply to this will depend upon how one sees the task of such comparative studies. If a comparative project is to have any usefulness at all, it must be able to draw some clear lines and distinctions, so it cannot just admit any group that has at some time been given the title—dolphins do not belong in a comparative study of fish just because a cursory glance would suggest that they do. At the same time, it cannot set its margins too narrowly, since the value of comparisons is in making clear the uniqueness of each phenomenon studied. Those who have applied the title *scholastic* to the Mu'tazilites and other *mutakallimûn* have often done so at least partly because they have wanted to see in this movement a rationality akin to their own.[23] In their desire hold up what they see as a rational systematic approach to religion against a tradition-bound legalism they have, perhaps, glossed over the often very narrow aims of the *mutakallimûn* more concerned with victory than with truth. The case of the *mutakallimûn* shows the value of the comparative project precisely because they show up the edges of the category, moving back and forth across them in the work of various thinkers and in different periods.

Juridical Theology as Scholasticism

Although it is the speculative theologians who are usually given the title of *scholastic*, the jurisconsults of the schools of law have perhaps a stronger claim to the appellation. As already noted, George Makdisi argues that they deserve the title not merely because they were associated with schools, but because it was within these schools that they developed the characteristic methodology and approach that was later taken up by those who are usually thought of as the original scholastics: Europe's medieval doctors in the schools of theology (1990a, 1990b, 1989, 1981, 1974).

Let us now examine briefly the emergence of Islam's classical jurisconsults and the characteristics of their method and organization. We may then ask whether they might qualify for the title under our comparative definition and also whether their case might suggest some useful refinements of that definition.

The balance in the continuing struggle between the Traditionists and the rationalists in Islam began to shift definitively in the latter half of the ninth century. We have already identified one of the causes of this to have been a certain disillusionment with rationalist speculation in theology, but much more decisive was that the Traditionist group established a power base of its own, such as the Muʿtazilites had enjoyed as the official theologians of the ʿAbbâsid regime. Although he had already died before the Muʿtazilites reached the height of their power, al-Shâfiʿî provided the theoretical basis for the juridical theology that was to supplant that extreme rationalism. From the time of Ibn Ḥanbal, personal schools of law began to emerge from and eventually replace the geographical affiliations that originally had grown out of regional variations in pre-Islamic customary law. The so-called school of law (*madhhab*) is a "school" in the sense of a school of thought; it is not a college of law (*madrasa*). However, in the tenth century it became common to endow a mosque (*masjid*) with a chair of law and perhaps an inn to house the students. There also emerged specially endowed colleges (*madrasas*) that, according to the law of *awqâf* (charitable endowments), could be controlled by the donor and his descendants in perpetuity. This allowed particular schools of legal thought to maintain their hold in individual institutions (Makdisi 1981, passim).

Through these perpetually endowed institutions with their highly developed curricula, a somewhat moderated Traditionism was able to establish a guild structure that gave it a lasting ascendancy in Islam. Indeed it was the purpose of these guilds to place exclusively in the hands of the jurisconsults the machinery for determining orthodoxy and orthopraxy in Islam (Makdisi 1989: 176). Although the colleges originally were seen as bulwarks against rationalism, it was virtually inevitable that the latter should have found a way into the thought of the schools, even if not always formally into the curriculum of the colleges. In the colleges, one was defined not by one's theology but principally by one's affiliation with a particular legal tradition (*madhhab*), so it was difficult for traditionally inclusive Sunni Islam to exclude the rationalists entirely, for they participated primarily as students and teachers of law, not of theology. (Makdisi 1990a: 39–43) Still al-Ghazzâlî could find much to criticize in the way the dialectical style of *kalâm* and its lack of concern for real knowledge continued to affect the colleges of law (Frank 1994a, passim).

Law as developed and practiced in the colleges succeeded in occupying a position between the extremes of Muʿtazilite rationalism and Traditionist literalism. It rejected the disputatious wordplay and logic chopping of the *mutakallimûn* as well as the literalist fideism of their opponents. In this way it placed itself more in the center of the range of phenomena to which we give the title *scholasticism*. In his enquiry into the origins of European scholasticism, George Makdisi introduces us to the fascinating figure of Ibn ʿAqîl, a late eleventh-century jurisconsult in whose work we find all the characteristic features of European scholasticism already in full bloom—the *sic et non* method (*al-khilâf* in Arabic), dialectic (*jadal*) and the disputation (*munâẓara*) as distinct from the lecture (*qirâ'a*) (1963; 1967; 1974: 648ff.). Ibn ʿAqîl makes it clear that he has combined consciously the rationality he learned from Muʿtazilites with respect for revelation characteristic of the Traditionists. However, neither group is spared his criticism for failing to strike the balance between these two factors (Makdisi 1974: 654–55).

Following al-Shâfiʿî's *uṣûl al-fiqh* (legal theory), law recognized the ultimate authority of scripture (again, Qur'ân and Traditions), yet reason had to be brought to bear to develop the hermeneutical principles by which such a large textual corpus was to be dealt with, and also to deal with situations not addressed. The extent to which rational concerns had become part of the stock-in-trade of Islamic legal theory (*uṣûl al-fiqh*) can be seen from a list of problems treated under this heading two centuries after al-Shâfiʿî: (1) the problem of the determination of good and evil (*al-taḥsîn wa-l-taqbîḥ*); (2) the relation between reason and revealed law (*al-ʿaql wa-l-sharʿ*); (3) the qualifications of acts before the advent of revelation (*ḥukm al-afʿâl qabla wurrûd al-sharʿ*); (4) prohibition and permission (*al-ḥaẓr wa-l-ibâḥa*); (5) the imposition of responsibility or obligation beyond one's capacity (*taklîf mâ lâ yuṭâq*); (6) the imposition of legal obligation on those who do not yet exist (*mas'alat al-maʿdûm*) (Makdisi 1990a: 4).

If the jurists were less rationalist than the *mutakallimûn*, they were not less rational. They saw no point to the word games or even the more advanced theological edifices of *kalâm*, since their juridical theology was in Frank Clooney's terms "performative" rather than "intellectualist." It was profoundly oriented toward practice and could recognize that there is a limit to enquiry, one imposed not by external authority but rather by the limits of the need to know. The need to know in turn was determined by the need to act and to interact. They were, to amend Cabezón's phrase, ever ready to answer a questioner's "what if?" With its extensive period (ten to twenty years) of professional training, Islamic law was, of course, strongly grounded in a tradition. Yet the whole edifice rested not only on the right but, indeed, on the duty of the jurisconsult to profess his own considered opinion rather than to follow the teaching of another: no religious or political authority could press him to give a particular response.

Scholasticism and the Determination of Orthodoxy by Consensus

If Islam's juridical theology indeed does qualify as scholasticism, perhaps its case might suggest some refinement of the working definition of this comparative category. The most important feature that Makdisi sees in the development of scholasticism in the schools of Islamic law is the method it evolved for determining orthodoxy. The guild schools' most lasting contribution both to Islam and to the West was the concept of the licence to teach and to profess one's personal opinions—the doctorate. Added to this was the notion of the consensus of the doctors as the standard of orthodoxy. This has determined right up until the present the understanding of authority and "orthodoxy" in the Western academic setting (Makdisi 1989: 176–77).

In the setting of the guild, the process began with a question put by a layman (*mustaftî*—seeker of a *fatwâ* or legal opinion) to a qualified jurisconsult (*muftî*). The *muftî* then would engage in *ijtihâd*—literally "exertion of effort." He would study the question, think of various ways of reformulating it, research the scriptural sources, and consider traditional responses. The layman was under no obligation to accept the opinion offered by the *muftî* and could ask any number of other jurists the same question. He was free to recognize as authoritative (*taqlîd*) any of the opinions he was given; the jurist on the other hand was not free to invest any other jurist's opinion with such authority. To be authoritative, he had to practice original scholarship. An act on the part of the layman that followed the opinion of one or another recognized jurisconsult was considered a lawful act for him personally. Orthopraxy on a broader scale was judged by the unanimous consensus of the professors on a particular point of law. The only way such a consensus could be known to exist was if there were no known authoritative dissent. This explains the importance in Islamic law of *khilâf* works, compilations of the dissenting opinions that rendered a question still open to the legal scholar's attempt to develop his own considered opinion—the process of *ijtihâd*.[24]

I propose that something of this guild-school aspect of scholasticism needs to be incorporated into our working definition. Scholasticism has at its very heart a commitment to professional competence in the field of study, and therefore it must develop a method of determining that competence. Since, as Cabezón points out, it is of its nature "proliferative," then in order for it to retain its cohesion it needs a mechanism of consensus for determining orthodoxy and so marking the boundaries of its inclusiveness.

Scholasticism's licence to teach and profess personal opinion along with its faculty of determining orthodoxy, although natural to the Islamic environment, is an anomalous element in the Christian West, since Christianity already has a magisterium, the episcopal college, which determines orthodoxy (Makdisi 1990b). The problem of a parallel magisterium of the professionally trained theologians has yet to be resolved in Christianity. This is a further reason why we should consider the teaching and defining function as part of the heart of scholasticism: it has remained inseparable from the other facets of the phenomenon even in a situation where it fits only awkwardly and where its presence is a threat to powerful interests. This should be taken as an indication of the organic unity of the scholastic method as it emerged in Islam and the West, and we should be alert for the manifestations of this important aspect when examining other scholastic discourses.

Conclusion

What I hope has been demonstrated in these pages is that, while the ascription of the title *scholasticism* to the rationalist theology of the *kalâm,* and especially to that of the Muʿtazilites, seems on the face of things unexceptionable, on reflection it is seen to be somewhat hasty and open to debate. This group cannot lay claim to a firm position in the center of the scholastic "field." Though *kalâm* began with reflection on urgent questions of community, politics, and morality, it gradually lost this performative focus. Yet it did not then develop into a fully intellectualist system either: its characteristic dialectical method was too tightly and artificially controlled to allow reason its full latitude. Furthermore, it was devoted to the *argumentum ad hominem* and showed more concern for a clever victory over a straw opponent than for the ascertainment of the fullest truth on any issue.

Still, we also have seen that some aspects of the work of the *mutakallimûn* place them within the scholastic fold. They move back and forth, as it were, across the margins of our category and thus help to delimit it. The fact that we are forced to situate this group at the edges can be taken as an indication of the prima facie validity of the analytical schema offered by José Cabezón for understanding scholasticism in different cultural and religious contexts. This is merely the familiar principle of falsifiability: if no rationalist theologians were able to be excluded from the category as Cabezón articulates it, then his definition might have proven a very blunt instrument indeed.

Following the extensive work of George Makdisi on scholasticism, we have identified another group that does seem to qualify for title: the juridical theologians of the legal *madhâhib* of Sunni Islam. We include them in the group for two reasons. Looked at historically it appears that the Muslim jurisconsult rather than the medieval school-man is in fact the paradigm case of the "scholastic." Considered even in isolation from that historical development, epistemology and methodology of the jurisconsults clearly place them in the company of those other groups identified in this project as scholastic. In joining that group, they bring their own refinement to its definition: they alert us to the importance of the role played in scholasticism by teaching and by the defining of orthodoxy (or orthopraxy) on the basis of a consensus of the professionals.

Notes

1. The terminology was not reserved for this group, however, and was used widely in translations from Greek philosophers to render terms that used the root *log-*: e.g. *physiologoi* (physicists) is translated into Arabic as *al-mutakallimûn fî al-ṭabî'iyyât*. Cf. Wolfson 1976: 1–2.

2. J. van Ess (1970:24) claims that the term *kalâm* "indubitably is derived from the Greek διαλεξις used by the Church Fathers."

3. Traditions are classified according to the reliability of their chain of transmission (*isnâd*): they may be *saḥîḥ* (sound), *ḥasan* (good) or *ḍa'îf* (weak). For a brief outline of the method of classification, see Juynboll (1953). The exegetical processes used by the jurists in dealing with *ḥadîth* are examined by Robert Brunschvig (1970: 14–16).

4. The original Khawârij defected from the army of 'Alî b. Abî Ṭâlib (fourth caliph) because he agreed to enter into arbitration with Mu'âwiya, leader of the rebel army that was opposing 'Alî's elevation to the caliphate in 656–57 after the murder of 'Uthmân; Mu'âwiya emerged from the arbitration as the new caliph (reigned 661–680). It was opposition to the perceived irreligiousness of this new dynasty (the Umayyads) that sustained the Kharijite sects. However, once the Caliphate had passed to the 'Abbâsids, who ruled from 750 through 945, the movement virtually died out.

5. For a discussion of the sources available for the study of this issue, see Watt (1948: 3–10).

6. This was edited by Helmut Ritter (1933). J. van Ess (1975:89 and n. 7) see it as validly dated and attributed to al-Ḥasan. However, this view has been disputed (for his own unique purposes) by John Wansbrough (1977: 161–63), and on separate grounds by M. A. Cook (1980: n. 5).

7. Translated from the edition of Ritter (1933: 70, lines 6–14).

8. See also van Ess (1976: 23–60).

9. See for example C. H. Becker (1912: 190ff.) and more recently van Ess (1977: 24; 1970: 24; and 1976 passim).

10. Griffith (1922) also has maintained that the *kalâm* style and practice owes more to the customs of the Syriac academies in Mesopotamia and Iraq than to the conventions of Greek theological writing.

11. See, for example, Nyberg (1953) and Brockelmann (1937–1949: 1, 206–7) who, however, points out that they have wrongly been considered the "freethinkers" or "liberals" of Islam.

12. They separated themselves from ʿAlî and refused either to fight for him or against him. (Nyberg 1953: 422–23).

13. Three summaries of agreed Muʿtazilite positions are given in an appendix to Seale (1964: 126–29). See also Brockelmann (1937–1949: Suppl. 1, 338β).

14. Van Ess (1976: 51) sees in this aspect of Muʿtazilite doctrine an echo of an early commitment on their part to missionary activity.

15. *Maqâlât al-Islâmiyîn*, quoted by Wensinck (1932: 75–76). This tortuous use of negations and double-negatives was intended to deal with the problem of the attributes of God. If God was creator, did this attribute begin with the act of creation or not? If so, then there must have been a time when He was not-a-creator; so when He began creating, God ceased to be not a creator. But God's ceasing to be anything posed a problem, because of the importance of eternity as the essence of the divine; the only attribute of God that they considered eternal was eternity itself. Richard Frank (1994b; 1968:296 n. 2) has pointed out that the awkward but unavoidable Arabic *lam yazal* (he has not ceased to be) would be better translated, with more awareness of its nature as a technical term, as 'he is eternally.'

16. The *Waṣîyat Abî Ḥanîfa* in Wensinck (1932:127). This creed claims to be the deathbed theological testament of the famous jurist Abû Ḥanîfa (d. 767) but Wensinck argues (186–87) for a later dating.

17. For the letter of the caliph instituting the Inquisition and outlining the dangers of the Traditionist position, see W. M. Patton (1897: 66–76).

18. A more detailed description of Muʿtazila positions and approaches is given in Gardet and Anawati (1948).

19. D. Gimaret (1965: 783–93) identifies its classical period as lasting till the mideleventh century C.E. and surviving among various Shîʿî groups. It even has modern revivals: see, for example, R. Caspar (1957).

20. *Iḥyâ' Ulûm al-Dîn,* book 2, quoted in Wensinck (1932: 100–101).

21. This characteristic style van Ess (1970:24) attributes to the peculiar situation of the origins of *kalâm* in which "there was no time for silent reflection about eternal truth; unequipped with systematic consistency, the *mutakallimûn* had to join the battle against Jewish, Christian, and Manichean intellectual skill." This is a less than convincing excuse, since many of the Muslims from the period of study were converts from those religions and often as well equipped as their former co-religionists. Furthermore, it is in the internal disputes of Islam that we find the bulk of *mutakallim* activity. As we have seen, those internal disputes were, initially at least, issues of ethics, politics, and community, where a great deal more hung in the balance than merely complacent advantage in an argument.

22. This is a quite critical review of Allard (1965).

23. Friedrich Niewöhner (1974: passim) has documented the manner in which European writers have re-created the *kalâm* theologians in their own image, seeing them as liberals, free-thinkers, and Enlightenment rationalists.

24. The parallel between this and the Western academy is clear. The professor, once having passed his doctorate, is free to profess his opinions, as is the student free to enquire and to make his own judgement on what he is being taught. Within his own discipline, the professor is not free merely to depend on the authority of another, and even less to copy the opinion of another; one may concur with another authority, but only on the basis of one's own research and judgment. "Orthodoxy" only emerges when something is debated over the years and no authoritative dissent is registered (Makdisi 1974: 649).

References

Allard, Michel.
1965 *Le Problème des attributs divins dans la doctrine d'al-Ash'arî et de ses premiers grands disciples*. Beirut: Imprimerie Catholique.

Arnaldez, R.
1965 "Falsafa." *Encyclopedia of Islam*. 2nd ed. 2: 769–75. Leiden: E. J. Brill.

Al-Ash'arî, Abu al-Ḥason 'Alî b. Isma'îl.
1979 *Maqâlât al-islâmiyîn wa-khtilâf al-muṣallîn*. Edited by 'Abd al-Hamîd. Al-Qâhirah: Maktabat al-Nahḍat al-Miṣriyya.

Becker, C. H.
1912 "Christliche Polemik und islamische Dogmenbildung." *Zeitschrift für Assyriologie und verwandte Gebiete* 26: 190ff.

Brockelmann, Carl.

1937–1949 *Geschichte der arabischen litteratur*. 2nd edition. 2 vols with 3 supplementary vols to the 1st ed. (1897–1908). Leiden: E. J. Brill.

Brunschvig, Robert.

1970 "Logic and Law in Classical Islam." In G. E. von Grunebaum, *Logic in Classical Islamic Culture*, 9–20. Wiesbaden: Otto Harrassowitz.

Cabezón, José Ignacio.

1994 *Buddhism and Language: A Study of Indo-Tibetan Scholasticism*. Albany: State University of New York Press.

Caspar, Robert.

1957 "Le Renouveau du Moʿtazilisme." *Mélanges de l'Institut Dominicain des Études Orientales*.

Cook, Michael A.

1980 "The Origins of Kalam." *Bulletin of the School of Oriental and African Studies* 43: 32–43.

Ess, Josef van.

1977 *Anfänge muslimischer Theologie: zwei antiqadaritische Traktate aus dem ersten Jahrhundert der Higra*. Beirut: Orient-Institut.

1976 "Disputationspraxis in der islamischen Theologie: eine vorlaüfige Skizze." *Revue des Études islamiques* 44:23–60.

1975 "The Beginnings of Islamic Theology." In *The Cultural Context of Medieval Learning*, 87–111. Ed. J. E. Murdoch and E. D. Sylla. Dordrecht and Boston: D. Reidel Publishing Co.

1970 "The Logical Structure of Islamic Theology." In *Logic in Classical Islamic Culture*, 21–50. Ed. G. E. von Grunebaum. Wiesbaden: Otto Harrassowitz, 21-50.

Frank, Richard M.

1994a *Al-Ghazâlî and the Ashʿarite School*. Duke Monographs in Medieval and Renaissance Studies 15. Durham, N.C. and London: Duke University Press.

1994b " '*Lam Yazal*' as a Formal Term in Muslim Theological Discourse." *MIDEO* 22: 243–70.

1989 "Knowledge and *Taqlîd*: The Foundations of Religious Belief in Classical Ashʿarism." *Journal of the American Oriental Society* 109: 37–62.

1968 "The *Kalâm*: An Art of Contradiction-Making or Theological Science? Some Remarks on the Question." *Journal of the American Oriental Society* 88: 295–309.

Gardet, Louis.
1965 "ʿIlm al-Kalâm." *Encyclopedia of Islam*. 2nd edition. 3:1141–50. Leiden: E. J. Brill.

Gardet, Louis and Georges Anawati.
1948 *Introduction à la Theologie Musulmane*. Paris: Librairie Philosophique J. Vrin.

Gimaret D.
1965 "al-Muʿtazila" *Encyclopedia of Islam*. 2nd ed. 7: 783–93. Leiden: E. J. Brill.

Griffith, Sidney J.
1992 "The Prophet Muḥammad, His Scripture and His Message, According to the Christian Apologies in Arabic and Syriac from the First Abbasid Century." *La Vie du Prophète Mahomet: Colloque de Strasbourg, 1980* (publ. 1983), 99–146. Reprinted Sidney J. Griffith, *Arabic Christianity in the Monasteries of Ninth Century Palestine*. London: Variorum Reprints, 1992.

Ibn Ḥanbal, Aḥmad.
1393 A.H. *al-Radd ʿalà al-Zanâdiqa wa-l-Jahmiyya*. Al-Qâhira: al-Maṭbaʿat al-Salafiyya.

Juynboll, Th. W.
1953 "Ḥadîth." *Shorter Encyclopedia of Islam*, 116–21. Leiden: E. J. Brill.

Makdisi, George.
1990a *The Rise of Humanism in Classical Islam and the Christian West*. Edinburgh: Edinburgh University Press.

1990b "Magisterium and Academic Freedom in Classical Islam and Medieval Christianity." In *Islamic Law and Jurisprudence: Studies in Honor of Farhat J. Ziadeh*, 117–34. Ed. Nicholas Heer. Seattle and London: University of Washington Press.

1989 "Scholasticism and Humanism in Classical Islam and the Christian West." *Journal of the American Oriental Society* 109: 175–82.

1981 *The Rise of the Colleges: Institutions of Learning in Islam and the West*. Edinburgh: Edinburgh University Press.

1974 "The Scholastic Method in Medieval Education: An Inquiry into Its Origins in Law and Theology." *Speculum* 49: 640–61.

1967 "Le Livre de la Dialectique d'Ibn ʿAqîl." *Bulletin d'Études Orientales* 20: 119–206.

1963 *Ibn ʿAqîl et la résurgence de l'Islam traditionaliste au XIe siècle.* Damascus: Institut Français de Damas.

Niewöhner, Friedrich.
1974 "Die Diskussion um den Kalâm und die Mutakallimûn in der Europäischen Philosophergeschichtsschreibung." *Archiv für Begriffsgeschichte* 18: 7–34.

Nyberg, H. S.
1953 "Al-Muʿtazila." *Shorter Encyclopedia of Islam.* Leiden: E. J. Brill.

Patton, W. M.
1897 *Aḥmad Ibn Ḥanbal and the Miḥna.* Leiden: E. J. Brill.

Ritter, Helmut.
1933 "Studien zur islamischen Frömmigkeit I: Ḥasan al-Baṣrî." *Der Islam* 21: 1–83.

Seale, Morris S.
1964 *Muslim Theology: A Study of Origins with Reference to the Church Fathers.* London: Luzac & Co.

al-Shahrastânî, Muḥammad b. ʿAbd al-Karîm.
1923 *Kitâb al-Milal wa-l-Niḥal.* Ed. W. Cureton. Leipzig: Otto Harrassowitz.

Wansbrough, John.
1977 *Qur'anic Studies: Sources and Methods of Scriptural Interpretation.* Oxford: Oxford University Press.

Watt, W. Montgomery.
1948 *Free Will and Predestination in Early Islam.* London: Luzac & Co.

Wensinck, Arent J.
1932 *The Muslim Creed: Its Genesis and Historical Development.* Cambridge: Cambridge University Press.

Wolfson, Harry Austryn.
1976 *The Philosophy of the Kalam.* Cambridge: Harvard University Press.

Chapter **3**

The First Meeting of Catholic Scholasticism with dGe lugs pa Scholasticism

Robert E. Goss

The neo-scholastic revival of Catholic scholasticism in the nineteenth and twentieth centuries by philosophers such as M. De Wulf allowed for the possibility of scholasticism as a social phenomenon existing in other religious traditions (1953: 57, 73). If method becomes the sole constituent structure for identifying a particular discourse or pedagogy as scholastic, then scholastic discourse can be considered to exist in a variety of cross-cultural settings and in a wide range of disciplines such as jurisprudence, philosophy, literary criticism, and theology.

De Wulf insists, however, that scholasticism can be comprehended only by its methodological features together with its particular doctrines. He restricts scholasticism to a specific set of methods and doctrines identified with particular religious systems (1953:19–144). De Wulf's adamant refusal to isolate methodological features from doctrine in his definition of scholasticism emerges from his own Catholic scholastic paradigm, including specific dialectical and systematic exigencies in the service of faith. He is correct to consider aspects of method and doctrine as definitional features of scholasticism, but his restricting definition to theistic doctrine while recognizing Jewish, Islamic, or Hindu intellectual movements as scholastic yet excludes the nontheistic Buddhist doctrinal system as scholastic.[1] While I agree with the general direction of De Wulf's definition of scholasticism as including specific methodological and doctrinal features, I disagree with his move to restrict the doctrinal content to theistic questions that emerge from Catholic scholasticism.

Recently, Panikkar, Adshead, Cabezón, and others have given serious consideration in identifying particular features of intellectual movements within the major world religious traditions that might be heuristically useful in characterizing these as scholastic. Adshead compared Buddhism to transcendental Thomism while Cabezón has made a strong case for applying scholasticism as a cross-cultural category to Indo-Tibetan philosophical tradition. This chapter explores the particular encounter of Catholic second scholasticism as it briefly engaged Tibetan dGe lugs pa scholasticism in the work of the early eighteenth-century Jesuit priest, Ippolito Desideri (1684–1734). Desideri, residing in Tibet from 1716 to 1721, studied Buddhist scholasticism in its Tibetan dGe lugs pa formulation and engaged it from his own Catholic scholastic point of view. Desideri recognized a resemblance of the Tibetan scholastic method to his own scholastic training and attempted to bring dGe lugs pa scholastics to an awareness of his own doctrinal tenets by a Jesuit pedagogy rooted in a revitalized Catholic scholasticism. Desideri acknowledged some foundational resemblances of Catholic and dGe lugs pa scholasticism on the levels of method and doctrine, though the two traditions diverge on the question of a creator God. For the Jesuit missionary, these resemblances in method and doctrine form a preamble for engaging in a scholastic disputation and a full exposition of Catholic faith. This first historical, albeit brief, encounter between the Catholic and dGe lugs pa scholastic traditions illustrates the limits of De Wulf's definition and points to the need for a revision of his particular understanding to include the case of Buddhist scholasticism.

First this chapter will examine Catholic medieval scholasticism as an investigative pedagogy and its apologetical engagement with other religious traditions. Then it will turn to second scholasticism and the Jesuit contribution to scholastic pedagogy, positioning us to assess Desideri's apologetic interaction with dGe lugs pa scholasticism.

Catholic Medieval Scholasticism: An Investigative Pedagogy

Bernard Lonergan, a twentieth-century, neo-scholastic Catholic philosopher and theologian, defines scholasticism as a "thoroughgoing effort to attain a coherent and orderly assimilation of Christian theology" (1974:309). Catholic scholasticism, a monumental achievement of the European Middle Ages, sought to reconcile the elements of faith and reason in a coherent intellectual system. As an intellectual movement, it is divided into three major developmental periods: medieval scholasticism (1050–1500), second or baroque scholasticism (1500–1830), and neo-scholasticism (1830–present). Medieval scholasticism created a conceptual system, giving coherent answers to all the possible questions concerning the textual traditions of Christianity and the ancient world. Scholasticism widened the authority (*auctoritas*) of Scripture and patristic teaching to include reason (*ratio*). Reason became authoritative because of its epistemological function in analyzing the content of faith and demonstrating its meaningfulness. The role of reason was extended to all philosophical and doctrinal questions and allowed for analytical and systematic thoroughness.

J. A. Weisheipl (1967:1145–46) describes the Catholic scholastic method as "essentially a rational investigation of every relevant problem in the liberal arts, philosophy, theology, medieval law examined from opposing points of view, in order to reach an intelligent, scientific scholastic solution that would be consistent with accepted authorities, known facts, human reason, and Christian faith." The scholastic method employed a particular form of reading (*lectio*) of Scripture and classical Christian texts. It differed from monastic theology in its use of logic in reading strategies of the Scriptures and classical Christian texts and by introducing new pedagogical methods for learning and research. Monastic reading of the Scriptures (*lectio divina*) was oriented toward meditation (*meditatio*) and prayer (*oratio*), while the scholastic reading of Christian texts culminated in scientific knowledge (*scientia*) (Leclercq, 1960:89). Monastic reading united an imaginative reading of the Scriptures with meditative prayer, and its objective was wisdom and appreciation (Leclercq, 1960:91ff.). Monastic reading was a contemplative activity centered directly on God (Vallet 1988). The scholastic strategy of reading differed in that it attempted to grasp the text rationally, to interrogate it, and to determine the exact meaning of the word of God.

Scholastic reading developed the oral form of question (*quaestio*) and disputation (*disputatio*), forming a pedagogical strategy for investigation and learning.[2] The scholastic method introduced questions to interrogate a particular text, to surface and to define clearly the problems obscuring understanding of that text. Study and interpretation maintained a dialectical form of question, provisional answer, objection, and final definition. This pedagogical strategy created "active methods, mindful to keep open, even under the dead-weight of school work, the curiosity of both the student and the master" (Chenu 1964:96).

This rigorous structure of questioning, answering, and objecting (*sic et non*) did not restrict the creativity of research but forced the scholastic to clarify those questions otherwise remaining hidden and unanswered, generating new approaches to solving the problem of understanding. The teacher (*magister*), or regent master in theology, would organize questions into a set of propositions for consideration and disputation: "From this starting point, the pro and con are brought into play, not with the intention of finding an immediate answer, but in order that under the action of dubitatio, research be pushed to the limit. A satisfactory explanation will be given only on the condition that one continue the search to the discovery of what caused the doubt" (Chenu 1964:94).

All arguments or points of view were examined in the disputation. The teacher resolved the doubts of the conflicting interpretations, authorities, or opinions. His resolution of conflicting interpretations presented in the disputation of the question were aimed at dispelling doubt and establishing certitude. The regent master in theology applied the certitude established by the lectio and disputatio to preaching (*praedicatio*) (Weisheipl 1967:1145). The communicative dimensions of this scholastic pedagogical strategy had a wider application than education in the university classroom. Catholic scholastics went beyond the difficulties of the text to understand the basic problems of the Christian life of faith. They investigated the meaning of the text and the meaning of Christian life by constructing a rational system of sacred doctrine. Their pedagogy had pastoral applications in establishing, constituting, and communicating the certitude of the Christian message through preaching and catechesis.

The questions and disputations detached themselves from the texts and were compiled into written collections. Monastic theology's expository technique of interlinear glosses on Scripture or classical Christian texts gave rise to the new literary genres of interlinear glosses of questions and objections in Catholic scholasticism. The glosses, interlinear questions, and comments were collated into sentences (*sententia*), or resumes, of diverse opinions on texts under interrogation and dispute. Collections of sentences were expanded into systematic commentaries, and commentaries evolved into the more comprehensive systems of the *summas* with their articles (See Roy in this volume). The minutely questioned, disputed, and defined questions, objections, and answers were organized into an orderly system. From these dialectical and systematic methods, the comprehensive systems of sacred doctrine were constructed.

The Protestant reformation and the humanism of the Renaissance precipitated a transformational shift from medieval scholasticism into second scholasticism. In turn, the Enlightenment, eighteenth- and nineteenth-century philosophical, scientific, and historical discourse challenged the metaphysical coherence of scholastic philosophy and theology. However, scholastic theology continued to provide the intellectual framework of Roman Catholic pontifical documents and conciliar decrees until Vatican II. For neo-scholastics such as Lonergan, scholasticism has been largely abandoned because of the inadequacy of medieval aims: "The Scholastic aim of reconciling all the elements in the Christian inheritance had one grave defect. It was content with a logically and metaphysically satisfying reconciliation. It did not realize how much of the multiplicity in the inheritance constituted not a logical or metaphysical problem but basically a historical problem (Lonergan, 1972:279–80).

Catholic Scholasticism and Apologetics: Dialogue with Other Religions

Medieval scholasticism considered unbelievers or non-Christians from the view point of the intellectual difficulties that they possessed concerning the truths of Christianity. Scholastic theologians applied scholastic philosophy with its problem-solving methods to confrontation and conversion of nonbelievers. Reason in scholastic philosophy demonstrated and validated the evidence of Christian revelation, but it also was extended to the defense of Christian faith against rival religious systems. Scholastic apologetics employed its philosophical method to search for a foothold of faith within non-Christian religious traditions so as to engage them in dialogue.

The basic structure of the dialogue took the form of the written text in which two or more persons engaged in rational argument. These apologetical texts were intended to establish a rational basis for communication between traditions and to enable opponents to learn about Christian doctrine and its superiority. From the scholastic perspective, apologetics created a rational language establishing the antecedences of faith in regard to issues such as the existence of God, the meaning of life, and morality. Reason established the truth of a proposition, and a proposition was demonstrated to be true only if it expressed the conclusion of a valid reasoning process, all of whose premises previously had been established as true. The Catholic apologist created a rational medium of communication in which the antecedences of faith could be uncovered rationally and from which the apologist could lead the dialogue partner through reasonable arguments to the truth of the revelation of the Triune God of faith.

For example, Thomas Aquinas understood that the purpose of dialogue with other religious traditions was to manifest the truth and refute the error of others (*Summa Theologiae*: 2.2, q.10, a. 6–10). Dialogue consisted for Aquinas and other medieval Catholic scholastics of an apologetical engagement with another tradition. It utilized a comparative method, first defining and refining the categories under consideration, and then demonstrating the relative superiority of one over the other. As an active disputation, dialogue was intended to establish a preamble to faith (*praeambula fidei*) and to demonstrate the superiority of Christian doctrine against rival religious traditions. Such public discourse with nonbelievers was not meant for the less educated Christian. Only those Christians with a strong foundation in the doctrine and who were well instructed in faith and scholastic reasoning could enter into dialogue with nonbelievers.

Aquinas' *Summa contra Gentiles,* written for missionaries confronting Islam in Spain, began with Aristotelian philosophical principles which he knew his opponents would acknowledge. He recognized that Gentile or Muslim philosophers did not accept the authority of the Christian Scriptures and that he had to establish mutually acknowledged principles prior to answering their objections to the content of Christian faith. The medium for dialogue between religions had to be natural reason, to which all rational persons are forced to give their intellectual assent. Aquinas indicates the first principle of natural reason, the wise man's task of ordering things rightly and governing them well. The wise man sees everything in light of the first principles from which all realities derive (*Summa contra Gentiles lib.* 1, c.2). The wise man can know about the existence of a personal God but cannot know more of God's internal life unless there is a revelation. Aquinas states his apologetic intention of showing what errors are excluded and how rationally demonstrable truth is in agreement with the principles of Christian religion (*Summa contra Gentile*s lib.: 1, c. 2).

There was limited dialogue between medieval scholastics and Muslims, Jews, Hindus, and other non-Christian traditions (Horvath, 1990). Scholastic writings about other religious traditions, mainly Islam and Judaism, were unquestionably polemical, and their objective was the refutation of their particular doctrinal errors and the acknowledgment of Christian revelation as unique and superior. Little fruit came from such attempts at dialogue in Spain when the Inquisition forced a monologue of Christian truth.

In the seventeenth and eighteenth centuries, the influence of non-Christian religions was progressively felt as a result of increased contact between Europe and Asia. Some Catholic missionaries—especially the Jesuit missionaries of the seventeenth and eighteenth centuries in Asia and the Americas—became sensitive to the questionings and reasonings of non-Christian believers. The Jesuits became open to the difficulties that nonbelievers faced when confronted with Christian doctrine and realized that there was a need to create a preamble to faith, a common language to rationally engage their dialogue partners on the question of the nature of God. One of these Jesuit missionaries was Ippolito Desideri, S.J., who traveled to Lhasa, the capital of Tibet, and engaged dGe lugs pa scholasticism.

Second Scholasticism: The Jesuits and the Ratio Studiorum

The sixteenth century witnessed Catholic attempts to revive and reinvigorate earlier medieval scholasticism. Several religious orders—the Benedictines, Dominicans, Franciscans, and the Jesuits—revived medieval scholastic philosophy and theology, creating an intellectual movement often labeled as "baroque" or "second" scholasticism (1530–1830). The focus of this chapter, however, will be on Jesuit scholasticism since it provides the background and the heuristic framework for Desideri's encounter with dGe lugs pa scholasticism in the early eighteenth century.

Ignatius of Loyola (1491–1556) fused the pedagogy of medieval Catholic scholasticism with his own spirituality manifested in the Spiritual Exercises and the Constitutions. He mandated that logic, natural and moral philosophy, metaphysics, and scholastic and positive theology be part of the curriculum of studies for Jesuit scholastics (Ignatius of Loyola 1970:188).[3] He prescribed St. Thomas' *Summa Theologiae* rather than Peter Lombard's *Sentences* as the basis for lectures in theology at the Roman College, a college established for the philosophical and theological education of Jesuits. Ignatius clearly set the direction for contemporary and future Jesuits in devoting themselves to the revival of medieval scholasticism. The fourth part of his *Constitutions of the Society of Jesus* is devoted to the subject of education of Jesuits in seminaries, colleges, and universities. Ignatius spells out his *Ratio Studiorum,* his educational code for Jesuit scholastics and collegiates (Ignatius of Loyola 1970:171–229). Jesuit training would include a rigorous three-year philosophical curriculum covering logic, natural and moral philosophy, metaphysics, rational psychology, and scholastic and positive theology. With a foundation in the study of classical languages, grammar, rhetoric, and Latin and Greek literature, the Jesuit student then pursued scholastic philosophy. Humanist classical studies was propaedeutic to the study of scholastic philosophy.

Jesuit educators employed the scholastic pedagogical method of reading (*lectio*) and disputation (*disputatio*) in training their own scholastics and students. For Ignatius, the *Ratio Studiorum* was a wonderful pedagogy for appropriating Catholic scholasticism. Such a scholastic pedagogy emerged primarily from the love and worship of God, which was the basis for all human learning, culture, and existence. The *Ratio Studiorum* enabled the Jesuit colleges and universities to become the most efficient educational institutions in Europe for the next two and a half centuries. By 1710, 612 Jesuit colleges implemented the *Ratio Studiorum* educational code. Ignatius' pedagogical code led to an explosion of Jesuit scholarship in philosophy, theology, the sciences, geography, ethnology, philology, and the literary arts.[4] In this way, the Jesuits became leaders in education in the sixteenth and seventeenth centuries.

Ignatius' *Ratio Studiorum* also inaugurated and directed the Jesuit revival of Catholic scholasticism. The Jesuit expression of second scholasticism attempted to restore established doctrines and defend them against attack. Leading Jesuit theologians—Robert Bellarmine, Francisco de Toledo, Francis Suarez, Gabriel Vasquez, and Luis de Molina—reinvigorated scholasticism by employing the scholastic method to respond to Protestant reformers and to the study of the natural sciences in which there was renewed interest. Jesuit scholasticism produced several prolific writers, modifying the medieval scholastic method to include the form of theses, proofs, and answers to objections that met contemporary catechetical and apologetic exigencies. Furthermore, Suarez, in fact, wrote ample commentaries on Thomas' *Summa* and treatises on diverse theological topics (Trentman 1982). Suarez pioneered a new style of scholastic manuals that simplified the teaching of medieval scholasticism and incorporated the new sciences. His *Disputationes Metaphysicae* was a systematic treatment of science, not based on Aristotle but upon the latest scientific evidence. It was read both by Catholic and by Protestant scholars. What is apparent in second scholastic texts is a methodological shift from the medieval quaestio to thesis and proof. The openness of the quaestio in Aquinas is replaced by dogmatic theses and proof, and this shift resulted from the challenges of the Reformation and the development of late Renaissance humanism. This apologetic syllogistic method of second scholasticism later would come to influence the developments of the early neoscholastic movement (Schüssler-Fiorenza 1991:29–35).

Robert Bellarmine systematized Catholic doctrine so as to respond to the Protestant reformers. His three-volume work, *Disputationes de Controversis Christianae Fidei adversus huius temporis haereticos*, was a critical work on Reformation theology, pointing out its strengths and weaknesses. Bellarmine's scholasticism lacked the calm speculative scholarship of the apologetic treatises of earlier scholasticism. He wrote two catechisms in Italian, *Dottrina cristiana breve* and *Dichiarazione piu copiosa della dottrina cristiana*. These catechical manuals, practical vehicles for teaching Catholic scholastic doctrine, remained normative for all catechisms until the Vatican I Council in the late nineteenth century. The catechism was the major pedagogical text for introducing Catholics and converts to the doctrines of Catholic Christianity.

By Bellarmine's time, practically all the professors at the Roman College were Spaniards, and the Roman College had been firmly established as a center for a reinvigorated Catholic scholasticism (Weisheipl 1987:118; Volloslada 1954:214–22). It was at the Roman College that Ippolito Desideri received his training in scholastic philosophy and theology. The practical dimensions of Jesuit scholasticism were expressed in implementing Ignatius' educational code, the apologetic defense of Catholic Christianity, the writing of catechisms for teachers and the laity, preaching, administering the Spiritual Exercises as a retreat movement, and missionary activities to the New World and Asia.

J. Gurr outlines the general characteristics of second scholasticism: (1) continuity with the past, (2) orientation of philosophy to the word of God, (3) systematic realism, (4) rational method, (5) adjustment to contemporary science and modern philosophy, (6) concern with ideology, and (7) the characteristic stresses of the different religious orders (Gurr 1967:1158). Second scholasticism modified and adapted medieval scholasticism to contemporary exigencies: the confrontation with the Reformation, the Enlightenment and scientific investigation, the discovery of the Americas, and a global world of diverse religious cultures. The Jesuits gave a rigorous articulation of second scholasticism, producing their texts in the defense of Catholic Christianity and the papacy. Many of these characteristics detailed by Gurr are found in Ippolito Desideri's Tibetan writings and his interaction with dGe lugs pa scholasticism. Many of these characteristics of Catholic second scholasticism overlap with the characteristics of Indo-Tibetan Buddhist scholasticism detailed in Cabezón's introduction to this volume.

Desideri's Earlier Scholastic Method

The Khoshot Mongol ruler of Tibet, Lha bzang Khan (1658–1717) summoned Ippolito Desideri, shortly after his arrival in Lhasa in 1716. The Jesuit missionary had mastered spoken Tibetan in Ladakh and on his long trip to central Tibet. The Khan and the dGe lugs pa scholars at court questioned him about his intentions to stay in Lhasa and about the nature of his religion (*chos*):

> I was asked the difference between our law (*chos*) and theirs. I did not venture to answer such delicate topics by word of mouth ex professo and in public, so long as I had not made a very perfect and prolonged study of the language, and so I pledged myself to

> explain the whole thing little by little in different books, in which one can speak more . . . to distract myself from my uninterrupted application to the study of the language, I had kept composing every day for some hours two booklets in Italian. In the first (*The Allegory*), I refute the widespread error that everyone can be saved in his law (*chos*), and I show that there is but one road to salvation, all the rest leading to perdition. . . . On the 8th of September (1716) I started by myself to translate into his language the first of my two said booklets and to make it still more attractive I did it in Tibetan verse. (Desideri 1938:649)

He presented his first exposition of Christianity to the Khan on the Feast of the Epiphany (January 6, 1717). Desideri titles his first Tibetan manuscript *The Allegory of Sunrise Dispelling Dawn's Darkness* (*Tho rangs mun sel nyi ma shar ba'i brda*). This Tibetan manuscript reflects Desideri's Catholic scholastic method and training in its philosophical arguments and shows only a cursory understanding of Tibetan Buddhist doctrines. *The Allegory* provides, however, a significant marker for measuring and judging the maturation of Desideri's understanding of Tibetan Buddhism and its doctrines in his last manuscript. According to Desideri, the text is written in Tibetan verse to stress the doctrinal content, since he thought Tibetan verse to be a more elegant style. Desideri eventually abandoned Tibetan verse for Tibetan philosophical prose. Nonetheless, this first text is written in verse as a dialogue between the "wise and holy person seeking truth" (*mi mkhas dag pas bden 'tshol ba*) and the "white-headed father (*padri*) who explains the dharma of pure truth" (*mgo skar dpa' 'dri dag par bden pa'i chos 'chad p*a). The form of the dialogue was a typical stylistic feature of apologetic texts of medieval and second scholasticism. The objections raised by the "wise and holy person seeking truth" are European, not Tibetan Buddhist objections.

The Allegory develops the genre of natural theology treatises, an apologetic form of scholastic philosophy demonstrating that the fundamental questions about existence depended upon God.[5] Desideri uses the image of light as a metaphor for truth and compares the person to a house. Light becomes the central metaphor of the text, and there are two forms of light reflecting in the world. There is the light of a lamp in the house that dispels a limited amount of darkness. This is compared to the truth that can be apprehended through natural reason. There is also the light of the sun which can dispel the darkness completely, and this type of truth can only be apprehended through revelation and reason. However, revealed truth does not contradict reason; in fact, reason opens the individual to the highest revealed truth. In *The Allegory*, Desideri repeats the arguments of scholastic apologetics: that natural reason is insufficient for salvation, that humanity cannot be saved through other religions, that God reveals the teachings of religion, namely within Christianity, and gives humanity precepts for right views and right moral action, and the necessity of one true religion.

The Allegory reflects a number of the salient characteristics that Gurr (1967) underscores as prominent in the writings of second scholasticism:

1. Orientation of philosophy to the word of God. Desideri makes the philosophical distinction between two types of knowledge: natural and supernatural knowledge. Natural knowledge is derived from reason while supernatural knowledge remains above the natural comprehension of reason and must be revealed by angels, prophets, and God's Son in the canonical scriptures. Revealed truth does not contradict reason but becomes intelligible through rational appropriation.

2. Rational method. *The Allegory* popularizes the Jesuit form of scholastic disputation, starting with a thesis and its defense, an explanation of the terms of the thesis, a list of contrary opinions, a proof of the thesis, and answers to opponents of the thesis. Reason provides the means for explaining the text and for reconciling the inconsistences between the canonical scriptures and classical Christian writers into a systematic whole.

3. Concern with ideology and the particular characteristics of the religious order: Desideri intended to refute Tibetan Buddhist errors and the false doctrine that any person could be saved through his or her religion. His intention was to engage in interreligious apologetics. The particular ideological characteristics of the Jesuit order included its devotion to the papacy, the taking of a fourth vow of obedience, and its service in the defense of the Church and Catholic doctrine.[6] Desideri's intellectual formation occurred in the culture of European Catholic Christianity where non-Christian religions were regarded as falsehood and the work of Satan. He understood that his mission in Tibet was to win souls for the standard of Christ.

The only extant sources that we have describing the reactions of dGe lugs pa scholastics to the Jesuit's Tibetan works are Desideri's own writings. The dGe lugs pa lamas accorded the Jesuit the respect of a European lama, treating him as a professed religious and scholar. According to Desideri, *The Allegory* was well received. Lha bzang Khan and the dGe lugs pa scholars at court remained open to his attempt to write a philosophical explanation for the existence of a Supreme Being who created everything. Desideri describes their reactions: "Their (dGge lugs pa scholastics') opinion was that the maxims and principles contained therein were well set forth and seemed to be well reasoned but were entirely opposed to their dogmas and opinions" (Desideri 1934:101). If Desideri's words are an accurate account, then the dGge lugs pa scholars perceived structural affinities between the moral maxims outlined by the white-headed lama and their own moral philosophical precepts. Perhaps what intrigued them about *The Allegory* was his scholastic method of presenting philosophical arguments for the existence of God. His scholastic method, systematic organization of tenets into a series of connected arguments to refute an opponent's position, was in accord with their own dGe lugs pa scholastic method of question and answer in philosophical disputation. (Perdue 1992:24–60, Cabezón, 1994:84–85, 142–50)

Tibetan scholastics appreciated a "well-reasoned" philosophical argument. Their educational formation occurred in a Tibetan intellectual climate where philosophical debate was an art and where scholastic reason was propaedeutic to religious practice (Cabezón, 1994). Desideri's argument for the existence of a creator God could be comprehended against the background of traditional Buddhist critique of the Hindu concepts of a 'creator God' and 'metaphysics,' and there would have been other sections understandable to dGe lugs pa scholars: on love and compassion, aids to overcoming obstacles and evils, the unicity of the law, the need for faith, and how to achieve the highest religious perfection. After reading *The Allegory*, Lha bzang Khan, prompted by his dGe lugs pa advisors, encouraged Desideri to immerse himself in the scholastic writings and pedagogical training of the dGe lugs pa lamas at Ra mo che monastery. Lha bzang Khan gave Desideri the opportunity to study firsthand dGe lugs pa scholasticism, its arguments, and its doctrinal tenets. To my knowledge, Desideri was the first European to study dGe lugs pa philosophy.

Desideri Immerses Himself in dGe lugs pa Scholasticism

At Ra mo che, a small but renowned dGe lugs pa monastery in Lhasa, Desideri studied the classical texts of dGe lugs pa scholasticism. He hoped to further develop a heuristic strategy for entering the dGe lugs pa scholastic system, rationally engage it, and argue persuasively for the truths of Christianity. This meant that he had to study dGe lugs pa scholasticism and to appropriate it through the traditional curriculum of dGe lugs pa studies. Desideri learned the Tibetan language, its philosophical vocabulary, and the method of Madhyamaka dialectics and argument. The Jesuit missionary read many of the important works of the scriptures (*bka' 'gyur*) and their commentaries (*bstan 'gyur*) found in the Tibetan Buddhist canon in order to better understand their doctrines and religious culture. At Ra mo che, he witnessed the frequent doctrinal debates of dGe lugs pa monks in the courtyard and even participated in some of these disputations. In his journals, Desideri notes that he began to make a separate dictionary of terms used in the doctrinal language (*chos skad*) of Buddhist scholasticism as a preamble for comprehending dGe lugs pa scholasticism.

After five months, Desideri moved to Se ra monastery, a dGe lugs pa monastic university of approximately eight thousand monks on the outskirts of Lhasa. The monastic university made available to him both a library and other scholarly resources. At Se ra, the Jesuit studied Madhyamaka dialectics under dGe lugs pa scholars, attended lectures, and participated in philosophical disputes in the courtyard. Desideri studied the writings on emptiness (*stong pa nyid*), particularly the relevant sections of the *Great Exposition of the* Stages *of the Path to Enlightenment (Lam rim chen mo*) of Tsong Kha pa (1359–1419).[7] Tsong Kha pa's *Great Exposition of the Stages of the Path to Enlightenment* was one of the central philosophical works of dGe lugs pa scholasticism. His classic work presents a synthesis of Indian Buddhist doctrines and practices and had a status similar to Thomas Aquinas' *Summa Theologiae* in Catholic scholastic theological education and practice. Desideri's notes from his study of the *Great Exposition of the Stages of the Path to Enlightenment* consist of a compilation of quotations from that work, texts on logic and philosophy, and Māhayāna scriptures. These Tibetan quotes, interspersed with interlinear glosses in Latin and Italian, indicate the breadth and depth of Desideri's study and his understanding of the classical dGe lugs pa curriculum in Māhayāna Buddhism. Tsong Kha pa's *Great Exposition of the Stages* provided Desideri with an outline of the basic philosophical teachings of Indian Māhayāna Buddhism and introduced him to the philosophical treatises of great figures of that tradition such as Nāgārjuna, Aryadeva, Candarkirti, Śāntideva, and others. *The Great Stages of the Path* functioned as a syllabus for studying the vast corpus of Buddhist scriptures and commentaries.

From his own training in Catholic scholastic philosophy and theology, Desideri recognized dGe lugs pa scholasticism as scholastic practice and appreciated its deep concern for authority and reason and its stress on logical argumentation. Much of dGe lugs pa scholastic philosophy was framed in syllogisms, and the respondent either challenges the reasons that support the syllogism or accepts the opponent's syllogisms. This form of dGe lugs pa philosophical argumentation reminded the Jesuit of his own scholastic training in philosophy and theology at the Roman College through the methods of *lectio* and *disputatio*.[8] For example, he describes Tsong Kha pa's great exposition as a "book in which is expounded with admirable method and clarity the dogmas of the Tibetan religion, and the treatises of emptiness (*stong pa nyid*)" (Desideri 1934:107). Ippolito Desideri respected the dGe lugs pa scholasticism of Tsong Kha pa, and he understood the role that rational inquiry, logic, and reasonable arguments played in dGe lugs pa pedagogy and philosophical investigation. Both the dGe lugs pa and the Jesuit stress on reason (Tibetan: *rigs pa;* Latin: *ratio*) provided each participant in this nascent Christian-Buddhist encounter with the foundational tools to engage in the art of interreligious polemics, the type of religious conversation to which both scholastic traditions were accustomed. For each tradition, reasoning was the means for ascertaining the precise meaning of a scriptural passage or a classical text and critically investigated the objections to doctrinal tenets. Reasoning and rational argumentation thus provided the medium for demonstrating the validity of one's own system and the lack of validity of other religious systems.

In his journals, Desideri reflects on his decision to engage dGe lugs pa scholasticism and fight for the "Standard of Christ" through rational argument: "Having by my aforesaid diligence discovered the site of the enemy's camp, the quality of their arms and their artifices, and provided myself with arms and ammunition, towards the end of November, I resolved to challenge them and begin war. In the name and by the aid of God, I commenced to confute the errors of that sect and declare the truth of our holy faith" (Desideri 1934:106).

Desideri engaged dGe lugs pa scholasticism by reading Indo-Tibetan Buddhist philosophical texts, studying dGe lugs pa scholastic method, and applying Catholic scholastic method to develop an interreligious apologetic.

Desideri's Scholastic Engagement with dGe lugs pa Scholasticism

The Essence of the Christian Doctrine represents Desideri's most mature engagement with and understanding of dGe lugs pa scholastic practice and doctrine. The manuscript is divided between the refutation of the Buddhist notion of emptiness (folios 1–13a) and the exposition of the Christian doctrine (folios 13a–50a). The division follows a Catholic scholastic pattern of the critique and refutation of the central truth claims of the adversary and presentation of the rational superiority of the truth claims of Christian revelation. The basic method of the text also follows a pattern similar to the rhetorical framework of dGe lugs pa argumentation: (1) invalidating the opponent's doctrines by demonstrating their logical fallacies and contradictions, (2) demonstrating the validity and consistency of one's own doctrinal system, (3) demonstrating the uniqueness and superiority of one's own doctrinal system vis-à-vis other systems (See Cabezón 1990:16ff).

The first section, refuting emptiness, is patterned after the rhetorical strategy of the invalidation of the opponent's doctrine. It surfaces the logical fallacies or inconsistencies inherent in the opponent's argument, a method employed by Tsong Kha pa's *Great Exposition of the Stages of the Path* and by Thomas' *Summa Theologiae*. The exposition of Christian doctrine in the second section is further divided into three subsections: "Faith" (folia 13a–28a), "Hope" (folia 28a–34a), and "Charity" (34a–50). Desideri's sections on Christian doctrine follow the typical catechetical content and method found in the Italian Jesuit Robert Cardinal Bellarmine's catechism, *Dottrina Cristiana*. Bellarmine's catechism became normative for Italian catechesis; it develops a catechical exposition of the doctrinal tenets of the creed, the Pater Noster, and the seven deadly sins. Instead of the dialogue between teacher (*magister*) and disciple (*disciplina*), Desideri composes a dialogue between the teacher, using the transliterated Sanskrit term *pandita,* and the "seeker of further wisdom" (*yang shes rab kyi snying po zhu ba po*), a term borrowed from the Perfection of Wisdom corpus of literature. Desideri's usage of "further wisdom" (*yang shes rab*) is significant in that he acknowledges a wisdom already present within the Buddhist tradition.[9] Part 2 of *The Essence* reflects the literary genre of Catholic apologetics and catechesis.

Part 1 of *The Essence* marks the first historical engagement of the Summa with the *Great Stages*, the interaction of scholastic method of Thomas Aquinas with the scholastic method of Tsong Kha pa. Desideri opposes Thomas' philosophy of being (*esse*) against Tsong Kha pa's philosophy of emptiness (S: *śūnyatā*, T: *stong pa nyid*). It is on the doctrinal level that the two scholastic traditions are most divergent. In his *Account of Tibet,* Desideri notes the primary difference between the two religious traditions to be doctrinal: "I explained that in every religion there were two principal facts: firstly, principles, maxims, or dogma to be believed, and secondly, precepts, counsels, or instructions as to what to do or not do. As regards the first, our religion and theirs were absolutely different, but in the second, the difference was slight" (Desideri 1934:99–100). Since the truth claims of Buddhist doctrines presented an obstacle to him, these had to be refuted prior to any acceptance of Christian truth claims by Tibetans. Desideri proposes to examine and compare the two doctrinal systems (*chos lugs*) in order to show the logical fallacies of the dGe lugs pa tenets, the coherence and superiority of the truth of Christian revelation. He qualifies Christian doctrine as a faith system (*dad lugs*) in addition to a doctrinal system, and this remains for the Jesuit an essential difference between the two forms of scholasticism.

In the opening folio of *The Essence,* he states the general dGe lugs pa position on emptiness:

> If one examines the scriptures and the philosophical systems of Tibet with a wisdom which remains honest, without partiality, and without hatred and attachment, they (their scriptures / systems) assert that there is not even one substance established as inherently existent. They understand that all existing substances are viewed as empty, the emptiness of inherent existence itself. (Goss II, folio 1)

Desideri claims to restate the primary thesis of dGe lugs pa scholasticism from a perspective of "wisdom which remains honest, without partiality." The Jesuit missionary understands that dGe lugs pa scholasticism equates its notion of emptiness with dependent origination, and this is apparent in the first section of *The Essence of Christian Doctrine,* as well as in comments in Italian journal writings and letters.[10] Desideri does not consider the Buddhist notion of emptiness to be nihilistic but rather radically relativist. Both emptiness and dependent origination exclude a self-existent creator as part of the more general deconstruction of any form of independent being or essence.[11] For the Jesuit, the truth claims of the Buddhist notion of emptiness require the falsity of the Christian doctrine of the self-existent God. There was no middle ground for him to reconcile the Buddhist notion of emptiness and the Christian notion of God.

Desideri rehearses the arguments for emptiness of all substances found in the *Great Exposition of the Stages,* focusing on the following topics: causality, the relationship of the relative to the absolute, the natural knowledge of the absolute, the birth of a person, the origin of substances, contingency and necessity, and the aggregates (folios 1a–12). According to his own journals, he uses arguments and rational disputations that conform to the form and method of Indo-Tibetan Madhyamaka philosophy and their canonical writers. He took seriously dGe lugs pa scholastic rhetoric, imitating its method and style of argumentation. When a flawed position has been advanced, the dGe lugs pa scholastic is ready to attack it by raising a series of logical fallacies to disprove the premise untenable. Desideri's strategy is to bring out what he perceives to be the contradictions within dGe lugs pa arguments for the notion of emptiness and then gives a common-sense example to demonstrate how the tenet is contradictory. For the Jesuit, the contradictions arise from what is not proven in dGe lugs pa arguments: the cause of causes, or first cause, and the necessity of a Supreme Being (folio 12a).

Ippolito Desideri disagrees with the dGe lugs pa arguments for the emptiness of inherent existence due to his own scholastic doctrinal presuppositions that are based on the notion of a creator God. Radical relativity without a first cause (*prima causa*) is the major error to be overcome if an explicit notion of God is to be introduced. From a Thomistic perspective, God's essence (*essentia*) is a pure act of being (*esse*). In other words, the "to-be" (*esse*) is to be within God's act of self-being; this means that everything, thus created, participates in God's act of being (*De Ente et Essentia* 1, 2; *Summa Theologiae* I-I, q.3, a.4; LaCugna 1991:150ff; Hankey 1987:57–80). The difficulty that Ippolito Desideri has with the notion of emptiness is neither its radical contingency nor its corollary, the interdependency of phenomena. Catholic scholastic philosophy's notions of potency and act allow for viewing reality as contingent, interdependent, and relational. Emptiness, however, excludes a first cause (*prima causa*) and thus excludes the creator God of Catholic scholastic theology.

Desideri demonstrates what he perceives to be the logical fallacies of the dGe lugs pa scholasticism from his own Thomistic perspective based on notions of being, essence, and potency. He retains the method of Madhyamaka argumentation to refute the notion of relativity without a first cause, arguing that the relative requires the absolute. He develops his scholastic argument for the need of natural knowledge of absolute truth as well as the necessity of a first cause (*prima causa*) to counter the pure relativity of the notion of emptiness. For dGe lugs pa scholastics, the relative does entail the absolute (emptiness), but relative, contingent, or conventional existence does not entail absolute or inherent existence, which is precisely the notion being refuted (*dgag bya*) in Madhyamaka arguments for emptiness.

For Desideri, the arguments for the existence of God emerge from the Thomistic tradition of construing God as "subsistent self-existence" (*ipsum esse subsistens*). Aquinas' metaphysical construal of God as "subsistent Being" provided the foundational basis for exposition of the question of the Trinity and other tenets of Christian doctrine. The Jesuit translates or mistranslates the Tibetan "jewel" (*dkon mchog*) for God. He misperceived the triadic significance of the Buddhist Three Jewels (Buddha, Dharma, and Sangha) that gave rise to the act of taking refuge for an incipient trinitarianism. As he read through the Tibetan scriptures and commentaries, Desideri realized that the Three Jewels was a not reference to the Christian triune God. He, nevertheless, translates the notion of the "self-existent God" into the Tibetan phrase "the self-existent jewel" (*rang grub dkon mchog*), attempting to create a triadic parallel of God and the "Three Jewels" in the act of worship. He lists the attributes of God as "independent, immutable, uncreated, non-dependent, free from another, perfect, eternal, free from fault, without sin, unrivalled." Desideri's scholastic method not only includes hermeneutical appropriation of dGe lugs pa scholastic techniques but also hermeneutical appropriation of Buddhist semantic terms. For example, he appropriates the Māhayāna Buddhist notion of "immeasurable compassion" *(thugs rje tshad med pa)*, often attributed to bodhisattvas and Buddhas, to explain the Christian notion of grace and God's salvific love. Desideri is not just literally translating Christian concepts into a Tibetan cultural milieu; rather, he is modifying a pre-existent doctrinal language and scholastic method that is hermeneutically significant to his Buddhist readers, so as to convey new meanings. Ippolito Desideri creates an interpretative medium, a rhetoric, for Buddhist-Christian communication and thus for polemical engagement of these two forms of scholasticism. Desideri describes how his three-volume work created an interest among the learned lamas in Lhasa. He writes, "My house suddenly became the scene of incessant comings by all sorts of people, chiefly learned men and professors, who came from the monasteries and universities, those of Se ra and 'Bras spungs, the principal ones to apply for permission to see and read the book" (Desideri 1934:106). Desideri notes that the learned lamas would read some of his statements, examine them with care, and specify further distinctions for consideration. The dGe lugs pa lamas provided corrections and refinements to his reasoned arguments. However, they would disregard the logical consequences of some of his arguments but would write their own corrections and solutions for explaining clearly the truth. The lamas were as much committed to the rational investigation and ascertainment of doctrinal truth as Desideri was. This interaction between dGe lugs pa scholars and Desideri proved to be a mutual learning process, forming a language for intercommunication and the preliminaries of the first Christian-Buddhist dialogue.

How the dGe lugs pa lamas and dGe bshes, in fact, understood Desideri's presentation of Christian doctrine is only speculation, yet their intellectual curiosity and openness brought them from their monastic universities to read the scholastic work of the "white-headed lama." Even if the dGe lugs pa scholastics would have disregarded Desideri's conclusions because they contradicted their own Buddhist tenets, they, nevertheless, would have found an appreciation for the rational philosophical argument and interreligious apologetics within *The Essence*. As for Desideri's doctrinal exposition of Catholic Christianity, the dGe lugs pa scholastics would have heard some of the elements of the story of Jesus in terms of the bodhisattva path. We catch a glimpse of such a reading in Desideri's journal. He notes, "Many a time when telling them what the image of the Crucifix meant they would prostrate themselves, beat their breasts and beg to hold it in their hands, when they would kiss and shed many tears on hearing that Jesus Christ had suffered for the redemption of their souls" (Desideri 1934:177). This Buddhist response of perceiving Jesus as a bodhisattva has been typical of even the current Buddhist-Christian dialogue (Lopez and Rockefeller 1987).

Interreligous Apologetics as Scholastic Dialogue

Apologetics is a form of religious discourse, attempting to demonstrate that the truth claims of one particular religion are superior to the truth claims of another religion. It is a systematic and argumentative form of scholastic discourse that aims at religious persuasion. Initially, apologetics relinquishes its primary and secondary sources of authority such as Scripture, revelation, or tradition in order to engage an adversary that would not accept such sources of authority. Apologists use methods, arguments, and criteria of knowledge acceptable to their adversary. When apologists present their own doctrinal truth claims as part of a coherent system, they necessarily rely on those initially excluded sources of authority along with the use of reason. In this fashion, apologists present their doctrinal system as rationally and cognitively superior to those of others that have, from their perspective, proven to be flawed. Recently, Paul Griffiths (1991) has argued for the necessity of interreligious apologetics as integral to interreligious dialogue. His premise certainly holds true in the particular case of Desideri's rhetorical encounters with dGe lugs pa scholasticism, a case of Catholic second scholasticism interacting with dGe lugs pa scholaticism.

Both Catholic and dGe lugs pa scholasticism considered the art of apologetics as integral to religious discourse. Both traditions understand that doctrine is based on intelligible principles and methods whose goal is to make evident a higher (theological or Buddhist philosophical) discourse. Both scholastic traditions strive to reproduce a systematic orderliness that is comparative, critical, consistent, and hierarchical. For both, reason is soteriologically necessary to their religious goals. The dGe lugs pa tradition uses rhetoric, logical argumentation, and rational dispute in pursuit of enlightenment, while logic and reasoning were essential to Desideri's pursuit of grace. Both traditions accept a rational method for critically analyzing adversarial positions and arguments, comparing and exposing them to logical principles, and arriving at a hierarchical system of doctrinal tenets.

Desideri's own Jesuit education prepared him in the tradition of scholastic philosophy, logic, metaphysics, and rhetoric. When Desideri immersed himself in the study of the philosophy of the dGe lugs pa tradition, he studied the Buddhist scholastic method of logic, dialectics, and the art of debate. The Catholic scholastic philosophy and theology at the Roman College served him in his study of the arguments of dGe lugs pa scholasticism and Tibetan philosophical language. He employed the method of *lectio*, reading, to understand Madhyamaka philosophy and method, and he utilized the method of *disputatio* to analyze the truth claims of both doctrinal systems. Both *lectio* and *disputatio* formed the heart of his pedagogical method, but they were also at the heart of Buddhist philosophical method. Desideri, therefore, learned the Tibetan language so as to learn the particular art of Tibetan philosophical dispute and argument. He further proposed to examine the two doctrinal systems (*chos lugs*) in comparison to each other to determine which doctrine is "pure and immaculate," or, that is, which is cognitively superior to the other. From the beginning of his interreligious apologetics, Desideri understood this to be Christian doctrine.

Desideri chose to introduce Christian doctrine by traditional Tibetan and Catholic scholastic practices: (1) the use of reason and dialectic argument in invalidating the dGe lugs pa notion of emptiness, (2) a coherent exposition of the Buddhist doctrinal system and the faith system of Christianity, (3) the demonstration of the uniqueness and superiority of Catholic doctrinal truth. Argumentation plays an important role in the learning process of both scholastic traditions, and it is equally vital for reaching consensus between two conversation partners. One dialogue partner either acknowledges the force of the reasons of the other's arguments or is forced to reply with critical counter-arguments. The point of the arguments is to convince the other dialogue partner to accept or refute the claims to truth of doctrinal statements. Reaching understanding or consensus between two dialogue partners depends on their mutual acceptance of the recognizable claims to truth of their statements.

Apologetic engagement was the only pedagogical method available to Desideri for carrying on a fruitful communication with the dGe-lugs-pa scholasticism, but it could take place effectively only in his learning of the Tibetan language and through hermeneutical appropriation of the dGe lugs pa philosophical terminology and scholastic method. Ippolito Desideri created an expanded language for argument and consensus between the two traditions and indicated the directions for future apologetic interactions between the two scholastic practices. Unfortunately, a territorial dispute between the Jesuits and the Capuchin-Franciscans forced Desideri to be recalled to Rome (Snellgrove and Richardson, 1986:224–26) He was, however, the most successful Christian to engage dGe lugs pa scholasticism until the modern era.

Notes

1. The comparativist philosopher Paul Masson-Oursel conceives of scholasticism as a cross-cultural philosophical category and stage within an evolutionary schema of human civilization that culminates in scientific and critical inquiry (1920:123–41). For Masson-Oursel, scholasticisms emerge as a philosophical response to sophism. He comprehends Buddhism as sophism and as a forerunner to scholasticism and something that prevents him paying serious attention to the development of Buddhist scholasticism.

2. Leclercq asserts that monastic theology perfected its writing in the obligations of silence. The literature of monastic schools was expressed in writing, whereas scholastic literature was created from the oral style of exchange between master and pupils. The question and disputation style of scholasticism emerged from the alteration of question and answer in dialogue. The scholastic oral style was more pedagogical than monastic writing. Leclerq, 1960:188–190. Weisheipl notes that both the lectio and disputatio employed three means: definition, division, and reasons. Weisheipl, 1967:1145. For a fuller exposition of scholastic method, see: Weisheipl, 1974:115–18 and de Wulf, 1954: 26–31.

3. The term *scholastic* was applied to all Jesuits who had taken vows and prior to their change of status with ordination to the priesthood and final vows.

4. See Harney's (1941:192–258) discussion of Jesuit education and learning and their achievements in the missions, as well as Volloslada's (1954:96–115) discussion of the *Ratio Studiorum* as implemented at the Roman College.

5. Sherburne calls *The Allegory* a "catechism." It lacks the typical catechical form of presenting the basic tenets of the Christian creed as Desideri does in the latter part of *The Essence of Christianity*. It is rather an apologetic text, more properly labeled as natural theology. See Sherburne 1989:298.

6. Ignatius' *Spiritual Exercises* provides an ideological framework for Desideri's scholastic method of apologetics. It divides the world into the standard of Christ and the standard of Satan, providing a combative spirituality. See "Two Standards" meditation in the *Spiritual Exercises* (Ignatius of Loyola 1992: 65–67). See Ganss' notes pp. 69–73, 167–69. The "Two Standards" meditation informs Desideri's apologetic by placing his encounter with Tibetan Buddhism as a form of spiritual warfare.

7. Desideri was the first non-Asian to translate the *Lam rim chen mo* into a Western language, Italian. His translation of this important Tibetan text has been lost.

8. Desideri's heuristic framework consists of more than the rational combativeness of the "Two Standards" of the Spiritual Exercises and Catholic apologetics in refuting the errors of Tibetan Buddhism. It also includes the positive valuation of created things in the Ignatian principle of "finding God in all things," lacking in Tibetan culture. The positive valuation of created things is found in the "Principle and the Foundation" meditation of the Ignatian Exer-

cises (Ignatius of Loyola 1992:32). See Ganss' note 17 on the "Principle and Foundation" (146–48). Desideri states, "Their (Tibetans) morality agrees with our own" (Desideri 1934:256). There was much in Tibetan Buddhist preceptual and moral practice that reminded Desideri of his own Catholic Christian practice of morality. Resemblances in preceptual practices and scholastic method provoked the Jesuit into a deeper investigation of Tibetan Buddhism, keeping him open to seeing its positive dimensions and resemblances. His writings constantly reflect the tension of refuting philosophical error for the "greater glory of God," while finding positive elements within Tibetan Buddhism and scholasticism with strong resemblances to his Catholic Christianity.

9. One could easily argue that Desideri is just adopting the "seeker of further wisdom" from the Perfection of Wisdom literature that he read. The notion of "further wisdom" is also congruent with a Catholic scholastic recognition of a wisdom already present in human rational inquiry. In *The Allegory*, Desideri uses the image of light of the lamp within a house that dispels limited darkness as a metaphor for natural reason.

10. In his *Account of Tibet*, he summarizes his understanding of the Buddhist notion of emptiness: "Nothing exists because nothing has any essence by itself, and therefore, nothing exists which is not dependently originated *(rten cing 'brel bas 'byung)* or unconnected, unfettered, and without correlativity"(Desideri 1934:249).

11. Desideri calls dGe lugs pa atheists but qualifies their denial of the existence of God: "Although the Tibetans theoretically and speculatively deny the existence of a divinity and the existence of an immortal soul . . . I only wish to make clear that these blind people unwittingly admit and confusedly recognize the Divinity which they persistently deny in words" (Desideri 1934:251). Desideri recognized an implicit notion of God within Tibetan Buddhism evident in Tibetan religious practices, faith, and morality. In another instance, he noted that the real aim of Madhyamaka philosophical treatises was "to exclude and absolutely deny the existence of any uncreated and independent Being and thus effectively to do away with any conception of God" (Desideri 1934:104–5).

References

Adshead, S.A.M.
1977 "Buddhist Scholasticism and Transcendental Thomism," *Downside Review*, vol. 95:297–305.

Beckwith, Christopher I.
1989 "The Medieval Scholastic Method in Tibet and the West." In *Reflections on Tibetan Culture: Essays in Memory of Turrel V. Wylie,*

307–13. Ed. Richard Sherburne and Lawrence Epstein. Lampeter, UK: The Edwin Mellen Press.

Cabezón, José Ignacio.
1994 *Buddhism and Language: A Study of Indo-Tibetan Scholasticism.* Albany: SUNY Press.

1990 "The Canonization of Philosophy and the Rhetoric of Siddhanta in Tibetan Buddhism." In *Buddha Nature: A Festschrift in Honor of Minoru Kiyota*, 7–26. Ed. Paul J. Griffiths & John Keenan. Tokyo: Buddhist Books International.

Chenu, M. D.
1964 *Toward Understanding Saint Thomas*. Chicago: Henry Regency.

Clooney, Francis X.
1990 "Roberto de Nobili, Adaptation and the Reasonable Interpretation of Religion." *Missology* xviii / 1:25–36.

Desideri, Ippolito.
1989 *Opere Tibetane di Ippolito Desideri*. Volume 4. Trans. & ed. G. Toscano. Roma: Instituto Italiano per il medio ed estremo.

1987 *Opere Tibetane di Ippolito Desideri*. Volume 3. Trans. and ed. G. Toscano. Roma: Instituto Italiano per il medio ed estremo.

1984 *Opere Tibetane di Ippolito Desideri*. Volume 2. Ed. G. Toscano. Roma: Instituto Italiano per il medio ed estremo.

1981 *Opere eTibetane di Ippolito Desideri*. Volume 1. Trans. and ed. G. Toscano. Roma: Instituto Italiano per il medio ed estremo.

1954 "Notizie Istoriche del Thibet." In *I Missionarii Italiani nel Tibet e nel Nepal*. Ed. Luciano Petech, volumes 5–7. Roma: Instituto Poligrafico Dello Strata.

1938 "Letters and Other Papers of Fr. Ippolito Desideri, S.J., a Missionary in Tibet (1713–21). Ed. and trans. H. Holsten. *Journal of the Royal Asiatic Society of Bengal*. 4:567–767.

1934 *An Account of Tibet*. Trans. Felippo de Felippi. London.

Gettleman, Nancy Moore.
1989 "Karma-bstan-skong and the Jesuits." In *Reflections on Tibetan Culture: Essays in Memory of Turrel V. Wylie*, 269–77. Ed. Lawrence Epstein and Richard Sherburne. Lewiston: The Edwin Mellen Press.

Gispert-Sauch, G.
1990 "Desideri and Tibet." *The Tibet Journal* 15 / 2:29–39.

Goss, Robert E.

Forthcoming I "Ippolito Desideri S.J. and the Beginnings of the Christian-Buddhist Dialogue."

Forthcoming II "The Essence of Christianity," translation of *Ke ri sti an gyi chos lugs kyi snying po.*

Griffiths, Paul J.

1991 *An Apology for Apologetics: On the Logic of Interreligious Dialogue*. Maryknoll, N.Y.: Orbis Books.

Gurr, J. B.

1967 "Middle Scholasticism, 1158–1165." In *New Catholic Encyclopedia.* Volume 12. New York, McGraw Hill.

Hankey, W. J.

1987 *God in Himself: Aquinas' Doctrine of God as Expounded in the Summa Theologiae*. New York: Oxford University Press.

Harney, Martin.

1941 *The Jesuits in History*. New York: The America Press.

Horvath, Tibor.

1990 "Apologetics as Dialogue in the Western Church from the Classical Period of Scholasticism to the Beginning of the Reformation." *Asian Journal of Theology* 4:136–61.

Ignatius of Loyola.

1992 *The Spiritual Exercises of St. Ignatious*. Trans. and commentary George E. Ganss. *St. Louis: The Institute of Jesuit Sources*.

1970 *The Constitutions of the Society of Jesus*. Trans George E. Ganss. St. Louis: The Institute of Jesuit Sources.

LaCugna, Catherine M.

1991 *God For Us*, San Francisco, HarperSanFrancisco.

1985 "The Relational God: Aquinas and Beyond." *Theological Studies* 46:647–63.

Leclercq, Jean.

1960 *The Love of Learning and the Desire for God*. Trans. Catherine Misrashi. New York: Fordham University Press.

Lonergan, Bernard.

1972 *Method In Theology*. New York: Herder and Herder.

Lopez, Donald and Steven Rockefeller (eds.).

1987 *The Christ and the Bodhisattva*. Albany, New York: State University of New York Press.

Lubac, Henri De.
1952 *La Recontre du Bouddhisme et de l'Occident*. Paris: Aubier.

Luca, Augusta.
1987 *Nel Tibet ignoto: la straordinario viaggio de Ippolito Desideri*. Bologna: EMI.

Masson-Oursel, P.
1920 "La Scholastique étude de philosophie comparée." *Revue Philosophique de la France et de l'Étranger* 90:123–141.

Panikkar, Raimundo.
1973 "Common Patterns of Eastern and Western Scholasticism." *Diogenes* 83:103–13.

Perdue, Daniel.
1992 *Debate in Tibetan Buddhism*. Ithaca, New York: Snow Lion Publications.

Sauch, G. Gispert.
1990 "Desideri and Tibet." *The Tibet Journal* 15/2:29–39.

Schüssler-Fiorenza, Francis.
1991 "Systematic Theology: Task and Methods."In *Systematic Theology: Roman Catholic Perspectives* vol. 1:1–87. Ed. Francis Schüssler-Fiorenza and John Galvin. Minneapolis: Fortress Press.

Sherburne, Richard.
1989 "A Christian Buddhist Dialogue? Some Notes on Desideri's Tibetan Manuscripts." In *Reflections on Tibetan Culture: Essays in Memory of Turrel V. Wylie*, 298–99. Ed. Richard Sherburne & Lawrence Epstein. Lampeter, UK: The Edwin Mellen Press.

Snellgrove, David and Hugh Richardson.
1986 *A Cultural History of Tibet*. Boston: Shambhala.

Trentman, John A.
1982 "Scholasticism in the Seventeenth Century." In *The Cambridge History of Later Medieval Philosophy*, 822–27. Ed. Norman Kretzman, Anthony Kenny, & Jan Pinboy. Cambridge: Cambridge University Press.

Vallet, Marie-Raphael.
1988 "Lectio according to Rance." *Liturgy, Order Cistercian of Strict Observance* 22/2:21–75.

Volloslada, Riccardo.

1954 *Storia del Collegio romana dal suo inizio (1551) all sopprewssione della Compagna di Gesu (1773)*. Roma: apud Aedes Universitas Gregorianae.

Weisheipl, J.A.

1987 "Scholasticism, 118." In *The Encyclopedia of Religion*. vol. 13. Ed. Mircea Eliade. New York: Macmillan.

1974 *Friar D'Aquino*. Garden City, New York: Doubleday.

1967 "Scholastic Method, 1154–1158." *New Catholic Encyclopedia*, vol. 12. New York: McGraw Hill.

Wessels, Cornelius.

1924 *Early Jesuit Travellers in Central Asia: 1603–1721*. The Hague: Martinus Hijhoff.

Wulf, M. de.

1956 *Scholastic Philosophy*. Trans. P. Coffey. New York: Dover Publications.

1953 *Philosophy and Civilization of the Middle Ages*. New York: Dover Publications.

Chapter 4

Scholasticism as a Comparative Category and the Study of Judaism

Michael D. Swartz

Introduction

A colleague tells a story of a conversation he had about twenty years ago with a senior scholar.[1] The older gentlemen was a product not only of European universities, but of the great rationalist Lithuanian talmudic academy—the Yeshivah. The conversation turned to current developments in Jewish studies and the burgeoning study of Jewish mysticism and spirituality. All this talk about mysticism, said the good professor, is silly. "I worship God with my mind."

There are, of course, responses to that statement. One might ask, quite seriously, what other part of the anatomy might be used to worship God. The heart is the seat of the intellect in classical Hebrew, and, therefore, is in fact the mind. Perhaps we can refer to the kidneys and related organs, which were the seat of the emotions for the ancients and which are said in Jewish tradition to praise God.[2] Or we could suggest that the proposition that scholars, unlike mystics, worship God with their minds implies a false dichotomy of intellect versus emotion.

But when we look further at our senior colleague's statement, it is not so simple as it appears. For when he said that he worshiped God with his mind, he was referring to specific patterns of behavior that constitute traditional Jewish learning in Rabbinic culture. The Yeshivah and similar institutions are highly ritualized environments in which thinking and learning take place within age-old conventions and social structures. Recently, these patterns of behavior have been studied closely and analyzed by Samuel Heilman and William Helmreich.[3] Thus our scholar might in fact have worshiped God with other parts of his anatomy—his body, which might sway, stand, or sit in a particular posture; his social self, which interacted with his companions, teachers, and forerunners in specific ways; and his feet, which placed him in institutions organized for the promotion of the sort of worship he cherished.

In this chapter it will be argued that scholasticism can have meaning as a comparative category if we examine precisely what social assumptions and behavior are involved in "worshiping God with one's mind." The study of scholasticism need not be limited to the comparison of the ideas of Christian scholastics with those formed in other cultures. By studying the living context of learning in scholastic cultures, a more encompassing comparison of varieties of scholasticism can take place. This proposition will be considered with regard to Rabbinic Judaism, the system of law, lore, reasoning, and religious practice developed by the Jewish sages of the first six centuries of the common era in Palestine and Babylonia.

The Study of Scholasticism

In our quest to understand premodern religious phenomena in their variety, historians of religion often focus on those activities, such as magic, that seem most alien to modern sensibilities, while paying less attention to the phenomenological aspects of types of scholastic behavior that seem closest to our own, intellectualist approach. Yet scholasticism and magic have something in common. The term *scholasticism,* like *magic,* often has been used pejoratively.[4] Moreover, scholasticism also shares with magic a past reputation as a kind of outmoded rationality. As scholasticism has been considered to be a rudimentary precursor to contemporary academic discourse, magic once was conceived as primitive science.[5] For these reasons, the recent call to establish scholasticism as a comparative category is a significant development.

In *Buddhism and Language* (1994: 11–26), José Cabezón argues for the "decontextualization" of the category of scholasticism and its use in religious studies.[6] According to Cabezón, scholasticism can describe social and intellectual movements in several complex religious cultures and is often characterized by several features. Among these are a belief in the basic intelligibility of the universe; an orientation to tradition; an investment in the value of intellectual argument for the self-conception of the group; and an interest in synthesizing large quantities of textual material into a coherent whole (20–21). Although scholasticism usually is associated with philosophical systems, Cabezón acknowledges that the scholastic interest in reconciling the intellectual and experiential dimensions of religious life can be applied to the study of ritual and law, as in Mīmāṃsa Hinduism, Judaism, and Confucianism (19).

To be interested in the idea of scholasticism is to be interested in the living context of learning. Dialectic, polemic, and commentary are inherently social activities. They presuppose interlocutors, opponents, forebears, and teachers. Furthermore, they usually are made possible by institutions realized both in society itself and in literary forms. To be sure, these partners in dialectic or opponents in polemic may exist largely on the page of the scholastic treatise; nonetheless, scholastics are expressing their social values as well as their theologies when they utilize these forms. Thus, while the exercise of decontextualization is a necessary step in the establishment of scholasticism as a comparative category, it also is important to carry out a comparison of those environments in which scholasticism as a process takes place—a decontextualization of context, so to speak.

In the same way, the study of Rabbinic Judaism is concerned not only with the theological and legal concepts developed by the ancient Rabbis, but also with how they sought to transmit them as well. Indeed, because of the primacy of the idea of Torah as embodied in the sage and his teaching, Rabbinic theology cannot be separated from the behavioral context in which it is carried out.

Earlier cross-cultural uses of the term *scholasticism* have referred to Judaism. P. Masson-Oursel (1920) included medieval Jewish philosophy among his examples in his early essay arguing for a comparative concept of scholasticism.[7] More recently, Anthony Saldarini implies the comparative possibilities of this term in giving the title *Scholastic Rabbinism* to his study of the Rabbinic manifesto *'Avot de-Rabbi Natan.* Saldarini's book, like earlier related studies by Henry Fischel (1973), places the Rabbinic ideals of study and tradition in their Greco-Roman context.[8]

In this chapter some of these features of scholasticism will be tested against aspects of Rabbinic Judaism in order to see to what extent the category as thus formulated applies. At the same time, we will ask what the study of Rabbinic Judaism offers to students of comparative scholasticism.

Rabbinic Judaism

Rabbinic Judaism is a product of a class of postbiblical sages that emerged in the aftermath of the destruction of the Second Temple in Judea in 70 C.E. These scholars, who traced their heritage to the Pharisees of Jesus' time, were not necessarily priests but laymen who held that by a life of study of Torah, observance of the commandments, and ethical action, the individual Jew could gain salvation in the form of resurrection in the messianic era. This system of everyday observance of what came to be known as the "halakhah" depended on its constant teaching and refinement by masters—the rabbis—who considered their extrabiblical traditions to have been handed down as Torah from Sinai.

The rabbis of late antiquity produced a series of texts and traditions that became a kind of second canon for Judaism. The Mishnah, compiled in 200 C.E., sets forth Rabbinic law and related matters in statements and formulae attributed to the sages of the Second Temple era and of the first two centuries C.E. While the rabbis considered Rabbinic law to be based on Scripture, the Mishnah does not generally frame its laws as biblical commentary but rather states them in independent, apodictic form. Rabbinic study of the Mishnah resulted in the redaction of the great compendia of Mishnaic commentary, tradition, and lore known as the Talmuds. The Palestinian Talmud was redacted in the early fifth century and the Babylonian Talmud in the early sixth century.

The Babylonian Talmud became the source of legal decision, intense study, and reverence for most of world Jewry in the Middle Ages and remains so for traditional Jews. As a result, when people speak of "the Talmud," they often are referring to the Babylonian Talmud. The Talmud's commentary to the Mishnah is called the "Gemara." Besides commenting on the meaning and implications of the Mishnah's laws, the Gemara discusses the relationship of the Mishnah to Scripture and extramishnaic sources and includes tales of the sages, biblical exegesis, and folklore. While it is a commentary to the Mishnah, the Gemara often takes the form of an ongoing conversation among sages, many of whom lived centuries apart from each other. This conversation is moderated, as it were, by an anonymous Aramaic text (called the "*stam*") that can take the role of a skeptical observer—asking questions regarding opinions presented, pointing out contradictions and logical inconsistencies, and arranging source materials for comparison. This method of presentation can be considered a kind of dialectical argumentation about traditional sources for exegetical purposes.[9] It is thus in the Talmud that many of the characteristics we can identify with scholasticism are best expressed in Judaism.

Rabbinic scriptural exegesis, Midrash, found its way into compilations that were completed from the fourth century to the early Middle Ages. These compilations, the most famous of which are collected in the *Midrash Rabbah,* contain specific elucidations of the biblical text, but also include postbiblical legends, homilies, and discourses on biblical themes. In Midrash we occasionally can find elements of the sort of theological speculation that might appear in systematic philosophical treatises in other cultures. So although ancient Rabbinic Judaism does not have a systematic philosophical literature equivalent to that of Christian scholasticism, the types of discourse found in its legal and commentarial literatures do lend themselves to comparison.

The following discussion will refer to current developments in the study of Rabbinic civilization and how they might bear on the questions being considered in this volume. Although a theme will be the evolution of Rabbinic scholasticism from the composition of the Mishnah in the early third century to the redaction of the Babylonian Talmud in the sixth, this chapter will be a composite portrait, spanning several centuries and places. The student of Rabbinic scholasticism who is looking for the interplay of ideas and their context is at a disadvantage. We have little external evidence for the social and historical milieu of Rabbinic Judaism, and the internal evidence consists of texts written centuries after the deaths of the sages they cite. For this reason, much that will be said about community and society will have to do with how these factors operate in the form, rhetoric, and transmission-history of literary texts.

Tradition and Authority

Scholasticism, like Rabbinic Judaism, does not rely on reason independent of authority but insists on traditions and dialectical practices that are passed down through a succession of teachers. This aspect of scholasticism is given particular prominence in an interesting essay by Raimundo Pannikkar (1973).[10] Chief among the features of scholasticism that he enumerates is the principle of authority. As a consequence, scholastics believe in the intrinsic value of tradition: "Truth or any other value is not reached by means of private and individualized tools, but by receiving from and handing over . . . the cultural deposit" (105).

The contribution of the individual is made in scholasticism through commentary and dialectic, the preferred modes of discourse (104–9). At the same time, a specific set of dialectical procedures can reinforce tradition by marking an adept member of a community, who stands in a line of specialists in those procedures. A given type of legal or philosophical reasoning can be accompanied by claims that its method was passed down from teacher to student and that those who follow it are expressing their solidarity with the tradition. Furthermore, dialectic can function to test, and finally reaffirm, the unity or validity of that tradition.[11]

We shall see that all of these elements feature prominently in Rabbinic Judaism. But to what end are teaching, tradition, and dialectic applied? Did the Rabbis believe in what Cabezón calls "the basic intelligibility of the universe?" It is difficult to give an unambiguous answer to that question. *Bereshit Rabbah,* the Rabbinic commentary to Genesis, quotes Ben Sira in this way:

> about what is concealed from you do not ask,
> but about what has been permitted, investigate,
> and do not concern yourself with hidden things.[12]

The Midrash takes this to mean that whatever happened before the creation of the world is not a subject for speculation, but from that point on, it is permitted. But while topics such as cosmology, anthropology, and theodicy are addressed in Rabbinic texts, they are not addressed systematically and with philosophical rigor.

There is, however, one "universe" that is considered wholly intelligible, and that is the universe of God's Torah. A saying in the tractate *Avot* says of the Torah, "Turn it over, turn it over, for all is in it."[13] Statements in the Babylonian Talmud tell of the literally cosmic dimensions of the Torah—said to equal the dimensions of the world itself.[14] This is important because it implies that philosophy is, in a sense, recourse to exegesis. Rabbinic literature was not the first to see Torah as inclusive of knowledge of the cosmos. In fact, several postbiblical texts written before the Rabbinic period, such as Jubilees and 4 Ezra, tell of a dual revelation: an exoteric one given to Israel at Sinai by the word of God, and an esoteric one given by an angel at the same time, representing the secrets of cosmology and history.[15] This conception of revelation, characteristic of apocalyptic literature, has greater affinities to early Rabbinic literature than we might think. Both literatures engage in what has come to be known as *listenwissenschaft*.[16] A well-known example is a passage in the Mishnah tractate *Shabbat,* where the "fathers of labor," the fundamental classes of prohibited work, are enumerated:

> The fathers of labor are forty save one:
>
> A. planting, plowing, reaping, binding sheaves, threshing, winnowing, cleansing crops, grinding, sifting, kneading, and baking;

B. shearing wool, washing it, beating it, dyeing it, spinning, weaving, making two loops, weaving two threads, breaking apart two threads, tying, untying, sewing two stitches, tearing in order to sew two stitches,

C. hunting a deer, slaughtering, flaying it, salting it, curing its skin, scraping it, cutting it up, writing two letters,

D. building, pulling down, extinguishing, starting [a fire], striking with a hammer, and taking something out from one domain to another. (*m. Shab.* 7:2)

The postmishnaic Rabbis, the Amoraim, recognized that this passage depicted sequences of individual actions involved in activities such as baking bread, making clothes, and writing on parchment. The traditional understanding of this passage is that these were the activities involved in making the Tabernacle. Modern commentators have pointed out that this passage is a step-by-step account of the actions that comprise civilization: the steps from nature to culture that result in the necessities of life.[17] This way of expressing its concerns has led Jacob Neusner (1981) to identify the Mishnah as a book of philosophy. Whether or not this term elucidates the purpose of the Mishnah sufficiently, it does alert us to the idea that one goal of the early Rabbis was to say something—although perhaps not everything—about what the universe of things and actions contains.

Somewhat before the advent of Rabbinic Judaism, the authors of apocalyptic psuedepigrapha cast their ideas in the form of purported revelations to biblical heroes, who were said to be shown the secrets of cosmos and history by an angel. In contrast, the Rabbis included themselves, their opinions, and their reasoning in the category of Torah. The chain of succession is marked by Fischel and Saldarini as a distinguishing feature of Greco-Roman scholasticism, and one that influenced Rabbinic rhetoric deeply.[18] The most famous example of this attitude is the introduction of the tractate *Avot*, the Sayings of the Fathers, composed shortly after the Mishnah in the third century and included in the Mishnaic canon. It presents what is considered to be the principal validating myth of Rabbinic Judaism: "Moses received Torah from Sinai, and handed it down to Joshua, and Joshua to the Elders, and the Elders to the Prophets, and the Prophets to handed it down to the Men of the Great Assembly" (*m. Avot* 1:1).

This myth is a dramatic illustration of the idea of tradition. Revelation is not given anew to each sage or generation. Rather, it has come to Israel from Moses and has been transmitted through the succession of masters and disciples. Yet the Torah is not simply a document passed from one pair of hands to another. It is associated with a process by which the Torah's wisdom is elaborated by each successive generation.[19] In the passage just quoted, the initial list of sages culminates in the Men of the Great Assembly. At this point the text introduces the sayings of that body and continues with statements of two of its members, Simon the Just and Antigonos of Sokho. From here on, chapters 1 and 2 consist of statements of the individuals who received the tradition. As Steven Fraade (1991: 69–70) observes, this device, by which each teacher "adds one or more teachings to what he has received," serves to emphasize that the texts of Rabbinic literature "not only transmit received traditions from an earlier time, but simultaneously and often subtly transform—for purposes of their own place and program in time—what they seek to transmit."

Human agency and wisdom thus play an essential role in the Rabbinic theory of revelation. But more than that, since the agency is that of a succession of sages, this wisdom is cumulative. This distinguishes the Rabbinic mode from the apocalyptic, in which the revelation is given by an angel to an individual, who is then charged to write it in a book that is made available to the community. By its inclusion of the sages from Moses to the later rabbis in its account of the transmission of Torah, *Avot* brings a community of mythic teachers into the classroom where the text itself is being recited and repeated by contemporary teachers. The authority of those teachers is thus reinforced by their place in the scholastic succession.

Commentary and Dialectic

Canon and commentary also are understood to be essential to scholasticism. The authority of past revelation is presupposed by scholastics' reliance on a canon as the source of discussion and their preference for commentary as a mode of discourse. As Panikkar puts it, "The best method to reach truth, to assimilate it, to attain the core of the matter and to express it, . . . is the commentary"(106). Commentary allows the canonical text to stand in its authoritative position while exegetical methods allow, in effect, for the scholastic's divergence from the text's point of view (106).

Commentary is likewise an emblematic Rabbinic activity. In Rabbinic Judaism, the claim that the opinions of the sages constitute Torah itself places a burden on commentary—both the Rabbis' commentaries to the canon and their students' commentary to their words. In fact, the preponderance of the Rabbinic canon consists of commentaries: the Talmud is a commentary to the Mishnah and Midrash is commentary on the Bible. The Mishnah stands out precisely because it is not framed as a commentary to the Torah, but as a collection of laws stated independently. David Weiss Halivni underscores this anomalous feature of the Mishnah in arguing for a "Jewish predilection for justified law." Soon after the composition of the Mishnah in the third century, the Rabbis turned to the compilation of the Midrashic commentaries of the fourth and fifth centuries and the interpretation of the Mishnah and cognate sources that became the Talmuds in the fifth and sixth centuries. Commentary thus became increasingly prevalent, and dialectic was called upon to negotiate between apparently conflicting sources. Michael Fishbane sees the history of ideas of authority from the biblical to the Rabbinic period as an evolution from "scribalism" to "Rabbinism"—that is, from what he calls "custodians of the letters of scripture" to privileged exegetes.[20] In a somewhat different way, Isaiah Gafni (1987) applies Weber's notion of the routinization of charisma to the development of the idea of the Rabbi from the Second Commonwealth of Judea to the talmudic period. Gafni sees this evolution as one from Second Temple authorities like Hillel, known only by name, to semiprofessional "rabbis" of the Talmud.

The scribe, then, is someone who teaches by his thoughts and deeds, on the one hand, and encompasses knowledge of a classificatory and systemic nature, on the other. The rabbi is an individual participating in a community of dialectical interpretation.[21] As methods of interpretation evolve, they are increasingly formalized and allow for the give-and-take[22] that a shared hermeneutic makes possible.

As Rabbinic literature developed, it increasingly incorporated dialectical arguments as a mode of commentary. In these, a passage of the canonical text is elucidated by posing questions about its applicability or consistency with the tradition and by drawing inferences from the answers to these questions. The dialectical principles in talmudic thinking were forged in the Greco-Roman period. However, whether they are historically related to Aristotelian dialectic is a matter of debate.[23] Recently, this debate has become part of a larger discussion over whether we can speak of the rationality of so-called "primitive" or premodern societies.[24] At any rate, Rabbinic culture became conscious enough of this dialectical process that several traditions attributed to early sages attempted to codify it in lists of hermeneutical principles.[25]

Cases and Voices

An illustration of these factors together—the peculiar way the Talmudic literature has of dividing up the world through specific cases; the importance given to the words of the sages, and the reliance on commentary to link those elements to Torah; and the use of dialectical arguments to reconcile apparent contradictions and to clarify nuances—can be found in another example from Sabbath law. The following passage from the Mishnah illustrates its use of cases to state principles. In the talmudic commentary to that passage we will see how dialectic and authority interplay in Rabbinic discourse.

Mishnah *Shabbat* 3:3, in the course of discussing the prohibition of cooking on the Sabbath, states:

A. An egg may not be placed beside a boiler so that it roasts,

B. nor may it be broken into a hot cloth,

1. but Rabbi Yose permits it.

C. Nor may one put it in the dust of the road so that it cooks.

On the face of it, this passage would seem to be regulating behavior that would rarely occur in the first place. However, the purpose of the rule is to express the boundaries of the prohibited act of cooking. The egg is a food in which readily visible changes occur in cooking and thus is a good measure of that act. The dust of the road and the hot cloth are examples of secondary sources of heat. These principles thus are not stated abstractly, but in the form of cases. But the report of Rabbi Yose's opinion is jarring to someone not familiar with Mishnaic form. None of the other cases is cited in a sage's name. In form, the citation of his opinion constitutes a gloss in an otherwise plain set of legal statements. Furthermore, Rabbi Yose seems to stand against the weight of the entire tradition. When we ask why this opinion is recorded, it shifts our attention to the statement about which he dissents. What is the difference between the hot cloth and the previous cases? It is the latter question and not that of the authority of Rabbi Yose to dissent that is asked by the Babylonian Talmud's commentary (*Gemara*) to his passage (*b. Shab.* 39a). The Gemara proceeds by citing a series of cases and asking if they would fall under the categories of actions that Rabbi Yose would permit.

It is decided that if the cloth has been heated by the sun and not direct heat, Rabbi Yose would disagree with the anonymous opinion. But would he disagree in the case of the egg in the dust of the road? The Gemara cites a further difference of opinion between two fourth-century authorities regarding why Rabbi Yose also would forbid it:

A. "Nor may one put it in dust:"

1. Let Rabbi Yose dissent from this as well!

a. Rabbah said: [he would agree in this case because] it is an injunction lest one bury it in hot ashes.

b. Rav Yosef said: It is because one might move dust from its place.

According to Rabbah, Rabbi Yose would forbid the action because it might encourage someone to bury the egg in hot ashes, thus subjecting it to direct heat—a clearly forbidden action. Rav Yosef's opinion is that it could entail moving earth from another place to cover the egg, another forbidden action.

We thus find ourselves in a discussion of two glosses on a gloss—that of the Mishnaic citation of Rabbi Yose's opinion. This results in a remarkable exchange on the part of the anonymous text:

2. What is the difference between them?

3. There is a difference between them: loose dirt!

The Gemara, in its famously elliptical way, is demanding, "Show me a case in which the distinction between the two opinions would make a difference." Its solution is to find such a case—if the dirt in which you bury the egg is loose, there would be no need to move earth from one place to another. Thus Rav Yosef's concern would not apply, but Rabbah's would.

What has the Gemara done by this line of argument? It has followed two principles of exegesis similar to those articulated by James Kugel and others as applied by Midrash to Scripture: the principles of the economy of Scripture and the omnisignificance of Scripture.[26] The first stage in the Gemara's program is to link Rabbi Yose's opinion regarding the hot cloth to the case of the dirt. It is assumed that he follows a system that would be relevant to the latter case. The second is to ask what nuances to the law beyond those specific cases Rabbi Yose has to teach us. The working assumption here is that Rabbi Yose's opinion cannot have been placed in the Mishnah arbitrarily; rather it is juxtaposed between the two opinions for a larger reason. Finally, the Talmud works through these problems by presenting its sources in a kind of dialectical deliberation. That is, it is through the constant questioning of the principles by which the statements express the law that its nuances are worked out. This questioning takes the form of a conversation among the talmudic sages, moderated by the anonymous voice of the Gemara. In A 1, the Gemara's questioning why Rabbi Yose does not dissent serves to explain the reason for his previous dissent. The exchange in 2 through 3 serves to refine this understanding further by asking the difference between the two opinions about the nature of Rabbi Yose's agreement. These texts, then, illustrate three important characteristics of scholasticism as enumerated above: commentary, dialectic, and the reconciliation of disparate sources.

However, another characteristic of scholasticism cited by Cabezón (1994: 21–22) is that of increasing abstraction. It is difficult to say if this criterion for identifying scholasticism is met by the process of talmudic argument. The Talmud's reconciliation of sources leads to a more complex web of application of legal cases and principles. But these are not expressed abstractly, but in terms of further cases.[27]

We also have seen that crucial to expressing this tension between dialectic and authority is the interplay of individual rabbis and the anonymous consensus within the text. Many forms in Rabbinic literature display sources and their relationships by means of a brief dialogue staged in the course of the argument or a brief tale of the origins of a statement. An example is the "dispute form," in which two rabbis, who may not have lived at the same time, stand for differing traditions or ways of interpreting a passage.[28] Another is the brief introduction, "when Rabbi X sat before Rabbi Y he taught, etc."[29] There has been much debate about whether these opinions, written down centuries after the rabbis to whom they are attributed, were in fact held by those rabbis.[30] More important to our purposes is the idea that these structures not only serve to represent various positions under discussion, but present as well a model of the proper interaction of scholars.

Brian Stock refers to "textual communities," in the Middle Ages, organized around an authoritative text and its interpreters.[31] Rabbinic society was clearly this; but in order to describe the *literary* form of the talmudic text, we might turn this idea inside out and use it to describe a fictive community which is depicted in a text for the purposes of illustrating the ethos of its authors.[32] In these communities, sages representing the positions the text wishes to present appear to engage each other on the implications of their opinions, directed by the anonymous questioner of the commentary, the Gemara.[33] This format is essential to the Talmud's rhetoric, for it not only states facts or theories, but it also calls forth an ideology of tradition and argumentation. A page of text and commentary creates such a community by its physical format. The classic example is the traditional page of the Talmud, dating from the Middle Ages, in which the Mishnah, Gemara, commentaries, and supercommentaries are placed concentrically. The reader faces a gathering of commentators almost literally sitting around the table of the text under discussion.[34]

Scholastics, Schools, and Scholastic Behavior

But what do these textual formats have to do with the real world of human beings, their societies, and their actions? The scholasticism of Rabbinic society had political consequences. Because their patterns of dialectic and tradition were applied to law and ritual behavior, the rabbis sought to create a class of scholarchs who had real influence and power over people's lives. The living institutions evolved from small circles of disciples to well-established academies headed by powerful legislators.[35] In looking at these we see other aspects of scholasticism worth noting: the practices of learning and discipleship that transformed a student into a scholastic; the creation of an elite that scholasticism facilitates; and the effect of the scholastic ethos on other classes of society.

Becoming a rabbi meant attaching oneself to a rabbi as a servant.[36] As the apprentice to a sage, one learned the Torah not only from his mouth, but from his actions. This does not mean simply that the disciple learned "by example" how an ethical person behaves. Rather, he learned his teacher's opinions on issues of ritual law by observing in what sequence he said his blessings, at what minute in the day he began the Sabbath, and so on. These observations are recorded in talmudic literature as full-blown opinions: The statement "When I served Rabbi X he did Y" is thus worked into the Talmud's discussion of the legal issue expressed by the teacher's action as if he had stated it explicitly.

The social and political implications of this system are apparent. The ideal of the Rabbinic estate was that every male Jew should be a sage, valuing the study of Torah as his highest vocation. That this vocation is not only meant for the wealthy is demonstrated by numerous stories depicting the humble social origins of great Rabbis.[37] Yet the specialized conditions and language of Rabbinic learning and dialectic also tell us that the Rabbinic estate sought to control the terms of the debate in such a way that the new disciple was dependent on his teachers and institutions for true understanding even as he learned argumentation. Once again, the Rabbinic ideology of tradition emphasized this dependence. A famous story tells of how a student came to Hillel asking to learn only the written Torah—not the Oral Torah.[38] Hillel taught him the alphabet one way the first day and the opposite way the next. When the student objected, Hillel demonstrated that the oral tradition—and by extension, the agency of the sage—was inseparable from the text.[39]

Other Scholasticisms

Behavioral norms of a somewhat different sort also were fostered by a literature of Rabbinic etiquette, known as *derekh 'ereṣ*, (the way of the world). These texts, compiled in the late talmudic period and outside of the talmudic canon, systematized statements scattered throughout Rabbinic literature.[40] On the understanding that a sage had a responsibility to deport himself differently from ordinary people, and perhaps on the understanding that this responsibility transcended the realm of what we would call the "ethical," this literature set out prescriptions for Rabbinic etiquette in sonorous maxims and enumeration sayings: "A Sage should not eat standing up, nor drink standing, lick his bowl, lick his fingers, or belch in the presence of his neighbor. He should be sparing [in saying] 'yes, yes' and sparing [in saying] 'no, no'" (*Derekh Ereṣ Zuta* 5:1).

Here table manners, social graces, and correct colleagueship are placed together as characteristics of a sage.[41] The warning to be sparing in assent and dissent may mean that a scholar should not be overly sycophantic or contrary, or that he should not be too quick to accept or refuse requests for help.[42] Other rules instruct the student in the protocol of deference to his teacher in actions such as entering rooms and climbing ladders.

These rules, however, did not have the status of *halakhah*, normative law. In fact, some of them deviate slightly from Rabbinic norms set forth in the Talmud.[43] These may indicate that although they seem to have been intended for the Rabbinic elite, they were taken up by a different class, of nonelite pietists who sought to adopt the ethos and charisma of the sage.

Another example of how social circles outside of the academy took up Rabbinic scholasticism and made it their own is a phenomenon that can be called "scholastic magic."[44] A set of remarkable texts written in the late talmudic and early posttalmudic periods (fifth to eighth centuries) concerns the cultivation of the scholastic virtues of Torah, memory, and acumen through ritual practices designed to attract an angel (known as the *Sar-Torah*, the Prince of the Torah), who then endows the practitioner with spectacular powers of learning and retention. In these texts, scholastic virtues of tradition, authority, and study were marshaled for the purposes of securing the intellectual and social benefits that came with being a sage. These texts, for example, present magical names or rituals in "chains of tradition" similar to the passage from *Avot* quoted above.[45] But instead of Torah, the heroes of the esoteric tradition hand down the magical means to learn it. The magicians thus sought a shortcut through the labor of learning and social process of discipleship that went into becoming a rabbi.

These phenomena are of considerable historical importance. They illuminate Rabbinic scholasticism by contrast and provide one of the few examples of how groups outside the academy saw the Rabbinic estate.[46] They remind us that scholastic communities affect not only their own class and history, but those of others. We are accustomed to thinking of religious communities as stratified by education and class in such a way that the leisured "elite" emphasizes the intellectual virtues, and the "populace" emphasizes folklore and piety.[47] Yet where members of a scholarchy have reputations as saints and holy people, it is reasonable that other members of the society should appropriate their values. Furthermore, in complex societies, nonelite intellectuals draw from a variety of sources in organizing their thinking.[48] Thus the cultural effects of a scholastic movement can go beyond its proximate social setting.

Conclusions

Is scholasticism, then, a useful category to describe Rabbinic Judaism? What has scholasticism gained by considering whether Rabbinic Judaism belongs among its members? This survey has touched upon several features of Rabbinic thought and praxis that bear on the "family of resemblances" that could comprise the category of scholasticism. It has been suggested here that several criteria for identifying scholasticism—commentary, dialectic, canon, and so on—are met by Rabbinic Judaism. However, there are a couple of characteristics of other scholastic cultures that are not as prominent in this case. One is polemic, which has been noted as important in scholastic societies for its function in defining the community and its own positions. There are a few places in Rabbinic lore where explicit polemic takes place. These are set pieces in which a Rabbi debates a stereotyped "heretic" or "heathen" about such controversies as divine design in creation, the necessity or naturalness of circumcision. But more common is the type of argument that is depicted as occurring *within* the academic setting in debate. That is, the text presents an opposing legal position within the Rabbinic estate in order to define a norm. At times the Babylonian Talmud sets up hypothetical objections in order to teach or define the parameters of what its position had been all along.[49]

A second issue concerns the subjects of Rabbinic discourse. Rabbinic literature abounds in scriptural exegesis, consideration of theological topics, and practical wisdom. But the processes of exegesis and dialectic described above are applied in Rabbinic Judaism most systematically in the area of law. This may be a contribution that the study of classical Judaism can make to the study of scholasticism. In Rabbinic Judaism, scholasticism gains an example of a civilization in which many of its characteristics—such as the tension between authority and reason, tradition and dialectic, and the tendency to systematization—are applied to actions more than to thoughts.[50] Key concepts, such as Torah and the Sabbath, refer to ritual and social actions. Moreover, they are elaborated in terms of ever more precise cases. We also have seen that the peculiar voice of Rabbinic discourse, which speaks as an ongoing conversation of scholars rather than a single, systematic disquisition, also expresses the idea that the tradition is embodied in the collective class of sages.

Cabezón (1994:190–91) suggests that the scholastic's goal is the reconciliation of reason and experience. Likewise, we must remember that Rabbinic scholasticism exercises its intellectual effort in the service of the *halakhah,* the system of actions and obligations that express the individual's covenental relationship with God. The scholar we met at the beginning of this essay indeed was engaged in the act of worship—by applying his knowledge and reason in devotion to the Torah. But the Rabbis insisted that wisdom was ephemeral without a foundation in works.[51] In this way as well, our scholar, who worshiped God with his mind, did so in order to worship with his body.

Notes

1. My thanks to Professor Michael Stone for this anecdote.

2. As for the heart as seat of the psyche, see Rosner (1978:104–5); for the kidneys see 108 and the liturgical prayer *Nishmat Kol Ḥai* (Birnbaum, 1948:333–34); cf. Prov. 23:16 and Ps. 103:1.

3. Heilman's *People of the Book* is an analysis of contemporary talmudic lay study groups from the standpoint of social interaction. Helmreich's *The World of the Yeshivah* is a study of the contemporary talmudic academy.

4. See, most recently, Steiner (1989:39–47), who sees in the scholastic heritage of the contemporary university many of its current failings. Even more dispassionate writers on scholasticism often have attributed these characteristics to later scholasticism. See for example Pieper (1960:24–25); cf. also Le Goff (1993), and compare his recent reconsideration of his earlier position (xxi–xxii).

5. On scholasticism, see the previous note. On the history of conceptions of magic as primitive science, see Jarvie and Agassi (1970) and Tambiah (1990).

6. My thanks to Professor Cabezón for making portions of his study available to me in advance of publication.

7. In particular, the philosophical system of Moses Maimonides has been labeled "scholastic," primarily because of its Aristotelianism and influence on Thomas Aquinas' thought. Pieper (1960:105) notes that Maimonides' *Guide for the Perplexed* has been called "a Jewish-Scholastic *Summa.*"

8. Steiner (1989:40–42) also includes talmudic dialectic and commentary in his description of the scholasticism that he opposes.

9. On characteristics of the dialectical argument in Rabbinic literature see the discussion in Neusner 1994:73–94.

10. My thanks to Professor David Carpenter for this reference.

11. Cf. Cabezón (1994:83–87), using examples from classical Judaism.

12. *Gen. Rab.* 8:2. Cf. also *b. Ḥag.* 13a, where the passage is taken to refer to speculation on Ezekiel's vision (*Ma'aseh Merkavah*). On its meaning in Ben Sira's time see Fishbane (1989:67).

13. *M. Avot* 5:22. Cf. *Avot de-Rabbi Natan* A ch. 12.

14. See Idel (1981/82:41) and Kook (1967).

15. See Stone (1990).

16. On the idea applied to apocalyptic literature, see Smith (1975) and Stone (1976). On the idea in the Mishnah see Neusner (1981) and Jaffee (1981).

17. See Hoenig (1978), Gilat (1979), and Goldenberg (1987). Indeed, the list, as Gilat and Goldenberg point out, is not definitive, as it omits classes of labor such as buying and selling.

18. See Swartz (1994).

19. Cf. *y. Sanh.* 10:1 (28a) (cf. *Eccl. Rab.* 12:11) which, quoting *m. 'Avot* 1:1, likens the Torah to a "girls' ball" or "shuttlecock" tossed from one player's hands to another's. See Braude (61–62n. 7). By use of Eccl. 12:11 as the prooftext, the Midrash equates the Torah with the "words of the sages."

20. For a cross-cultural collection of studies of the ancient idea of the sage, see Gammie and Perdue (1990), which also includes Fishbane's essay.

21. In his very suggestive study of the development of intellectual patterns in the Babylonian Talmud, Kraemer follows Halivini's findings on the stages of redaction of the Talmud by showing that while the juxtaposition of sources and the working out of their implications characterized early post-Mishnaic activity, argumentation as such is largely the product of the latest stage of talmudic redaction (the *stam*).

22. Known in talmudic vernacular by the Aramaic term *shaqla ve-tarya*, meaning business negotiation or dialectical argument.

23. See, for example, Kraemer (1990) and Daube (1949, 1953).

24. See Eilberg-Schwartz (1990); cf. Janowitz and Lazarus (1992).

25. For these, see the discussion and bibliography in Strack and Stemberger (1991:17–34).

26. On this concept see Kugel and Greer (1986).

27. As the Babylonian Talmud became canonical for world Jewry in the Middle Ages, a Franco-German school of interpretation, the Tosafists, emerged which extended this process of comparison of disparate sources well beyond what the

Talmud had done. The effect was to develop further legal categories which were subjected to an increasing process of reification and reconciliation.

28. On this form see Neusner (1971 3:5–6, 16–17); cf. the discussion in Kraemer (1990:99–100).

29. On this form see Gafni (1990:180 n. 12), citing *Ḥiddushe ha-Rashba* to *b. Nid.* 20b.

30. For an account of the general problem see Green (1978).

31. See Stock (1983:90).

32. Cf. also the phrase *virtual community*, used in computer terminology to refer to the community that takes place in a network of interconnected users. Again, in both cases, the locus of the "community" is a text. The difference is, of course, that a real user sits behind each computer terminal.

33. Kraemer (1990:99–107) discusses this format in comparison with Greek philosophical dialogues and theories of argumentational discourse. Cf. Martha Nussbaum (1986, especially 122–35), on the relationship of Platonic dialogues to the various voices in Greek drama. Boyarin (1990:23–26) refers to Mikhail Bakhtin's *The Dialogic Imagination* in his discussion of the interplay of voices in the citation of the canonical Torah in Midrash.

34. Cf. Panikkar (1973:106): "Scholasticism is humble vis-à-vis the original; even typographically the commentaries are marginal."

35. It is not certain when the permanent institution of the Yeshivah became the primary setting of Rabbinic learning. See Gafni (1990:177–236) and Goodblatt (1975).

36. For some features of Rabbinic discipleship, see Goodblatt (1975:267–80) and the sources cited there.

37. See especially *Avot de-Rabbi Natan* A chs. 6–7.

38. *B. Shab.* 31a, *Avot de-Rabbi Natan* A ch. 15.

39. There has been much interesting discussion of the historical implications of the ideology of Oral Torah and how deeply it infused Rabbinic Judaism. For excellent recent discussions of the issues, see Strack and Stemberger (1991:35–49); and Jaffee (1992:53–72), who takes full account of the contemporary study of orality in traditional societies; cf. also the studies cited in both.

40. On this literature see Sperber (1985, 1990), Higger (1935), and van Loopik (1991).

41. Cf. *Derekh Ereṣ Zuta* 5:3: "By four things a sage is recognized: by his purse, his cup, his anger, and dress" (*be-khiso, be-khoso, be-kha'aso, u-ve-'aṭifato*) based on an earlier three-part saying found in b. *Erub.* 65b. See Sperber (1990:29–35).

42. See Sperber (1990:23–24).

43. See, for example, the matter of the priority of prayer over study in the synagogue, discussed in Sperber (1990:44–45).

44. See Swartz (1996).

45. On these and their social implications see Swartz (1994).

46. For a provocative recent account of several sectors of ancient Judaism that takes both Rabbinic and esoteric expressions of "transformative knowledge" into consideration, see Jaffee (1997, especially 213–43).

47. For a critique of this tendency see Brown (1981:12–22) and Davis (1982).

48. For an example of such a case see Ginzburg (1982).

49. On this function of the talmudic discussion see especially Jacobs (1961).

50. Cf. Clooney (1990).

51. See m *Avot* 3:17.

References

Bakhtin, M. M.
1981 *The Dialogic Imagination. Four Essays*: Austin: University of Texas Press.

Birnbaum, Philip.
1948 *Daily Prayer Book*. Trans. and annot. Philip Birnbaum. New York: Hebrew Publishing Company.

Boyarin, Daniel.
1990 *Intertextuality and the Reading of Midrash*. Bloomington: Indiana University Press.

Braude, William G.
1968 *Pesikta Rabbati*. New Haven and London: Yale University Press.

Brown, Peter.
1981 *The Cult of the Saints: Its Rise and Function in Latin Christianity*. Chicago: University of Chicago Press.

Cabezón, José Ignacio.
1994 *Buddhism and Language: A Study of Indo-Tibetan Scholasticism*. Albany: State University of New York Press.

Clooney, Francis X.
1990 *Thinking Ritually: Rediscovering the Pūrva Mīmāṃsa of Jaimini.* Vienna: Gerold & Co.

Daube, David.
1953 "Alexandrian Methods of Interpretation and the Rabbis." In *Festschrift Hans Lewald,* 27–44. Basel: Helbing and Lichtenhahn.

1949 "Rabbinic Methods of Interpretation." *HUCA* 22:239–65.

Davis, Natalie Zemon.
1982 "From 'Popular Religion' to Religious Cultures." In *Reformation Europe: A Guide to Research.* Ed. Steven Ozment. St. Louis: Center for Reformation Research.

Eilberg-Schwartz, Howard.
1990 "Myth, Inference, and the Relativism of Reason: An Argument from the History of Judaism." In *Myth and Philosophy,* 247–85. Ed. Frank Reynolds and David Tracy. Albany: State University of New York Press.

Fischel, Henry.
1973 "The Uses of Sorites (Climax, Gradatio) in the Tannaitic Period." *HUCA* 44:119–51.

Fishbane, Michael.
1989 "From Scribalism to Rabbinism." In *The Garments of Torah,* 64–78. Bloomington: University of Indiana Press.

Fraade, Steven D.
1991 *From Tradition to Commentary: Torah and Its Interpretation in the Midrash Sifre to Deuteronomy.* Albany: State University of New York Press.

Gafni, Isaiah.
1990 *Yehude Bavel bi-Tequfat ha-Talmud.* Jerusalem: Merkaz Zalman Shazar.

1987 *"Shevet u-Meḥoqeq—'Al Defuse Manigut Ḥadashim bi-Tequfat ha-Talmud Be'Eres Yisrael u-Vavel.'"* In *Kehunan u-Malkhut—Yaḥase Dat u-Medinah be-Yisra'el u-va-'Amim,* 79–91. Ed. Israel Gafni and Gabriel Mutzkin. Jerusalem: Merkaz Zalman Shazar.

Gammie John G. and Leo G. Perdue.
1990 *The Sage in Israel and the Ancient Near East.* Winona Lake, IN: Eisenbrauns.

Gilat, Yitzhaki D.
1979 *"'Al L"Ṭ'Avot Mal'akhot Shabbat."* *Tarbiṣ* 48:222–28.

Ginzburg, Carlo.
1982 *The Cheese and the Worms: The Cosmos of a Sixteenth-Century Miller*. New York: Penguin.

Le Goff, Jaques.
1993 *Intellectuals in the Middle Ages*. Trans. T. L. Fagan; Oxford: Basil Blackwell.

Goldenberg, Robert.
1987 "Law and Spirit in Talmudic Religion." In *Jewish Spirituality from the Bible to the Middle Ages*, 232–52. Ed. Arthur A. Green. New York: Crossroads.

Goodblatt, David.
1975 *Rabbinic Instruction in Sasanian Babylonia*. Leiden: Brill.

Green, William Scott.
1978 "What's in a Name? The Problematic of Rabbinic 'Biography.'" In *Approaches to Ancient Judaism: Theory and Practice*, 77–96. Ed. William Scott Green. Missoula: Scholars Press.

Halivni, David Weiss.
1986 *Midrash, Mishnah, and Gemara: The Jewish Predilection for Justified Law*. Cambridge, MA: Harvard University Press.

Heilman, Samuel C.
1983 *The People of the Book: Drama, Fellowship and Religion*. Chicago: University of Chicago Press.

Helmreich, William.
1982 *The World of the Yeshivah: An Intimate Portrait of Orthodox Jewry*. New York: The Free Press.

Higger, Michael.
1935 *The Treatises Derek Erez*. New York: Debe Rabanan.

Hoenig, Sidney.
1978 "The Designated Number of Kinds of Labor Prohibited on the Sabbath." *JOR* 68:193–208.

Idel, Moshe.
1981/82 "*Tefisat ha-Torah be-Sifrut ha-Hekhalot ve-Gilguleha ba-Qabbalah*." *Meḥqere Yerushalayim be-Maḥshevet Yisrael* 1:23–84.

Jacobs, Louis.
1961 *Studies in Talmudic Logic and Methodology*. London: Cambridge University Press.

Jaffee, Martin S.

1997 *Early Judaism*. Upper Saddle River, NJ: Prentice Hall.

1992 "How Much Orality in 'Oral Torah'? New Perspectives on the Composition and Transmission of Early Rabbinic Tradition." *Shofar* 10:53–72.

1981 "Deciphering Mishnaic Lists: A Form-Analytical Approach." In *Approaches to Ancient Judaism* 3:19–34. Ed. William Scott Green. Chico, CA: Scholars Press.

Janowitz, Naomi and Andrew J. Lazarus.

1992 "Rabbinic Methods of Inference and the Rationality Debate." *Journal of Religion* 72:491–511.

Jarvie, I. C. and Joseph Agassi.

1970 "The Problem of the Rationality of Magic." In *Rationality*, 172–93. Ed. Bryan Wilson. Oxford: Basil Blackwell.

Kook, S. H.

1967 "*Godel ha-Torah ve-Yaḥasah le-Godel ha-'Olam.*" In *'Iyyunim u-Meḥqarim*, 108–19. Jerusalem, Mosad Harav Kook.

Kraemer, David.

1990 *The Mind of the Talmud*. New York: Oxford University Press.

Kugel, James L. and Rowan Greer.

1986 *Early Biblical Interpretation*. Philadelphia: Westminister Press.

Loopik, Marcus van.

1991 *The Ways of the Sages and the Way of the World*. Tübingen: Mohr.

Masson-Oursel, P.

1920 "La Scholastique." *Revue Philosophique* 45:123–41.

Neusner, Jacob.

1994 *Introduction to Rabbinic Literature*. New York: Doubleday.

1985 *Torah: From Scroll to Symbol in Formative Judaism*. Philadelphia: Fortress Press.

1981 *Judaism: The Evidence of the Mishnah*. Chicago: University of Chicago Press.

1971 *The Rabbinic Traditions About the Pharisees Before 70*. 3 vols. Leiden: Brill.

Nussbaum, Martha.

1986 *The Fragility of Goodness*. Cambridge: Cambridge University Press.

Panikkar, Raimundo.
1973 "Common Patterns of Eastern and Western Scholasticism." *Diogenes* 83:103–13.

Pieper, Joseph.
1960 *Scholasticism: Personalities and Problems of Medieval Philosophy*. London: Faber and Faber.

Rosner, Fred (ed. and trans.).
1978 *Julius Preuss' Biblical and Talmudic Medicine*. Brooklyn, NY: Hebrew Publishing Company.

Saldarini, Anthony.
1974 "The End of the Rabbinic Chain of Tradition." *JBL* 93:97–106.

Schechter, Solomon.
1887 *'Avot de-Rabbi Natan*. London / Vienna / Frankfort.

Smith, Jonathan Z.
1975 "Wisdom and Apocalyptic." In *Religious Syncretism in Antiquity: Essays in Conversation with Geo Widengren*, 131–56. Ed. B. Pearson. Missoula: Scholars Press.

Sperber, Daniel.
1990 *A Commentary on Derek Ereẓ Zuta*. Ramat Gan: Bar-Ilan University Press.

1985 "Rabbinic Manuals of Conduct." In *Scholars and Scholarship: The Interaction between Judaism and Other Cultures*, 9–26. Ed. Leo Landman. New York: Yeshiva University Press.

Steiner, George.
1989 *Real Presences*. Chicago: University of Chicago Press.

Stock, Brian.
1983 *The Implications of Literacy*. Princeton: Princeton University Press.

Stone, Michael.
1990 *Fourth Ezra: A Commentary to the Book of Fourth Ezra*. Minneapolis: Augsburg Fortress.

1976 "Lists of Revealed Things in the Apocalyptic Literature." In *Magnalia Dei: The Mighty Acts of God*, 414–52. Ed. F. Cross, W. E. Lemke, and P. D. Miller, Jr. Garden City: Doubleday.

Strack H. L. and G. Stemberger.
1991 *Introduction to the Talmud and Midrash*. Edinburgh: T&T Clark.

Swartz, Michael D.

1996 *Scholastic Magic: Ritual and Revelation in Early Jewish Mysticism*. Princeton: Princeton University Press.

1994 "Book and Tradition in Hekhalot and Magical Literatures." *Journal of Jewish Thought and Philosophy* 3:189–229.

Tambiah, Stanley Jeyaraja.

1990 *Magic, Science, Religion and the Scope of Rationality*. Cambridge, England: Cambridge University Press.

Chapter **5**

Taoist Scholasticism: A Preliminary Inquiry

Livia Kohn

Introduction

The Taoist religion grew in the Chinese Middle Ages (c. 200–900 C.E.) under the heavy influence of Buddhism, then newly introduced and the first and foremost model for organized Chinese religion. Beyond that, religious Taoism had its original base in a combination of ancient Taoist philosophy, the thought of oneness with the Tao and harmony with the universe as described in the works of Laozi[1] and Zhuangzi, and a variety of ascetic practices that served to extend life and allow adepts to reach higher mental states and spiritual immortality.

This base was firmly in place in the second century C.E., when the first Celestial Master (Tianshi) Zhang Daoling experienced an ecstatic vision of the Highest Venerable Lord, the deified Laozi and personification of the Tao. He received the Covenant of Highest Unity and founded the first messianically oriented Taoist community, limited then to southwestern China. Further revelations, notably those of Highest Clarity[2] (Shangqing) in 364, Numinous Treasure (Lingbao) in the 390s, and the new Celestial Masters under Kou Qianzhi in 415, together with the ever increasing Buddhist impact strongly furthered the development of Taoism as a religion (see Robinet 1991).

These various revelations and traditions were integrated into a coherent whole toward the late fifth century, and by the Tang dynasty

(618–906 C.E.), the heyday of traditional Chinese culture, served as the dominant organized religion of the country. This was the scholastic period of religious Taoism, a time when the originally tangled growth of the religion, more like a jungle than a forest, had already been basically integrated under the umbrella of Highest Clarity and organized in the system of the Three Caverns (major vehicles or schools). It was now ready for a more subtle and more complex form of analysis and exegesis.

The Tang, moreover, which succeed the short-lived Sui that favored Buddhism (see Wright 1978), elevated Taoism to high status not only because of its overall political usefulness but also because of the identity of the imperial surname Li with that of the philosopher and later god Laozi. Taoism at the time was further tamed and made more subtly coherent, controlled both administratively through a well-defined hierarchy of priests, and doctrinally by an increasingly scholastic system under the dominant teaching of Highest Clarity and with an ever increasing Buddhist dimension.

Scholasticism with its "formal nature, its systemacity, its preoccupation with scriptures and their exegesis in commentaries, its rationalism and its reliance on logic and dialectics in defense of its tenent, its penchant for lists, classification and categorization, [and] its tendency toward abstraction," as José Cabezón characterizes it in his recent study (1994: 15), could flourish particularly well in such an organized and centrally structured environment. Such an environment, moreover, made it politically and organizationally necessary to create coherence and general accessibility to a wide variety of doctrines, scriptures, and rituals.[3] Taoist scholasticism, then, was a direct function of the political unification and elevation of Taoism to the status of the major religious teaching under the Tang. At the same time, it is a case in point for the argument offered by Masson-Oursel, who maintains that scholasticism emerges as a response to "sophism," a period of chaotic creativity without order and discipline (1920, cited in Cabezón 1994: 14). Taoism grew wildly and with great variance during the Six Dynasties, from the fourth to the sixth centuries, then was integrated and systematized under the Tang, seventh to ninth centuries, in a format that can be described only as scholastic.

This is not to say that Taoism was in a state of utter chaos before the Tang. The basic doctrines, rituals, and hierarchies of the Taoist religion in its major schools existed fully by the midfifth century. Even then eminent Taoists such as Lu Xiujing (406–77), Wang Daoyi (447–510), and Tao Hongjing (456–536) made every effort to integrate the religion and make it coherent in a plausible system both of priestly organization and religious doctrine. What distinguishes these earlier efforts from the scholasticism of the Tang is the intellectual thrust of the former. Pre-Tang Taoists strove to authenticate and canonize scriptures, to establish a basic ethical code and ordination hierarchy, to create a religious organization on par with the flourishing Buddhist church. They had a concrete goal in mind, a goal more often than not linked with immediate political influence on the ruler of the day.[4] Nevertheless, they succeeded in the creation of a basically organized Taoist religion.

Scholastics of the Tang, then, not only were secure in their imperial favor but already had a fundamentally integrated, if very complex, religious system at their disposal. This freed them to turn to speculation, to intricate theoretical questions, to the exegesis of scriptures, the codification and logical interpretation of rituals. As Barbara Hendrischke (1993: 139) points out, one of the new developments of Taoism under the Tang was the tendency to make Taoist rituals useful to the court and Taoist teachings intelligible to a wider audience. For this, critical self-reflection and analysis were needed, a leisurely speculation on doctrines and practices that led, in due course, to the flourishing of full-blown Taoist scholasticism, a truly innovative and unique development in the history of Taoism.

Systematics, Logic, and Exegesis

Scholasticism flourished throughout the Tang dynasty and began fairly soon after its founding in 618. The most prominent scholastic activities in the seventh century, besides the creation of more sophisticated new "Māhāyana"-style scriptures,[5] were the systematization of the Taoist teaching in relation to its Buddhist antecedents, exercises in Buddho-Taoist logic, and the reinterpretation of earlier texts, notably of the *Daode jing*, but also of religious scriptures, such as the *Duren jing* (Scripture of Universal Salvation; *DZ* 1).[6]

The Daojiao yishu

An example of a the systematic description of the teaching is found in the *Daojiao yishu* (The Pivotal Meaning of the Taoist Teaching; *DZ* 1129) by Meng Anpai of the late seventh century. Responding to Buddhist criticism, the text outlines the major tenets of the Taoist teaching in thirty-seven sections (see list 5.1).[7] Each section, in turn, provides a detailed account of the various doctrines relevant to its topic, integrating in a most sophisticated manner various Taoist views with corresponding Buddhist concepts. Doing so, the variety of Taoist doctrines, as they developed in the many different schools and lineages, are systematized and integrated actively with the current, well-known, and already integrated Buddhist visions of the time. Taoism as a religious doctrine becomes more encompassing and more sophisticated in

List 5.1
The Thirty-seven Sections of the Pivotal Meaning

1. The Tao and Virtue
2. The Body of the Law
3. The Three Jewels
4. Positions and Results
5. The Three Caverns [of the Canon]
6. The Seven Sections [of the Canon]
7. The Twelve Classes [of the Canon]
8. The Two Sides [Senses and the Tao]
9. Intention toward the Tao
10. The Ten Good Attitudes
11. Cause and Effect
12. The Five Covers [Forms of Consciousness]
13. The Six Feelings
14. The Three Conditions [of Karma]
15. The Ten Evil Deeds
16. The Three Ones [Bodily Deities]
17. The Two Kinds of Observations
18. The Three Vehicles [to Salvation]
19. The Six Supernatural Powers
20. The Four Necessities
21. The Six Ferries
22. The Four Virtues
23. The Three Worlds
24. The Five Destinies
25. Primodial Chaos
26. Principle and Teaching
27. Mental States and Wisdom
28. Spontaneity
29. Tao-Nature
30. Fields of Blessedness
31. The Pure Lands
32. The Three Periods
33. The Five Deteriorations
34. Movement and Serenity
35. Impulse and Response
36. Being and Nonbeing
37. Illusion and Reality

the process. The scholastic enterprise serves to create wholeness and fullness out of partiality and doctrinal discrepancies.

The human body, for example, discussed in section 2, played a central role in religious Taoism since its early emphasis on physical practices and longevity (see Kohn 1991a). The body accordingly appears in the *Daojiao yishu* immediately after the most basic concepts of *daode*, 'Tao' and 'Virtue.' The discussion, however, does not stop with the practical relevance and immortal potential of the body, but also integrates the Taoist concepts with the Buddhist "body of the law" (*dharmakāya*). In Buddhism, this refers to the spiritual or true body of the Buddha, the essence of Buddhahood, and the ultimate nature of the universe. The scholastic Taoist vision then merges the traditional Chinese view with the Buddhist concept and takes the body of the law as referring to the cosmic nature of the human body, which appears both as the original body of the Tao and as the body in the world (Kohn 1992: 149).

A similarly systematic and even contrived mixture of theories is found in section 17, "Observation," or insight meditation. Here two fundamental kinds of observation are described, based on the Taoist distinction between energy and spirit:

> The two kinds of observation are the observation of energy and the observation of spirit. The two terms "energy" and "spirit" refer to the inner constituents of body and mind.
>
> The body belongs to the realm of being; it is subject to the delusions of the World of Form. Thus the term "energy" is used to refer to concentration.
>
> The mind belongs to the realm of nonbeing; it is difficult to fathom. Thus the term "spirit" is used to refer to the insight of emptiness. (5.3b; Kohn 1993: 224)

In a second step, however, this basically Chinese system is further and more subtly distinguished as it is linked with the Chinese Buddhist—specifically Tiantai—analysis of contemplation:

> One does not reach enlightenment and perfection of body and mind through the two major kinds of observation alone. Rather, there are five different sets of three levels of observation.
>
> One such set of three is:
>
> 1. Observation of apparent existence
> 2. Observation of true existence.
> 3. Observation of partial emptiness
>
> Another set of three levels of observation consists of the following:
>
> 1. Observation of being.
> 2. Observation of nonbeing.
> 3. Observation of the Middle Way. (5.4b and 5b; Kohn 1993; 225)

This section on observation unfortunately has not survived in its entirety, but the first two sets cited here are instructive. Buddhist notions of emptiness and concepts of illusory existence, as well as Mādhyamika ideas of the Middle Way, are thoroughly and logically integrated into the Taoist vision, listed as different models and variants of the Way.

The *Daojiao yishu* evinces its scholastic nature in its high degree of systematization, its tendency to make lists for clearer distinction, its application of logic, and its tendency to be all inclusive. The goal of the text, even if it was originally molded in a polemical environment, is less the practical establishment of a teaching or the refutation of an opponent's argument, than the creation of a theoretically comprehensive system of doctrines and interpretation of practices that merges all major lines of thought current at the time. It creates a scholastic reformulation of the teaching as a whole.

Mādhyamika Logic

Taoist scholastics of the Tang also believed in the importance of logic. Their main model of thinking in this respect is called by the same name as the major school of *Daode jing* exegesis: Twofold Mystery. The expression goes back to the line "mysterious and again mysterious" in the first chapter of the *Daode jing*. In the Tang, the word *mysterious* appears as a verb in the sense of 'to make mysterious'," making the phrase *mysterious and again mysterious* parallel with *decrease and again decrease* (*Daode jing*, chap. 48; see Robinet 1977). The idea is not only that one discards all desires in two steps. It also implies the theoretical approach to the Tao in a twofold movement of making mysterious and decreasing.

This theoretical structure goes back to the Buddhist theory of the two truths, which in turn is part of traditional Mādhyamika thinking. The two truths were formulated first in China by Jizang (549–623). According to him, truth was realized in three distinct stages: first, through a passage from worldly truth to the absolute truth of emptiness; second, from emptiness, now understood as another form of worldly truth, to a new level of absolute truth now understood as complete nonduality—neither being nor nonbeing; third, from duality and nonduality to neither duality nor nonduality.

This structure of two levels of truth and its application to three stages of mystical progress leads logically to the analytical method of the "Four Propositions," part of the traditional Mādhyamika:

affirmation of being;

affirmation of nonbeing;

affirmation of both, being and nonbeing;

negation of both, being and nonbeing.

(Robinson 1967: 57; Robinet 1977: 117).

In Taoist scholasticism this is reformulated in terms of origin and traces and is applied immediately to practice and the immortal state of mind. As Cheng Xuanying of the seventh century says in his commentary on the *Zhuangzi*:

> There are four levels of meaning:
> First, the wonderful origin is empty and concentrated, one is serene and without movement.

> Second, the secondary traces develop through impulse and response, one is active and not serene.
> Third, origin and traces coincide, one is active and serene at the same time.
> Fourth, origin and traces are both forgotten, one has discarded both movement and serenity. (*DZ* 745, 9.13b)[8]

The Taoist thinking of the period, as exemplified mainly in the philosophy of Twofold Mystery, is therefore an adaptation of Buddhist Mādhyamika logic and two-truths theory. At the same time it is also an active effort to integrate Taoist conceptions of the universe, the self, and realization into one logically coherent whole. The scholastic reliance on logic and the tendency toward unification and theoretical coherence clearly are evident.

Daode jing *Commentaries*

The main body of texts, to which this logic was applied, consisted of the ancient philosophical works: the *Daode jing* and the *Zhuangzi*. Especially the former underwent a great renaissance in the seventh century, when it was formally named the primary text of the religion (Kohn 1992: 141). Commentaries on the text—by scholars, recluses, even emperors—abound, going into ever more subtle details of intricate speculation, until Du Guangting (850–933), in his comprehensive commentary work, the *Daode zhenjing guangsheng yi* (Vast Sagely Meaning of the True Scripture of the Tao and the Virtue; *DZ* 725), summarizes them according to five distinct tendencies or schools:

> 1. the Liguo school, which placed most emphasis on the "regulation of the country";
>
> 2. the Lishen school, which concentrated on self-cultivation and the "regulation of the body";
>
> 3. the Shili yinguo school, which dealt primarily with the "cause and effect in the interrelation of affairs and principle";
>
> 4. the Chongxuan school, centering their interpretation around the "mysterious and again mysterious" of the text;
>
> 5. the Xuji wuwei lijia liguo school, which strove to "rule clan and country through utmost emptiness and non-action." (Xu.1a; Kohn 1991: 189)

In all these different ways, then, Taoist scholastics of the Tang integrated and organized their teaching into a comprehensive whole.

They combined various views through the use of sophisticated theoretical structures and developed elaborate listings. They applied formal logic to establish an active link between the purely abstract formulations of the doctrine and the practice of the active seeker and commented on the major scriptures of the time to explore, in ever more intricate detail, the depths of the divine words.

Major Scholastics of the Tang

Tang scholastics were court Taoists. They were trained in a monastic setting, and each had a home monastery, but their institutions as well as their activities were court-sponsored. They moved freely and actively in the intellectual circles of the capital. Their roles and thinking, though similar in their overall pattern, were not static but changed over time, just as their outlooks were influenced by the evolving cultural and political climate and differed according to individual character. To provide a first impression, I shall describe the lives and works of three main thinkers: Li Rong of the seventh, Sima Chengzhen of the eighth, and Du Guangting of the ninth centuries.

Li Rong

Li Rong, of the seventh century, also was called "Renzhenzi" (Master Who Follows Perfection). Few concrete details of his life are known, since he does not have an official or Taoist biography. According to gleanings from a variety of sources and anecdotes, he came originally from Sichuan, more particularly from a district northeast of Chengdu. Here he became a Taoist monk in his early years and received basic training on Mount Fule. By the middle of the seventh century, he was already in the capital and engaging actively in court debates with famous Buddhists.[9] He also was a poet of some renown and a respected member of the literati, a friend of the famous poets Lu Zhaolin and Luo Binwang. They both wrote poems about him, in which he is stylized as a close friend of the immortals on high, having easy access to the peaches of immortality and continuing his existence in the various spheres of cosmic life forever.

In addition to being an active contestant in the debates and a poet in literary circles, Li Rong was the author of two major Taoist commentaries, one on the *Daode jing*, the other on the *Xisheng jing* (Scripture of Western Ascension; *DZ* 726). The latter text dates from the fifth century and purports to contain the oral instructions Laozi gave to Yin Xi when he transmitted the *Daode jing*. It is a mystical text of some importance in medieval China (see Kohn 1991).

In both commentaries, Li Rong subscribes fully to Twofold Mystery philosophy and Mādhyamika logic, insisting on the necessity of increased forgetfulness in attaining the Tao. In addition, he combines Buddhist and Taoist thought by equating enlightenment with the natural spontaneity of the Tao and by developing subtle distinctions among knowledge, wisdom, and insight. A Confucian, state-supporting element enters his thought when he defines the sage as a realized person who has the pleasure and the duty of leading others to salvation and saving the human community. In addition, a formalized ritual aspect of Li Rong's teaching is found in the Dunhuang manuscript *Xiyu shenxin jing* (Scripture of Cleansing and Purification of Body and Mind; S. 3380; Ōfuchi 1979: 132), attributed to him (Sunayama 1980: 36).

A short text of only four pages, the *Xiyu jing* is set in the Seven-Jeweled Gold-Towered Palace of Purple Tenuity in the Jade Capital of heaven known as Mystery Metropolis. The Heavenly Venerable of Primordial Beginning addresses an assembly of the sages, emperors, kings, nobles, and commoners of the ten directions, including all kinds of spirits, dragons, demons, and so on. The sermon consists of a series of instructions on how to purify oneself properly for interaction with the divine: upon entering the meditation room known as the "chamber of silence," one should scatter flowers, burn incense, and thoroughly cleanse one's body and mind. Doing so, one matches the activity of the celestials above:

> Every year, as the last days approach, the immortals, realized ones, and sages of the upper eight ranks as well as all the men and women in the universe bathe and cleanse their physical bodies in an effort to exhort all living creatures to return to proper accordance with the Tao and eventually go beyond the sufferings of life and death. (Ōfuchi 1979: 133)

To summarize, Li Rong was a devout and active Taoist, a prominent participant in the aristocratic life of the capital, a court debater, a poet, and a philosopher. He lived the life of an established court figure, not that of a reclusive mountain dweller. Although firmly embedded in his religious beliefs and practices, he participated actively in the intellectual and political life of his times and formulated his scholastic ideas and treatises with the goal of contributing not only to a better understanding of the Taoist teaching but also to creating a more powerful integrative doctrine that would benefit the human community as a whole.

Sima Chengzhen

A century later, Sima Chengzhen (647–735) also was an important public figure. The twelfth patriarch of Highest Clarity Taoism, he was in fact the leading Taoist figure of his time and has merited various biographies, both in dynastic histories and in Taoist hagiographies, beginning with a stele inscription composed seven years after his death (Engelhardt 1987: 26–33). Born in Henan, the son of an aristocratic family of long-standing official service, he underwent Taoist training on Mount Song under Pan Shizheng, the eleventh patriarch of Highest Clarity. Succeeding the latter after his "transformation" in 684, Sima traveled to various famous mountains of Taoist repute to settle eventually, upon imperial command, on Mount Wangwu, at an easy distance from the capital. Serving at court as ritual master and teacher of doctrine, he was well regarded by the emperor and had much contact with the leading literati of his time. Throughout his life, he was a court Taoist in good standing (Engelhardt 1987: 36–61; Kirkland 1986: 43–71).

Sima Chengzhen was a prolific writer, but not all his works have survived. Among those extant are various devotional works that include listings and descriptions of famous mountains and Taoist sages, as well as a well-known inscription on the sacred sword he had made as a present for the emperor (see Fukunaga 1973; Schafer 1979). His major works, however, are instructions: treatises that systematize the Taoist teaching in its theoretical and practical aspects and make it accessible to a wider audience. Repeatedly he emphasizes in his prefaces that he saw his main task as being that of formulating the salvific teachings of the Tao for all those ready to listen and practice. One of his works, the *Zuowang lun* (Discourse on Sitting in Oblivion; *DZ* 1036), describes the seven-step meditational transformation of the mind and body into immortal emptiness. It survives also in an early inscription of 829 and can be traced back to lectures Sima gave to his disciples, possibly literati of the capital who joined him for a time on his mountain (Kohn 1987: 40).

The scholastic character of Sima Chengzhen's writings, his systematization of the Taoist teaching, thus is closely related to his pedagogical concerns. A speaker for the Tao, he made the doctrines practically accessible to an audience of literati. Many of his surviving works fit into this pattern. In his *Daoti lun* (On the Embodiment of the Tao; *DZ* 1035), he patiently explains the nature of the Tao and its role in the world to an ignorant student who continues to ask questions, both complicated and foolish. In his *Fuqi jingyi lun* (On the Essential Meaning of Energy Absorption; see Engelhardt 1987), he outlines the various kinds of physical and respiratory practices necessary to bring the body into line with the Tao and to ready it for the higher stages. His *Tianyin zi* (Master of Heavenly Seclusion; *DZ* 1026; Kohn 1987a), moreover, provides a comprehensive description of the Taoist path as a whole, dividing it systematically into five stages.

Between the seventh and eighth centuries, therefore, the main emphasis of the scholastic endeavor underwent a change. Li Rong still worked in an atmosphere of debate and defense of the teaching, striving, like the *Daojiao yishu*, to give a comprehensive logical picture of the Taoist teaching that also did justice to its Buddhist elements and served to convince the rivals of its validity. Sima Chengzhen, on the contrary, addressed primarily disciples of the Tao and intellectuals who came to learn about a deeper, more meaningful level of life. He had no need to justify, and instead worked toward systematization, giving lists and logical explanations, interpretations, and rational outlines. His goal was to develop a simplified, more accessible, and eminently practical form of the Taoist teaching, motivated, as he himself states, by his desire to help the suffering people of his time.

Du Guangting

Du Guangting (850–933) again worked in a completely different environment. Where Li Rong was part of the consolidation of Tang power and Sima Chengzhen lived during its heyday under Emperor Xuanzong, Du Guangting was active during its decline, working in Sichuan, on the periphery of the empire, and serving the local ruler after the downfall of the Tang. He has not merited a biography in official sources but is mentioned honorably in Taoist hagiography and has left behind a large number of works that allow a detailed reconstruction of his career (see Verellen 1989).

Born in the environs of the capital of Chang'an, Du failed the imperial examination and turned to the Tao, which he studied on Mount Tiantai under Ying Yijie (Verellen: 1989: 13; Cahill 1986: 129). First called to court under Yizong in 875, Du became a palace resident and editor of imperial memoranda, serving as counselor and participating in controversies with the Buddhists. Eventually, he was promoted to commissioner of Taoist ritual. After the capital was sacked by rebels in 881, he withdrew to Sichuan, where he edited and compiled Taoist texts and liturgies (Verellen 1989: 86; Cahill 1986: 129). Following the court, he returned to Chang'an in 885 and with it fled back to Xingyuan in Sichuan a year later. In 901 the Tang exile government was overthrown by a local king, and Du joined the new ruler as royal tutor. He continued to be promoted by the Sichuan king until he retired from official service to Mount Qingcheng, where he compiled, edited, and composed Taoist texts until his death in 933 (Cahill 1986: 130).

Du Guangting wrote a large number of works, which Verellen classifies according to eight different groups: mirabilia, saints' biographies, liturgies, inscriptions, editions and commentaries, memoranda and official writings, poetry, and miscellanea. His scholastic efforts are found mainly in the first three and the fifth categories. His collections of mirabilia, for example, give a detailed and systematic record of various wondrous events documenting the power of the Taoist gods and their teaching, especially as it was evident in the Tang dynasty and in Du's own lifetime.[10]

Hagiographies and the biographies of saints and immortals form another venue for Du's systematization of the Taoist tradition (Verellen 1989: 208–11). Here, his most famous extant work is the *Yongcheng jixian lu* (Record of Assembled Immortals of the Walled City; *DZ* 783), a collection of the lives of divine ladies—goddesses, immortals, and active Taoist practitioners.[11] His numerous works on liturgy, moreover (Verellen 1989: 212–15), are the most extensive collection of practical and formal manuals on Taoist ritual remaining from medieval China. Here Du Guangting's vibrant awareness of the changing times and the threats of shifting patterns of power to the Taoist tradition finds its most powerful expression. He compiled and systematized the practices as they were still undertaken in his time, creating a comprehensive corpus of hitherto unknown proportions.

In addition, Du edited and wrote commentaries on a number of Taoist scriptures, including the *Shenzhou jing* (Scripture of Spirit Spells; *DZ* 335), the *Duren jing* (Quan Tangwen 932), the *Suling jing* (Scripture of Immaculate Numen; *DZ* 389), and others (Verellen 1989: 217–19). His commentary and summary of commentaries to the *Daode jing* in his enormous *Daode zhenjing guangsheng yi* (Wide Sagely Meaning of the Perfect Scripture of the Tao and Virtue; *DZ* 725), consisting of fifty scrolls, is a masterpiece of scholastic systematization and integrative interpretation. In addition, before treating the text proper, Du outlines the pursuits of the cosmic deity Laozi (chaps. 2 and 3), thereby laying the foundations for the standard Laozi hagiographies of the Song (Boltz 1987: 131–36).

Du Guangting, the greatest and most prolific among the Tang scholastics, thus was motivated in his endeavor by the political unrest and ongoing decline of the dynasty he served. He was a court Taoist, working for most of his life at court under a formal appointment and compiling his many Taoist works in an official context. His primary concern was the rescue of the Tao as he knew it and the documentation of the power of the gods and the teaching. His powerful systematizations, editions, and new interpretations make him a truly eminent scholastic but they also stand in direct relationship to the upheaval of his time. He created order in the face of overarching disorder, theoretical systems to last where social patterns crumbled.

In all three phases of the Tang dynasty, Taoist scholasticism thus played a significant role. Carried by Taoists active in literati society and at court, it was an expression of the dominant intellectual climate and thus a direct outcome of the political situation of the time. Li Rong and the philosophers of Twofold Mystery established an integrated Taoist teaching, set up the predominance of the *Daode jing*, and interpreted its thinking in terms of Mādhyamika logic just when the Tang rulers were actualizing their claim to power. Sima Chengzhen created systematic descriptions of the teaching and organized paths to Taoist realization when Emperor Xuanzong was using the veneration of Laozi to strengthen his hold over the empire and to establish strong unified structures (see Benn 1987). Similarly Du Guangting, in his own time, compiled Taoist miracle tales, hagiographies, liturgies, and commentaries in immediate reaction to the evident destruction and disorder that grew all around him.

The Scholastic Vision

These three main scholastic thinkers, though different in time and style, share certain basic concerns, which they express in their own ways. In all cases the main focus of their work is on finding ways of expressing the reality of the Tao on earth and in human life. They all concentrate on defining the Tao in its various aspects and on giving an impression of the ways in which it can be realized by human faculties and through human actions.

Li Rong in this context defines the Tao as nature (*ziran*, spontaneity or so-being) and delineates three different levels of knowing or realizing it. Sima Chengzhen presents a lengthy speculative discussion on the "Embodiment of the Tao" that is couched as a dialogue between teacher and disciple. Du Guangting, in his turn, excels in explaining the role of Laozi, highest deity of the Tao and also known as "Laojun" or "Venerable Lord," and gives lists and analyses of the god's names in his efforts to better understand the Tao and bring it closer to humanity.

Knowledge and the Tao

In giving an account of the Tao, Li Rong follows the *Xisheng jing*, which says that "the Tao is nature" (*DZ* 726, 1.3a). He then proceeds to define nature.

> Nature has no specific character within itself. It is free from all causes and dependencies on the outside. Clear and empty, in mys-

> terious serenity, one cannot fathom its origins. Thus it is called "nature."
>
> The within and without of nature cannot be distinguished on the basis of self and other. The form and material substance of nature cannot be defined on the basis of being and nonbeing. The energy and symbols of nature cannot be fixated on the basis of yin and yang. The root and branches of nature cannot be penetrated on the basis of cause and effect.
>
> This is the great Tao of emptiness and nonbeing. This is nature. (1.3a; Kohn 1991: 203)

The Tao as nature for Li Rong therefore is utterly beyond the limitations of human understanding and the definitions of human language. It is free from the bounds of ordinary life and represents the state of permanent serenity sought by the adept of the Tao.

Though beyond all, this spontaneous nature is realized within the perfected human mind. Called "sagacious virtue," it is beyond ordinary knowledge and understanding. Always active, it is yet deeply at rest; always radiant, it is yet intensely dark.

> Sagely virtue is broad and encompassing, there is nothing it does not accord with. Its knowledge can illuminate all mental states, yet despite its brightness it is always dark. Its substance can give rise to all kinds of functions, yet despite its activity it is always at rest.
>
> Thus one who is wondrously joined with names and principle, skilled at entering aloneness, concentrated and imbued with nonaction, is called one with the Tao and nonaction. For him, there is nothing that is not done. (1.1a; Kohn 1991: 203)

Realization of the Tao is the actualization of the basic state of natural so-being in human life and mind. The limitless and ever changing, always active, yet serene way of the world becomes the inherent mental function of the realized Taoist. Still, even within the realm of perfection, there are differences in degree. Li Rong proceeds to distinguish different kinds and levels of knowledge. In his commentary on chapter 33 of the *Daode jing,* he says,

> Knowing it by hearing is called sageliness. Knowing it by seeing is called wisdom. What is hard to know on the outside are other people. What is hard to know on the inside is oneself.
>
> Reflecting on others and knowing their good and evil is called wisdom. Illuminating oneself and learning about one's good and bad points is called enlightenment.

> Knowing goodness is to come closer to being a superior person. It is like acquiring the fragrance of an orchid. Knowing evil is to distance oneself from being an inferior person. It is like removing the stench of a fish-shop. Knowing how to acquire and fulfill goodness, one will develop a sense of loyalty. Knowing how to reject and abandon evil, one will find feelings of repentance. This is enlightened knowledge. (Yan 1983: 831; Kohn 1991: 203–4)

Here Li Rong describes two approaches to realization that go together with two levels of knowledge: analyzing the outside world and observing the life within. Either way, conceptions are found to be mere constructs without solid reality. Nothing is permanent, and while both approaches ultimately must go together, the inner realization that the self is not solid is more important and leads closer to realization of the Tao. More elementary, and underlying these two levels of knowing, is the correct understanding of good and evil, the knowledge how best to accumulate good and remove evil in one's life.

Sageliness, according to Li Rong, thus is divided into three levels: the knowledge of good and evil and its correct application in life; the knowledge of the outside world and the understanding that all conceptualizations are constructs without solid reality; and the knowledge of oneself as a floating immortal entity, the fully realized embodiment of no-self.

Li Rong then distinguishes these three terminologically as knowledge, wisdom, and insight. "Insight reflects emptiness, wisdom illuminates being," he says in his *Xisheng jing* commentary (2.15b). His views seem strongly Buddhist at first sight, depicting an increase in wisdom by throwing things open to light and "awakening" illuminated insight. Nevertheless, a traditional Taoist element remains in Li Rong's description of the ultimate state as the darkness of unknowing. Oblivion is the final characteristic of perfect nature or so-being; it is reached at the deep, dark center of the Tao. Commenting on the *Xisheng jing* statement "To know without knowledge, this is the pivot of the Tao," he says:

> Following the teaching without words, relying on the principle of nonaction, one spontaneously awakens to the Tao and wisdom becomes omniscient. Although then there is nothing that is not known, one is yet in a state of unknowing. Only upon forgetting all knowledge does one attain the pivot of the Tao. (3.15b; Kohn 1991: 205)]

Also, in discussing the definition of the Tao as "invisible and inaudible" (*Daode jing* 14), he comments,

> One goes beyond beings and returns to where there are no beings. In a state without beings there are no forms to be seen or sounds to be

> heard. Thus one joins with the invisible and inaudible. With these, one reverts to complete serenity (Yan 1983: 777; Kohn 1991: 205)

Knowledge for Li Rong thus means a number of different things. On the lowest level, it is the superficial division of affairs into good and evil and is easily applicable in the outside world. In a second step, it becomes enlightened wisdom and means the understanding that all conceptualizations of self and world are constructs without a reality of their own. On the third level it is insight, the realization that one is without a permanent identity, and thus the active embodiment of no-self. In addition, the highest knowledge of all is unknowing, sensory oblivion and utter merging with the Tao (Kohn 1991: 204).

Li Rong's scholastic interpretation of the Taoist scriptures integrates the logic of the Mādhyamika and the Buddhist understanding of the progress toward enlightenment into the traditional Taoist world view. He systematizes and explains, delimits stages, and levels and makes clear distinctions in terminology and understanding. His analysis is succinct and logical, and his integrative interpretation is a good example of early Tang scholastic thinking.

The Tao and Its Embodiment

More complex and intricate, looking at problems from many different sides and defining terms in phrases such as *both* or *neither*, Sima Chengzhen's *Daoti lun* (On the embodiment of the Tao; *DZ* 1035) is a lengthy and highly abstract dialogue on the original nature and active presence of the Tao. The text is divided into three parts, focusing in turn on the *Daode jing*, the nature of the Tao, and the embodiment of the Tao.

The text begins with a basic distinction between the Tao and Virtue, the underlying cosmic power of the universe and its active principle in the world.

> The Tao is all-pervasive; it transforms all from the beginning. Virtue arises in its following; it completes all beings to their end. They thus appear in birth and the completion of life. In the world, they have two different names, yet fulfilling their activities, they return to the same ancestral ground. They are two and yet always one. (1a; Kohn 1993: 19)

It then moves on to discuss the different qualities of the two, the Tao as the creative potential, and Virtue as the nurturing quality of life, which again are "two and yet always one." Following logically, the question arises whether the Tao is "the same or different from beings"? The text answers,

> The Tao is always there, yet eternally other. Beings need the Tao to embody themselves. At the same time, the Tao needs beings to em-

> body itself. Beyond the inherent oneness of all, there are good and evil, right and wrong, life and death, opposition and conformity. (2a; Kohn 1993: 20)

The Tao and beings need each other and depend on each other just as the Tao and Virtue are two aspects of the creative power of life. They are different yet the same, separate yet one, nameless yet named, at rest yet in constant motion.

Names and reality, in particular, raise the problem of epistemology and knowledge of the Tao. Both names and reality ultimately belong to the same underlying structure that essentially never can be grasped. But they are also an active part of the world. This means that as practitioners of the Tao strip off names and classifications in their minds, the "Chaos Perfected" nature of the Tao emerges (*Daoti lun* 4b).

The term *chaos* here means "without distinctions," something, not a thing, that cannot be called by any name. *Perfected* means "total and centered in itself," some not-thing that has no referent outside of itself. Speaking of self or beings as "Chaos Perfected" thus creates a dichotomy that is not there originally. Any name, even that attached to the human body, arises from a conscious self and is mere projection. The concept is a formal expression of a perceived difference—it is unrelated to the being as being, as Chaos Perfected (5a).

Knowledge of the Tao is thus a contradiction in terms, yet that is precisely what Taoism is all about, what the practictioner strives to realize. It can be attained only in utter so-being, a state that is both empty and serene, and not empty and not serene at the same time. In that it equals the Tao, which both embodies emptiness and rests originally in serenity, and is also actualized in the living world and moves along with beings and things (5b).

In its second part, the discussion of the *Daoti lun* concentrates especially on the Tao. Although ineffable and empty, it is yet the beginning and mother of all things, manifest both in the nameless and in the named (7b); both negative and affirmative, elusive and visibly embodied (8a). The discussion here leads to the question of why "if there is no difference between all beings and the Tao, one should cultivate it?" The answer given is that "cultivation makes up for the discrepancy, however minor, between the root and its embodiment, and leads back to original nonbeing" (8b).

The third part, then, focuses on the embodiment of the Tao and its reality in the world and among living beings. Again, the basic nature of the Tao is discussed, new and additional terms are defined, and the problem is looked at from yet more and different angles. For example, we find,

> Question: But if beings are the Tao that means that the Tao also lives and dies. Or doesn't it?
>
> Answer: Living and dying or not living and dying are both attained naturally. That is to say, if the Tao embodies itself in beings, then beings are the Tao.
>
> Since beings live and die, the Tao also lives and dies. As the Treatise says, "It shares the same pattern with beings, active and resting, empty and full." So it ends and begins anew. The text also says, "When spirit radiance joins the hundred transformations, it goes along with the living and dying of beings. Square or round, nobody knows its root."
>
> Good and evil, life and death can be compared to the way fishes both live and die in water. Life and death happen to the fish, but the water does not change.
>
> Again we may say, once there are distinctions, there is life and death, but the Tao contains all equally, and so it is free from life and death. In yet other words: Life and death happen to beings, but what destruction could ever touch the Tao? Thus the Tao is free from living and dying. (10b)

Looking, therefore, at the problem from the perspective of beings' living and dying, the Tao is inherent yet beyond, changes as beings change yet stays always and ultimately the same. In life, beings are with the Tao as they continue to change, yet they also are permanent in and through their transformation as the Tao is one and eternally the same.

The same perspective is clarified again in terms of separateness and ubiquity, of difference and identity.

> The embodiment of the Tao widely encompasses all. This means that it is everywhere. Being everywhere, it is wondrously beyond individual bodies and names, yet at the same time it is fully embodied in the myriad beings. This gives rise to the inherent principle of identity and difference.
>
> The principle of identity and difference, in its perfection, culminates in the absence of identity and difference. Identical and different, the Tao in beings wondrously goes beyond all and is widely encompassing. Neither identical nor different, it wondrously goes beyond while at the same time actively encompassing all. As it goes beyond all, it realizes its fullest embodiment. This is wondrous complete pervasion. This is the Tao. (8b–9a)

The subtle scholastic vision of Sima Chengzhen thus formulates the differences and similarities in understanding the basic notions of the Taoist religion. With great philosophical exactness and in painstaking detail it formulates the logical and paradoxical dimensions of realizing the Tao. Sima's reading and explanation of the doctrine—theoretically subtle and in full command of the scholastic methods and faculties—never loses sight of the practical dimension, of the application of the doctrines in the lives and aspirations of Taoist adepts. Realization of the Tao remains Sima Chengzhen's ultimate goal, even in his most intricate and paradoxial analyses of various doctrinal and theoretical aspects.

The Names of Laozi

A different approach to the same essential problem of the Tao in the world and its accessibility to human beings is offered by Du Guangting in his commentary to the *Daode jing*, *Daode zhenjing guangsheng yi* (*DZ* 725, hereafter abbreviated *Guangsheng yi*) in which he makes several notes on the deity Laozi and his names.

Historically, Laozi is the name of the philosopher associated with the *Daode jing* and its transmission to Yin Xi, the Guardian of the Pass. His name means "Old Master" and has been understood as the polite title of the ritual master Lao Dan (Old Dan), a teacher of Confucius later linked with the *Daode jing* (Graham 1990: 113). Once integrated into religious Taoism as a full deity and active personification of the Tao, however, Laozi became more exalted and came to be called by different names.

Du Guangting mentions Imperial Heavenly Sovereign as his appellation when in heaven, and Highest Venerable Lord as his title when teaching the Tao on earth. In addition to these, the deity had 1,200 titles and 180 names. Among others, he was called the "Father of Nonaction" and the "Mother of All Beings." However, in his deepest foundation he is like the Tao itself: so enormous and so unfathomable that he cannot possibly be named (*Guangsheng yi* 2.2ab).

Moreover, the name Laozi itself took on a much deeper significance. From "Old Master," its emphasis was changed to "Old Child," a name given to the god by his mother upon birth because he had spent seventy-two (in later versions, eighty-one) years in the womb and was born with white hair like an old man (*Shenxian zhuan* 1; Kohn 1996). Du gives a much more sophisticated and scholastic interpretation of the name.

> As to the name given to the sage, Laozi, "Old Child," it is usually assumed that it refers to the fact that he remained in the womb for eighty-one years and had white hair when he was born. The Holy Mother Goddess thus named him to show his wonderful nature to the world.
>
> In addition there are five theories regarding this problem:

> First, as the appearance of sages on earth is different from that of ordinary man, the Holy Mother wanted to call him "Old." But as he had only just been born, she also wanted to call him her "Child." Therefore she decided to combine these two words and call him Laozi.
>
> Next, the name "Old Child" was chosen to illustrate the nature of the sacred Tao as opposed to the profane. "Old" usually means aged, whereas "child" commonly denotes a young person. Normal people are first young, and gradually grow old, but Laozi started out being old and gained youth. Thus it was intended to clarify the fact that he lived and thereby returned to the root.
>
> Third, "old" refers to Laozi's position as supervisor of the many sages, whereas "child" indicates his creative power over the myriad beings. Laozi combines both names because he is the teacher of the sages and the creator of all beings. He is therefore called "Old Child." This name was given to him when he was born on earth. His real name Laojun, Venerable Lord, on the other hand, stems from times unknown in the past.
>
> Fourth, he is called Old Child to demonstrate his rejection of ending and his continuous return to the beginning. "Old" represents the end of life; "child," on the other hand, is its beginning. Normal people start at the beginning and gradually proceed toward the end. But the Venerable Lord rises from the end and gradually proceeds to the beginning. He wants to make all people practice the Tao, repel old age, and return to youthfulness. This is why he took the name "Old Child."
>
> Fifth, Laozi radiates the light of harmony to spread the Tao among humanity. He is called "old," because he had white hair when he was born. He is "child" or "master," because this is a common appellation for philosophers. For instance, Kongzi, Mengzi, Zhuangzi, and Liezi all use their surname together with this suffix. Laozi, Heguanzi, Baopuzi, and Huainanzi call themselves after some special characteristic using the same word. (*Guangsheng yi* 2.16a; Kohn 1989a: 76–78)

With this detailed and multivalent scholastic explanation, Du therefore claims that the very name Laozi or "Old Child" symbolizes the full powers of the deity as the divine child, the creator, the returner, the eternal, the newly born. Both old and young at the same time, simultaneously transforming and eternal, divine and human in one body, the same being both growing and declining—Laozi in his human form combines and incorporates all the different aspects of life on earth, just as his name reflects his power and his supernatural stature among humanity.

The god Laozi in Du Guangting's work, just as the doctrine of the Tao in Sima Chengzhen's analysis and the concept of knowledge in Li Rong's discussion, is thus the subject of a detailed and sophisticated scholastic interpretation. The Taoist teaching, systematized into a coherent whole, is analyzed in one particular aspect with ever-increasing subtlety, making the multifaceted complexity of the religion shine forth with concentrated power in a single aspect. The thinkers add dimensions of meaning and intricacy to one point to reveal the fullness and power of the entire edifice. Du Guangting in particular, continuing the tradition of earlier Tang thinkers while working in a politically less stable environment, pushes the scholastic enterprise to further heights and, both in his analysis of Laozi's names and in his ritual and hagiographic work, achieves an intensity of vision that both penetrates and encompasses the religion to its very foundations.

Conclusion

When viewed against the background of scholasticism as a comparative category, the Taoism of the Tang dynasty, as represented by the texts and figures discussed above, appears as another valid example of the scholastic world view. It shows how a fully developed religion comes to terms with its teachings and organization and reflects back upon itself after a healthy period of growth.

Tang Taoism shows many classical characteristics of the scholastic approach. It is highly systematic and systematizing, focuses on the scriptures and their exegesis, and uses commentaries, logical argument, definition of terms, and complex lists to clarify its meaning and the issues with which it is concerned. Coming to the fore at a time when Taoism not only is a well-developed religious system but also enjoys state support, Taoist scholasticism plays an important role in the intellectual climate of the time and participates actively in its formation and development.

Like Taoism as a whole, the three representative scholastics whose lives and views we have presented above respond to the call of the era in the concerns they address and the methods they utilize. Li Rong, poet and commentator on the scriptures, exercises his logical skills in epistemology to develop a better philosophical understanding of how one can know the Tao. Sima Chengzhen, a century later, uses scholastic logic both to obscure and to illuminate the being and nonbeing of the Tao in his students' minds. He addresses practical questions, remaining foremost and always the teacher of the unenlightened, but his approach is characterized by highly sophisticated questions and answers, paradoxes, and logical twists. Du Guangting, finally, following both earlier masters in his extensive commentary and ritual works, adds a new component by actively integrating the myth of the hightest deity into the scholastic discourse. Laozi and his different names, to focus on the example described above, come to represent yet another model of the reality of the Tao in the world. In his lists and analyses, Du shows yet another way the true embodiment of the Tao can be known by humanity.

The three thinkers, with their common concern with systemacity and the accessibility of the Taoist teaching, are at the same time the product of their respective ages. Taoist scholasticism, far from being an unworldly exercise of speculation and mere theoretical organization, emerges as a relevant activity in and contribution to the intellectual life of the time. It begins as a call for inherent order after the Six Dynasties' period of vigorous growth, and proceeds, through the vagaries of the Tang's political and intellecutal climate, to bring forth a large number of highly sophisticated and speculative materials.

A thorough and continuing effort to systematize, classify, organize, and interpret the teaching, Taoist scholasticism, as it flourishes first and foremost during the Tang dynasty, not only occupies an important position in the history of Taoism, but can also can add to our evolving knowlege of the general category of scholasticism. While it shows many of the characteristics found typical of scholasticism so far, it also differs from the Western-defined picture in its continued emphasis on religious practice and active soteriological concerns. This, futhermore, implies a greater accessibility and spread of the scholastic vision not only to Taoist specialists but also to interested lay literati, if not to the common people of the time. Scholasticism in this time and culture, not unlike Chinese mysticism as opposed to its Western counterpart, is less divided from society as a whole and is apparently non independent of political climates and concerns. Scholasticism, we can see, has a distinct social and cultural function, one that goes beyond the glass-bead games commonly associated with it. Studying the Taoist form of scholasticism thus gives us another vantage point and new information, on the basis of which a truly comparative category can be constructed and further developed.

Notes

1. On the importance of Laozi in the founding of the Tang dynasty, see Hendrischke (1993: 113). For more on his various roles in legend, cult, and myth, see Graham (1990), Seidel (1969), Kohn (1989).

2. Highest Clarity at this time was formerly named the dominant Taoist school. Its second patriarch, Wang Yuanzhi, became the founding saint of the dynasty, an inspired Taoist who not only foretold the victory of the Tang but also gave practical help to their generals. For a general outline of Tang patriarchs and the status of the school under the dynasty, see Schafer (1980). For more details on Wang Yuanzhi, see Yoshikawa (1992).

3. Not only did the political integration promote an intellectual systematization typical of scholastic activity (Panikkar 1973: 112), but the political push toward integration necessitated the kind of monopolized knowledge based on which scholasticism thrives. For an enlightened discussion of this topic, see the contribution by David Carpenter in this volume.

4. This also holds true for the various debates among Buddhists and Taoists at the time. Although sophisticated and formal, dialectical and logical, arguments in these debates served the concrete aim of discrediting an opponent and had little or nothing to do with a systematic understanding of the doctrines. On the contrary, in many cases, the apparently well-structured analysis of certain concepts and ideas hides an intentional distortion of the opponent's views. See Kohn (1995) for more details.

5. The most famous of these were the *Benji jing* (Scripture of Original Time) and the *Haikong jing* (Scripture of Master Haikong). Both placed in the mouth of the Heavenly Venerable, preaching from a lotus-throne in the heavenly realm, they not only integrate the teachings of the various Taoist schools but also heavily rely on Buddhist doctrine and logic. For a brief summary, see Kohn (1992: 140).

6. Texts in the Taoist Canon (*Daozang*, abbreviated *DZ*) are given according to the number of the reduced sixty-volume edition published in Taipei and Kyoto. These numbers coincide with those found in Schipper (1975).

7. For a detailed summary, see Yoshioka (1959: 309–50). A brief outline of its mystical teachings is found in Kohn (1992: 149–54).

8. For a more detailed discussion, see Robinet (1977), Kohn (1992: 143), and Kohn (1991: 190).

9. Since the debates are reported in Buddhist sources, Li Rong often is depicted as dumbfounded or driven to mindless rage (Kohn 1991: 196–99).

10. See Verellen (1989: 206) for a list of texts with brief descriptions. A more detailed study of the *Daojiao lingyan ji* (*DZ* 590) with partial translation of miracle tales is found in Verellen (1992).

11. For a study of the Queen Mother of the West in this text, see Cahill (1993). For a more general discussion of women's practices in medieval Taoism as documented by Du Guangting, see Cahill (1990).

References

Benn, Charles D.

1987 "Religious Aspects of Emperor Hsüan-tsung's Taoist Ideology." In *Buddhist and Taoist Practice in Medieval Chinese Society*, 127–45. Ed. David W. Chappell. Honolulu: University of Hawaii Press.

Boltz, Judith M.

1987 *A Survey of Taoist Literature: Tenth to Seventeenth Centuries.* Berkeley: University of California, China Research Monograph 32.

Cabezón, José Ignacio.

1994 *Buddhism and Language: A Study of Indo-Tibetan Scholasticism.* Albany: State University of New York Press.

Cahill, Suzanne.

1993 *Transcendence and Divine Passion: The Queen Mother of the West in Medieval China.* Stanford: Stanford University Press.

1990 "Practice Makes Perfect: Paths to Transcendence for Women in Medieval China." *Taoist Resources* 2.2: 23–42.

1986 "Reflections on a Metal Mother: Tu Kuang-t'ing's Biography of Hsi-wang-mu." *Journal of Chinese Religions* 13/14: 127–42.

Engelhardt, Ute.

1987 *Die klassische Tradition der Qi-Übungen. Eine Darstellung anhand des Tang-zeitlichen Textes Fuqi jingyi lun von Sima Chengzhen.* Wiesbaden: Franz Steiner.

Fukunaga Mitsuji.

1973 "Dōkyō ni okeru kagami to ken" (Mirror and Sword in Taoism). *Tōhō gakuhō* 45: 59–120.

Graham, A. C.

1990 "The Origins of the Legend of Lao Tan." In *Studies in Chinese Philosophy and Philosophical Literature,* 111–24. Ed. A. C. Graham. Albany: State University of New York Press. Originally published 1981.

Hendrischke, Barbara.

1993 "Der Taoismus in der Tang-Zeit." *Minima sinica* 1993/1: 110–43.

Kirkland, J. Russell.

1986 "Taoists of the High T'ang: An Inquiry into the Perceived Significance of Eminent Taoists in Medieval Chinese Society." Ph.D. Diss., Indiana University, Bloomington.

Kohn, Livia.

1995a *Laughing at the Tao: Debates among Buddhists and Taoists in Medieval China.* Princeton: Princeton University Press.

1995b "Laozi: Ancient Philosopher, Master of Longevity, and Taoist God." In *Religions of China.* Ed. Donald S. Lopez. Princeton: Princeton University Press.

1992 *Early Chinese Mysticism: Philosophy and Soteriology in the Taoist Tradition*. Princeton: Princeton University Press.

1991a *Taoist Mystical Philosophy: The Scripture of Western Ascension*. Albany: State University of New York Press.

1991b "Taoist Visions of the Body." *Journal of Chinese Philosophy* 18: 227–52.

1989a "Die Emigration des Laozi: Mythologische Entwicklungen vom 2. bis 6. Jahrhundert." *Monumenta Serica* 38: 49–68.

1989b "The Mother of the Tao." *Taoist Resources* 1.2: 37–113.

1987a *Seven Steps to the Tao: Sima Chengzhen's Zuowanglun*. St. Augustin/Nettetal: Monumenta Serica Monograph 20.

1987b "The Teaching of T'ien-yin-tzu." *Journal of Chinese Religions* 15: 1–28.

Kohn, Livia (ed.).
1993 *The Taoist Experience: An Anthology*. Albany: State University of New York Press.

Masson-Oursel, Paul.
1920 "La Scolastique, étude de philosophie comparée." *Revue Philosophique de la France et de l'Étranger* 90: 123–41.

Ōfuchi Ninji.
1979 *Tonkō dōkei: Zuroku hen* (Taoist Scriptures from Dunhuang: The Texts). Tokyo: Kokubu shoten.

Panikkar, Raimundo.
1973 "Common Patterns of Eastern and Western Scholasticism." *Diogenes* 83: 13–113.

Robinet, Isabelle.
1991 *Histoire du Taoisme: Des origins au XIVe siècle*. Paris: Editions Cerf.

1977 *Les commentaires du Tao to king jusqu'au VIIe siècle*. Paris: Memoirs de l'Institute des Hautes Études Chinoises 5.

Robinson, Richard.
1967 *Early Madhyamika in India and China*. Madison: University of Wisconsin Press.

Schafer, Edward H.
1980 *Mao-shan in T'ang Times*. Boulder: Society for the Study of Chinese Religions Monograph 1.

1979 "A T'ang Taoist Mirror." *Early China* 4: 387–98.

Schipper, Kristofer M.
1975 *Concordance du Tao Tsang: Titres des ouvrages*. Paris: Publications de l'École Française d'Extrême-Orient.

Seidel, Anna.
1969 *La divinisation de Lao-tseu dans le Taoïsme des Han*. Paris: Ecole Francaise d'Extrême Orient. Reprinted 1992.

Sunayama Minoru.
1980 "Dōkyō chugenha hyōi" (The Tradition of Twofold Mystery in Taoism). *Shūkan tōyōgaku* 43: 31–44.

Verellen, Franciscus.
1992 "Evidential Miracles in Support of Taoism: The Inversion of a Buddhist Apologetic Tradition in Tang China." *T'oung-pao* 78: 217–63.

1989 *Du Guangting (850–933)—taoiste de cour à la fin de la Chine medievale*. Paris: Collège de France, Memoires de L'Institut des Hautes Études Chinoises 30.

Wright, Arthur F.
1978 *The Sui Dynasty*. New York: Knopf.

Yan Lingfeng.
1983 *Jingzi congzhu* (Collected Classics and Philosophers). Taipei: Xuesheng.

Yoshikawa Tadao.
1990 "Ō Genshi kō" (On Wang Yuanzhi). *Tōhō gakuhō* 62: 69–98.

Yoshioka Yoshitoyo.
1959 *Dōkyō to bukkyō* (Taoism and Buddhism), vol. 1. Tokyo: Kokusho kankōkai.

Chapter 6

Tibetan Gothic: Panofsky's Thesis in the Tibetan Cultural Milieu

José Ignacio Cabezón

Tibetan Buddhist temples are not Gothic cathedrals, but for all their differences (and there are many) there is a level at which semblance can be explored. The locus of this comparison—the site of the exploration of the pattern of similarities and differences—is the relationship of the scholastic world view of each culture (medieval Tibetan and European) to its respective architectural forms. I do not expect such a pattern to be immediately evident even to those conversant with the intellectual and architectural histories of these two very different cultures. My goal is not to uncover superficial similarities of architectural style, iconography, or even function. The comparability I wish to explore is more complex than this, involving as it does the relationship of an ideology—what, fittingly I think, is sometimes referred to as "a mode of thought"—to architecture. Stated briefly, my thesis is this: there is an isomorphism between medieval European scholasticism and Gothic architecture on the one hand, and Buddhist scholasticism and Tibetan architecture on the other, which is to say that both medieval Western and Tibetan Buddhist scholasticism are reflected in their respective material cultures. *How* material artifacts (in this case architectural ones) act as mirrors of the scholastic world view may well differ from one society to the next, but *that* the prevailing ideological idioms of these two premodern societies filters down—or perhaps siphons up—to the realm of material production seems to me to be invariant across the two cultures.

Of course, it is the *how* (and not the *that*) of the relationship between the ideological and the material—between scholasticism as an intellectual movement and architecture—that is of primary interest. The purpose of this chapter, then, is to suggest that *how* in the Tibetan case. To repeat, my goal is not to attribute to a mythic common scholasticism the superficial similarities we may find in the religious architecture of medieval Europe and Tibet. Mine is not a search for the Tibetan equivalent of the flying buttresses of Notre Dame or of the motives of the great windows of Chartres. Nor is it, essentialistically, to attribute these—even assuming they could be found—to some common ideology. Instead, it is my purpose to demonstrate that, in a way homologous to the Christian West, the scholastic method—as the intellectual world view of Buddhist Tibet (at least from the twelfth century on)—is reflected in Tibet's religious architecture. Hence, the objects of comparison here are neither architectural styles nor ideological world views. To the extent that this work is comparative, the comparanda are the *relationships* between the distinct scholastic methods and the religious architectural styles of two cultures.

The original inspiration for this project came as a result of reading the work of the great medievalist Erwin Panofsky. Though perhaps not the first to suggest a link between the medieval scholastic method and Gothic architecture, his was the most systematic and developed argument for this view. Unlike Panofsky, however, I wish to remain neutral on the question of causal influence. Although I believe the question to be answerable in principle, I am not interested here in whether scholastic thinking is the causal source of certain architectural artifacts (or, conversely, whether those artifacts created an ambience that promoted a nascent scholasticism as a method). But even apart from this issue (more on which below), it seems to me significant simply to establish how scholasticism as an ideology is mirrored in another aspect of culture (in this case a material aspect, to wit, architecture); or perhaps more accurately, that these two aspects of culture—one conceptual and abstract, the other visual and concrete—mirror, reflect, and recapitulate each other.

Panofsky's Thesis

In his Wimmer lecture of 1948, subsequently published under the title *Gothic Architecture and Scholasticism* (1951, 1957),[1] the eminent scholar of medieval Europe, Erwin Panofsky, put forward a thesis that has influenced medieval studies to this day. Briefly, it is that there exists a historical correspondence between the rise, evolution, and demise of European scholasticism and Gothic architecture, and that this parallelism, far from being accidental, is rather "a genuine cause-and-effect relation . . . that comes about by diffusion rather than by direct impact . . . by the spreading of what might be called, for want of a better term, a mental habit" (Panofsky 1957:21–22). Although equivocal at points, Panofsky for the most part concedes that there is little evidence to suggest that architects and builders had actual firsthand knowledge of scholastic philosophy. He argues, nonetheless, that the fabric of medieval society was so imbued with the scholastic ethos, and especially with the scholastic method, that the latter affected, causally, the nature and evolution of Gothic architecture. As B. B. Price notes (1992:138–41), Panofsky's thesis has not gone unchallenged, and yet, despite the controversy surrounding it, his rather detailed argument concerning the "homology" between Gothic architecture and scholasticism is still influential today.

A detailed overview of Panofsky's study is of course beyond the scope of the present chapter. Nonetheless, a summary of some of the more salient points is in order:

1. Panofsky sees a parallelism between the evolution of scholastic literature—from the simpler *libri senteniarum* to the more comprehensive *summa*—and the the evolution of Gothic architecture—from its origins in Suger's St. Denis to its culmination in high Gothic style.

2. The scholastic insistence on lucidity in exposition, which Panofsky refers to as *manifestatio* or "the postulate of clarification for clarification's sake" (Panofsky 1957:39) he sees to be reflected in the Gothic visual arts (e.g., in the representational scenarios found in portals) "through an exact and systematic division of space" (1957:39). The tendency to greater organization and clarity is for Panofsky the result of scholastic influence.

3. The Gothic cathedral, in its imagery, seeks to "embody the whole of Christian knowledge, theological, moral, natural and historical with everything in its place" (1957:44–45), thereby evincing the principles I have called "completeness" and "systematicity" (see the Introduction).

4. And just as the scholastic seeks to order the disparate parts of tradition through systematic synthesis, Panofsky sees the structural design of the Gothic edifice as a synthesis of "all major motifs handed down by separate channels" (1957:45). Hence, the authority of the architectural tradition as much as that of the intellectual tradition is preserved through the reconciliation of disparate elements, that is, through the principle of *concordantia* (1957:64 et passim).

5. The tendency to divide and subdivide texts for greater clarity, says Panofsky, "is most graphically expressed in the uniform division and subdivision of the whole structure" (1957:45), first into the three main parts (nave, transept, and chevet), and further into subparts (high nave, side aisles / apse, ambulatory and hemicycle of chapels / fore choir, and choir proper).

6. Finally, just as the primary purpose of the scholastic treatise was to uphold the validity of doctrine, the primary purpose of Gothic architecture was functional: the stability of the edifice. Nonetheless, Gothic architectural form, claims Panofsky, went further than was necessary for mere stability. "Just as the membrification of the *Summa* permitted [the scholastic] the re-experience of the very process of cogitation," through the contemplation of structure, so too did the "panoply of shafts, ribs, buttresses, tracery, pinnacles, and crockets . . . [allow for] a self-analysis and self-explication of architecture" (1957:59). The aim, both in the case of the scholastic *summa* and in that of the Gothic cathedral, was twofold. There were the first-order goals of (a) validity / stability, and (b) making the content explicit; and there was the second-order goal of making the very process and principles of reasoning / architecture manifest by bringing the very structure of the work to the fore, a principle I have referred to above as self-reflexivity.

The Analogical Argument

As we already have mentioned, Panofsky formulates his argument as a historical one. There exists for him a clear causal relationship between scholasticism as an intellectual world view and Gothic architecture. Such a formulation of the argument makes it necessary for Panofsky to find actual instances of influence, that is, specific cases of the conscious use of scholastic principles in the design of Gothic cathedrals.

Whether or not historical proof of this kind is forthcoming in the medieval European setting—and Panofsky himself seems to vacillate on this—in Tibet detailed proof of this kind is difficult to find. Tibetan Buddhist scholastics did have an important role to play in the construction of religious buildings and monuments; this much we know (see below). But our knowledge of the historical minutiae necessary to make the kinds of connections necessary to defend such a thesis in all its complexity—connections between Tibetan intellectual, institutional, political, and architectural history—is simply too limited, lacking as we do the details of the interactions between scholars, artisans, monks, and workers in medieval Tibet. This is to say nothing of questions concerning the dates of the construction of particular free-standing temples and the variety of structures within monasteries, their historical evolution, patterns of patronage, and so forth.

Part of the problem lies in the fact that the archival records of Tibet's great religious institutions are not yet fully accessible to scholars outside of China and Tibet. Only when this material, the inscriptions found in temples and the other sources (principally historical and auto/biographical) are fully examined can we hope to determine the direct causal impact of the Buddhist scholastic world view on religious architecture and other modes of cultural production. Until then our conclusions concerning the actual historical links between scholastic philosophy and architecture will be restricted to those that can be gleaned from the few texts in the public domain that make reference to the building activities of scholars (on which see below).

Even apart from determining the actual historical role played by scholastics in the construction of religious edifices, however, there is an alternative way of formulating Panofsky's hypothesis that circumvents the difficulty that results from our dearth of knowledge concerning historical detail. Formulating the argument not historically but analogically allows us to point out instances of structural similarity without having to suggest specific causal/historical influence. This is the tack I shall take here in arguing for the relevance of Panofsky's thesis to the Tibetan cultural sphere. Approaching the problem in this way vitiates the need to make a case for specific historical influence, allowing for the possibility both of scholasticism's influence on art and architecture and, conversely, the influence of the visual arts and architectural technique on the Tibetan intellectual tradition. In short, by avoiding the question of determining unidirectional influence, we extricate the argument from the realm of history proper and free ourselves to consider a wider range of semblance. In the Tibetan case, adopting such an approach represents not only a judgment call related to scholarly style, but, given the dearth of historical detail available to us, it is in fact a practical precondition for the task at hand.

Evidence of a Scholastic Link to Architecture

The history of Tibetan architecture has yet to be written,[2] and for the reasons just outlined above, this is not likely to occur in the near future. Nonetheless, a few texts available to us (as well as the inscriptions that have been studied to date) do give us clues as to the processes and personages involved in the building of religious monuments and monasteries. Among the more important texts for our purposes are:

1. The autobiography of the first Paṇ chen bla ma bLo bzang chos kyi rgyal mtshan (1570–1662) (Ngawang Gelek Demo 1969; Paṇ chen bLo bzang ye shes 1981, 1990; see also Cabezón, 1995), a work that describes in general terms the multitude of architectural and artistic projects undertaken by one of Tibet's most renowned scholastic polymaths, both at his home monastery of bKra shis lhun po, and throughout central and western Tibet generally.

2. The biography of Thang stong rgyal po (1385–1481?) (Lo chen 'Gyur med bde chen 1982; see also Vitali 1990:123–36). An accomplished yogi, but also a renowned architect, he is known popularly as Tibet's great builder of iron bridges. His greatest architectural undertaking, however, was the magnificent Ri bo che *stūpa* in La stod byang (western Tibet). Though not that of a scholastic in the classical sense, his autobiography is important because of the rich sociological detail related to the construction of this monument.

3. The *History of Myang* (MCB:1983; see also Ricca and Lobue 1993; and Vitali 1990:39 et passim), a text that contains a wealth of information concerning the erection of temples, monasteries, and other religious monuments during the high scholastic period.

4. 'Jigs med grags pa's fifteenth century history of the rGyal rtse princes, which contains invaluable information concerning the construction of one of the great centers of scholastic learning in western Tibet, the monastery of dPal 'khor chos sde and its great *stūpa* ('Jigs med grags pa 1987; see also Ricca and Lobue 1993).

From these and other sources we can glean, albeit impressionistically, some important facts relevant to the present study:

1. Famous scholars often played an important part in the architectural process. Those with power and wealth at their disposal (e.g., the first Paṇ chen bla ma and the fifth Dalai bla ma) often commissioned the construction of monasteries and religious monuments directly. Those who did not have such means at their disposal sometimes found the necessary funds and support from local rulers, as mKhas grub rje (1385–1438) did from the rGyal rtse prince Rab brtan kun bzang (see Cabezón 1992:17–18; and Ricca and Lobue 1993:20, 22). In a few instances scholars were enticed to move to a different location by a local ruler with the promise of a monastery; this was the case, for example, with Rong ston Shākya rgyal mtshan (1367–1449) (see Jackson 1988).

2. Whatever the means of support, monks with scholastic training often had a substantial role in the design and supervision of

building construction and in the renovation of existing structures. The great Bu ston rin chen grub (1290–1364), for example, supervised the building of a retreat at Ri phug and a chapel at the Zhwa lu gSer khang, and he oversaw a great deal of the interior decorative restoration at Zhwa lu.

3. In rare cases, great scholars were themselves artists and were responsible for murals, statues, or other works of art that adorned the interiors of temples (see, e.g., Ricca and Lobue 1993:20, 25).

4. It is more common, however, to find senior figures in the scholastic tradition not in the role of artist but as supervisors of the artisans[3] who decorated chapels or entire temples. When other duties prohibited their direct participation, they sometimes delegated the responsibility to more junior monks (Vitali, 1990:111). The art work in the great circumambulatory pathway (*skor lam*) at the Zhwa lu gSer khang, for example, is said to have been executed under the direct supervision of the third Karma pa, Rang 'byung rdo rje (1284–1338). (Vitali 1990:107)[4]

Thus, even though the minutuae of historical detail may escape us, we can at the very least infer from this admittedly impressionistic evidence that in some cases the great figures of Tibetan scholasticism had a direct hand in the architectural process.

Two Examples

In the case of Buddhism, most of the literature on the relationship between ideology / world view and art / architecture has tended to focus on East Asia—a good deal of it on Ch'an / Zen. In the case of Zen, numerous popular and scholarly works have convincingly shown the link between an aesthetic of absence as expressed in artistic and architectural minimalism, on the one hand, and Zen ideology and practice, on the other hand (see, e.g., Suzuki 1993).[5] Little, however, has been done to explore the link between intellectual world view and art in Tibet. In what follows, we turn our attention to two specific examples of Tibetan architecture in the hope of establishing the homologies that exist between architectural / artistic artifacts, and the Buddhist scholastic ideology of Tibet.

dPal 'khor sde chen or dPal 'khor chos sde

Before the final Chinese occupation of Tibet in 1959 this was one of the most important monastic centers of western Tibet.[6] Although a small temple seems to have existed at the site from as early as 1370, it was not until the third decade of the fifteenth century, during the reign of the rGyal rtse prince Rab brtan kun bzang, that serious building began. By 1425 two wings had been added to the original structure and three chapels to the upper story (Ricca and Lobue 1993:20, 23; see also figure 6.1). On the first floor, the central chapel contains as its principal image a statue of the Buddha; to its left was a chapel dedicated to the deities of the *yogatantra* (the second highest class of *tantra* in the standard fourfold schema; see below); to its right was the chapel of the *Dharma* kings of Tibet. On the second story above the central chapel we find the *gzhal yas khang* or "divine palace," a chapel that contains a variety of tantric *maṇḍalas*, the central one of which belongs to the deity Kālacakra, the chief deity of the monastery; to its left we find the *Lam 'bras lha khang*, dedicated to the deities and important lineage figures in the Sa skya practice known as "The Path and Its Result" (*lam 'bras*); the chapel of the sixteen arhants (practices related to whom are meant to insure long life, stability, and prosperity) is to the right of the central chapel on the upper story (Ricca and Lobue 1993:23–25).

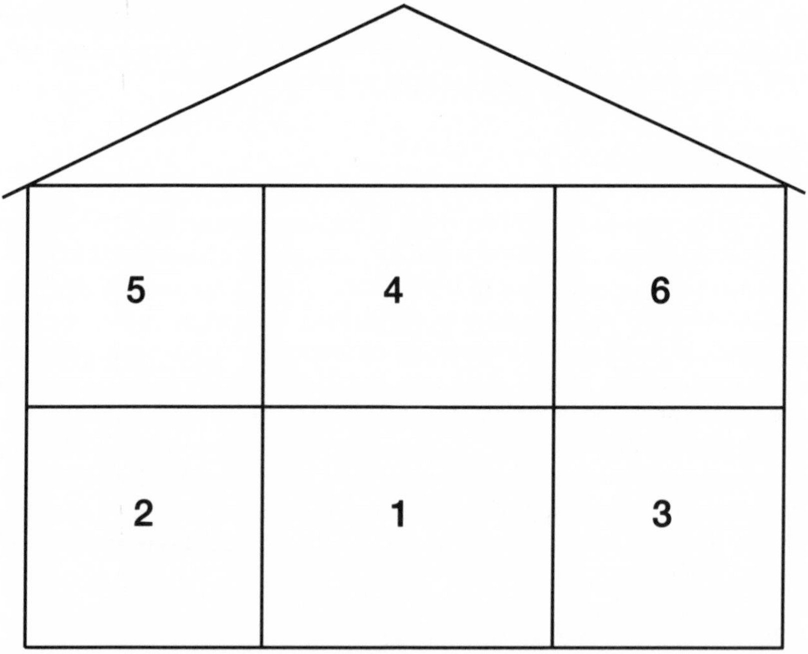

Figure 6.1. Schematic (frontal view) of the dPal 'khor sde chen temple (not to scale). (1) central (Buddha) chapel, (2) Yogatantra chapel, (3) Dharma King chapel, (4) Kālacakra chapel, (5) Lam 'bras chapel, (6) Sixteen Arhants chapel.

Those familiar with the systematics of the Buddhist scholasticism of this period will not find it difficult to see these reflected in the spatial organization of this temple. Fittingly, the historical Buddha, as the source of the exoteric teachings, is found in the central chapel of the first floor. But it is the Buddha in his esoteric, tantric form—as the deity Kālacakra, the source of the highest teachings—who is appropriately situated in the central and uppermost chapel, above that dedicated to the historical Buddha. As a practice belonging to the *anuttarayoga* (highest yoga) class, it is significant to find Kālacakra not only above the Buddha in his exoteric form, but above the deities of the *yogatantra* class as well (located on the first floor to the left of the central, Buddha chapel). The same logic explains the positioning of the chapel of the *Lam 'bras* tradition—a tradition of practice also belonging to the highest yoga class, though one not as central to this monastery as that of Kālacakra—above the *yogatantra* chapel. Finally, just as Tibet's great Dharma kings have insured order, stability, and prosperity through their manifestation in the physical realm that is the "Land of Snows," the sixteen arhants (located directly above them) are the guarantors of this stability in the nonphyiscal realm they inhabit.

Thus, the systematicity—the internal, hierarchical logic—of the Buddhist scholastic world view is reflected in what we might call the "spatial semantics" of the main temple of dPal 'lhor sde chen. It should not be surprising that mKhas grub dGe legs dpal bzang—one of the greatest scholastic minds of the time (see above; and Cabezón, 1992:13–19)—served as Rab brtan kun bzang's consultant in the building of this architectural masterpiece.

This sort of spatial semantics—the use of space in such a way that the juxtaposition of elements mirrors scholastic systematicity—is even more explicit in another structure at dPal 'khor sde chen, the *sku 'bum* or "great stupa" (see figure 6.2), an incredible eight-storied monument with dozens of chapels whose contents recapitulate the systematic ordering of the Buddhist Tantra into four tantric classes, with the *kriyā* and *caryā* represented at the lower levels, the *yoga* and *anuttarayoga* at the higher levels, and the Kālacakra at its highest point. Ricca and Lobue (1993) have provided us with the details of the spatial semantics of this edifice, demonstrating conclusively the way that the building mirrors the four-fold classification scheme developed by Tibetan Buddhist scholastics as a way of ordering the Tantras.[7] In their words:

> The seventy-five temples and chapels distributed on the eight storeys of the sKu-'bum, representing the deities of all the chief tantric cycles and the spiritual lineages who propagated them, afford a global view of the world as conceived in the Indo-Tibetan Buddhist culture of the 15th century, a visual *summa* of all the

Figure 6.2. The sKu 'bum or "Great Stupa" at dPal 'khor sde chen (photo by K. Mortensen).

> knowledge of the time, as well as a true pantheon (*sku-'bum*) of images, which for years to come will be an inexhaustible reference source for students of Tibetan art and religion. (1993:32)

The Monastery of Se ra

Anyone who has ever visited the great monastic universities of central and western Tibet—Sa skya, dGa' ldan, 'Bras spungs, Se ra—cannot but be struck by their size and vastness. Usually having started out as small retreats for the study and practice of Buddhism, these monasteries grew over time. Se ra, as paradigmatic of the great dGe lugs pa[8] seats of learning (*gden sa*), began in just this way, that is, as the residence of a small community of monks. Founded by Byams chen chos rje Shākya ye shes in 1419, it evolved into a monastic university with four colleges which were eventually consolidated into three: the colleges of Byes, sMad, and sNgags pa (the latter being the Tantric College). The larger colleges were further subdivided into *khang tsan* or "regional houses." The Byes College, for example, had in 1959 a monastic population of close to seven thousand monks and was divided into seventeen regional houses that ranged in size from sixty to over three thousand monks.[9] The houses were further subdivided into "households" (*shags*), and households in turn consisted of several senior monks, most of whom were responsible for a group of younger ones. It takes little imagination to see in the hierarchical arrangement of the colleges the analogue of the system of textual subdivisions (*za bcad*), with its branches and subbranches. This same type of systematic and treelike arrangement can be seen as well in the administrative structure both of the monastery and of the colleges. And of course it is recapitulated in the architecture of the monastic quarters.

The proliferative character of scholasticism and its tendency to "completeness" also has an institutional and architectural analogue. It was a fundamental policy of the colleges never to turn monks away. This policy of open admissions is of course what gave rise to the huge monastic populations of the great dGe lugs pa monasteries. It also led to a tremendous disparity in the quality of monks; hence the saying that the great seats of learning (*gden sa*) were like the ocean, in which everything from precious gems to trash could be found. Just as scholastic philosophers of Buddhist Tibet opened their canons for fear of missing some essential Buddhist truth, so the scholastic monasteries opened their doors for fear of turning away the one great scholar or practitioner who might become a master of the doctrine and who would thereby enhance the monastery's reputation.

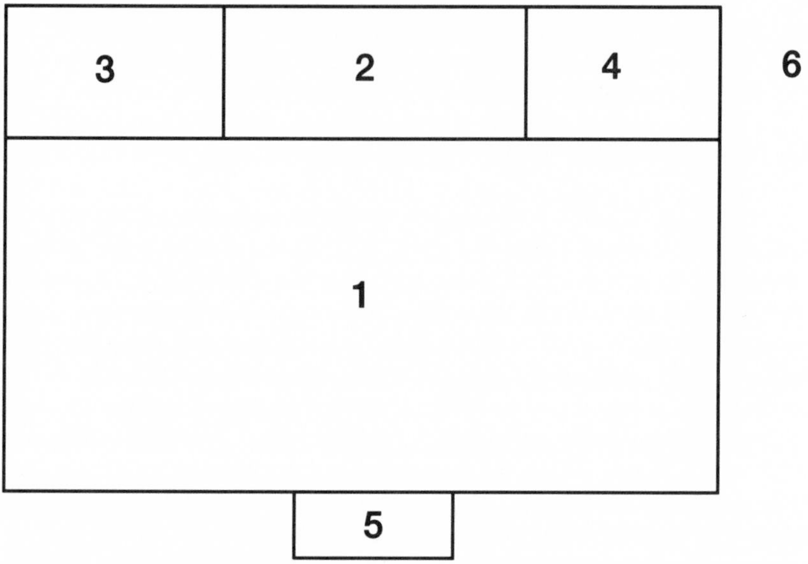

Figure 6.3. Schematic (as viewed from above) of the first floor of the Congregation Hall of the Byes College of Se ra Monastery (not to scale). (1) main meeting hall, (2) Tsong kha pa chapel, (3) Maitreya chapel, (4) Mañjuśrī chapel, (5) front portal, (6) debating courtyard.

As the number of monks grew, so too did the monasteries that housed them. Both temples (the meeting places for the congregation and subcongregations of monks) and monastic quarters were expanded consistently over hundreds of years. In keeping with the scholastic principle of synthesizing and reconciling rather than eliminating, few structures were destroyed. Instead, temples often were expanded. For example, the main, forward (and largest) portion of the present congregation hall of the Byes College (see figure 6.3, no. 1) is actually an addition, the original meeting place being what is today the smaller rear chapels of the building (figure 6.3, nos. 2, 3, and 4). And when the sheer number of monks necessitated the construction of a new building, as was the case with the Great Assembly Hall (*tshogs chen*) of Se ra in the eighteenth century,[10] the previous building was put to another use, in this case as the headquarters for the Se ra Tantric College, which dates from this time. As in the great commentarial traditions of scholastic philosophy, monks opted for building onto an already existing base, rather than starting from scratch.

In addition, the tradition-centeredness and conservatism of the scholastic mind-set finds its analogue in the consistency and uniformity of architectural style, with relatively little being introduced by way of innovation. Finally, proliferativity as a principle finds expression in the rambling character of monastery buildings: not only in the layout of the monasteries as a whole, but also in the structure of individual buildings. It is as easy to get lost in one of the great *gden sa* as it is to get lost in a Tibetan scholastic treatise, and it takes equal amounts of skill to find one's way through each.

The organization of temples and their decoration also reflect scholastic principles. To take the meeting hall of the Byes College as an example (see figure 6.3), it is no exaggeration to say that one is, even from the portal, bombarded by the history, cosmology, and philosophical doctrines of Buddhist scholasticism in visual form. On the left wall of the portal (figure 6.3, no. 5) one finds a mural of the wheel of life, the pictorial representation of the process of transmigration and its causes. To its left, above the door leading to the second story, is a mural of the founders of Buddhism in Tibet (*mkhen slob chos gsum*), and to the left of that, facing the façade, are pictorial representations of the garments and accoutrements permitted to monks according to the Vinaya's code of discipline. Flanking the portal at either side are *bskal bzang khor lo-s*, intricate cross-word murals on religious themes that are one of the Tibetan scholastics' favorite forms of wordplay. On the front portal wall, and covering virtually every inch of the interior walls of the temple are extremely intricate murals on a variety of iconographic themes, ranging from depictions of protector (*srung ma*) and tutelary (*yi dam*) deities to scenes from the life of the Buddha. Statues and reliquaries (*stūpa, mchod rten*) of every size and dimension fill the altars of the main hall and chapels, and extremely ornate brocade hangings and canopies adorn the pillars and roof. To say that the temples of the great colleges exemplify the principles of proliferativity, completeness, and scholastic totalism would be an understatement.[12]

As we have seen in the case of dPal 'khor sde chen, the scholastics' schematic organization of Buddhist doctrine often finds material expression in architecture. Tibetan Mahāyāna scholasticism divides its doctrines (and therefore its texts) into two: those that deal primarily with method (*upāya, thabs*) and those that deal primarily with wisdom (*prajñā, shes rab*). Such a division also finds its way into the curriculum, where it constitutes the basis for the two longest and most important classes (*'dzin grwa*): those of the Prajñāpāramitā and the Madhyamaka. In the visual arts of the dGe lugs pa school, this textual/curricular distinction finds expression in paintings known as *tshogs shing* or "assembled field," where a central figure (usually the Buddha or Tsong kha pa, the founder of the school) is flanked by Maitreya (the reputed author of the chief Prajñāpāramitā commentary that forms the basis for the "method" side of the curriculum) on the left, and by Mañjuśrī (the embodiment of wisdom, and the "patron" of the Madhyamaka philosophy of emptiness) on the right.

It is interesting that we find this same motif to be reflected in the arrangement of the earliest, aft chapels of the main temple of the Byes College (see figure 6.3).[12] There, the rear central chapel (figure 6.3, no. 2) is dedicated to Tsong kha pa and houses an immense statue of the founder of the school that is, according to tradition, said to be a simulacrum (*nga 'dra ma*) of the "Precious Lord" (rJe rin po che), as he is known to his followers.[13] To the left is the Byams pa lha khang, the chapel to the future Buddha Maitreya (figure 6.3, no. 3), and to the right (closest to the debating courtyard, figure 6.3, no. 6) is the 'Jam dbyangs lha khang, the Mañjuśrī chapel (figure 6.3, no. 4), whose main representation of Mañjuśrī is said actually to preach the doctrine ('Jam dbyangs chos 'khor gsung byon). Hence, temple layout recapitulates curriculum, which recapitulates the organization of the textual corpus and of the doctrine.

The scholastic philosophical concern with sacred texts is reflected socially in a variety of practices: the most common is called *chos klog*, or "the reading of the doctrine," in which a portion of the canon (bKa' 'gyur) will be divided among the monastic congregation and each individual portion read aloud simultaneously in assembly; this can take several days (depending on the number of monks in the community). Another is a ritual practice in which the canon is taken on procession into the fields in spring to bless them and to insure fertility.

In terms of architectural design, most of the larger temples have chapels in which the canons are housed. There the volumes will be supported above the floor on shelves, usually with an ambulatory beneath the shelving for devotees to walk (usually in a crouched position of respect) so as to receive the blessing of scriptures located above them. In the temple of the Byes College (see figure 6.3) there are two sets of the canon: one (a bKa' 'gyur) is housed in the Maitreya chapel, the other (a set of both the bKa' 'gyur and the commentarial texts that comprise the bsTan 'gyur) is housed in the Mañjuśrī chapel. This latter set of scriptures is highly revered as it is said to have been extracted as "treasure" (*gter*) from a statue of Vaiśravaṇa, the god of wealth, housed today in a corner of the Hayagrīva chapel in the Byes Meeting Hall.

In addition, of course, most of the larger monasteries in Tibet had separate library buildings, in which the blocks for the printing of textbooks were housed. Hence, the scholastic preoccupation with scripture finds expression both in social/institutional practices and in the structural layout of monasteries and temples.

Conclusion

Of course, other kinds of reasons can always be adduced as explanations for the phenomena I have dealt with here. The vast and rambling character of the great monastic universities is certainly as much a response to the need to house ever-increasing numbers of monks (a social fact) and as much the result of the financial patronage of those in power (an economic one) as it is a reflection of the Tibetan scholastic concern with quantity. The extreme elaboration of detail and symbol in decorative motives is undoubtedly influenced by the fact that Tibetan Buddhism is the child of Indian tantric Buddhism, which is in its own right highly proliferative in character. Likewise, psychological factors having to do with living in the barrenness that is the Tibetan landscape perhaps can be adduced to explain the Tibetan propensity for decorative detail and love of color. The analogical argument I have put forward here is not meant as a challenge to these more causal explanations. But whatever other factors may come into play in explaining the phenomena I have discussed above, it is my belief that scholasticism as an intellectual world view mirrors these phenomena, and that they, in turn, reflect the character of the Buddhist scholastic mind-set that was, and to this day continues to be, the all-pervasive intellectual idiom of Tibetan religious culture.

Notes

The author would like to express his thanks to Dr. Anne Chayet for her kindness in making available to him several of her published works on architecture. Research for this essay was supported in part by a grant from the Alexander von Humboldt Stiftung (Bonn).

1. Hereafter, reference will be made to the 1957 edition in its seventh printing (1963).

2. The *most* detailed, scholarly work on the subject are in French: Chayet (1994) and Mortari Vergara and Beguin (1987), which also contain the most complete bibliographies. For a brief and general overview with some useful bibliographical references see White (1990:139–54). Among the more scholarly works available in English are Vitali (1990) and Ricca and Lobue (1993).

3. Few artisans attained the kind of reputation that warranted their mention in the textual sources, but there are exceptions. One of the most famous artisans of his day was the Newari architect and master craftsman Aniko (1244–1306), who is mentioned in several sources; and both the first Dalai bla ma (1391–1474) and Thang stong rgyal po are said to have competed in 1461 for the services of a certain bKra shis rin chen, the "supreme artist of the La.bstod Byang school" (see Vitali 1990:103, 133; and also Ricca and Lobue 1993:17).

4. On the supervisory role played by Bu ston in the religious decoration of Zhwa lu, see Vitali (1990:110).

5. But see also LaFleur (1983) for a more general treatment of the relationship of medieval Buddhism to the literary arts of that period in Japan.

6. The most detailed study of this monastery in a Western language is Ricca and Lobue (1993), on which I base most of the remarks that follow.

7. This scheme seems to have been set forth and elaborated from the twelfth century on (Ricca and Lobue 1993:47). One of the most popular texts on the subject, the *rGyud sde spyi rnam,* was written by mKhas grub dGe legs dpal bzang (Collected Works, vol. *nya,* Tohoku no. 5489; translated in Lessing and Wayman 1959), who, as we have seen, was a consultant to Rab brtan kun bzang in his building of dPal 'khor sde chen.

8. The dGe lugs pa is the youngest and politically most powerful of the four main schools of Tibetan Buddhism, founded by Tsong kha pa bLo bzang grags pa (1357–1419).

9. These figures are based on interviews I conducted in Tibet in 1991 with monks from each of the *khang tsan* of Se ra.

10. It is interesting to note that the present monastery of Se ra in exile, in the Bylakuppe settlement of Karnataka, South India, recently has undergone a similar expansion of its Great Assembly Hall. The Byes College meeting hall presently faces the same problem. Since there is no place for further expansion, however, in this case a new hall is being built.

11. One other point is worth mentioning as regards iconography and the arrangement of statuary. We have seen that for Tibetan Buddhist scholastics quantity (that is, proliferativity in numbers) is as important as quality. We find this principle best exemplified in the literally hundreds of statues of Tsong kha pa that constitute the main altar of the re-established Byes College of Se ra in the Bylakuppe settlement in south India. More—at least as it applies to explanation, categories, and religious imagery—is always better.

12. Again, the central temple of the monastery of bSam yas (the dBu rtse), one of the earliest and most important structures in all of Buddhist Tibet, is flanked symmetrically by two smaller temples, to the west and east, dedicated, respectively, to Maitreya (Byams pa gling) and Mañjuśrī ('Jam dpal gling). See Buffetrille (1989:373–76), and Chayet (1988:25).

13. The oral tradition has it that this statue was said by Tsong kha pa himself to be the one that most resembled him from among all the statues of himself he had seen.

References

Buffetrille, Katia.

1989 "La restauration du monastère de Bsam yas: un exemple de continuité dans la relation chapelain-donateur au Tibet." *Journal Asiatique* 277.3–4:363–411.

Cabezón, José Ignacio.

1995 "On the *sGra pa Shes rab rin chen pa'i rtsod lan* of Paṇ chen bLo bzang chos rgyan." *Asiatische Studien/ Études Asiatiques* 44.4:643–69.

1994 *Buddhism and Language: A Study of Indo-Tibetan Scholasticism.* Albany: State University of New York Press.

1992 *A Dose of Emptiness: An Annotated Translation of the* sTong thun chen mo *of mKhas grub dge legs dpal bzang.* Albany: State University of New York Press.

Chayet, Anne.

1994 *Art et Archéologie du Tibet.* Paris: Picard.

1988 "Le monastère de bSam-yas: sources architecturales." *Arts Asiatiques* 43:19–29.

Jackson, David.

1988 "Introduction." In *Rong ston on the Prajñāpāramitā Philosophy of the Abhisamayālaṃkāra: His Commentary on Haribhadra's Sphuṭārthā.* Kyoto: Nagata Bunshodo.

'Jigs med grags pa.

1987 (ed.) *rGyal rtse chos rgyal gyi rnam par thar pa dad pa'i lo thog ngos grub kyi char 'bebs.* Lhasa: Bod ljong mi dmangs dpe skrun khang.

LaFleur, William.

1983 *The Karma of Words: Buddhism and the Literary Arts in Medieval Japan.* Berkeley: University of California Press.

Lessing, Ferdinand and Alex Wayman.

1959 *Fundamentals of the Buddhist Tantras.* The Hague: Mouton.

Lo chen 'Gyur med bde chen.

1982 *Grub pa'i dbang phyug chen po lcag zam pa Thang stong rgyal po'i rnam thar ngo mtshar kun gsal nor bu'i me long gsar pa.* Si khron mi rigs dpe skrun khang.

MCB.

1983 *Myang chos 'byung = Myang yul stod smad bar gsum gyi ngo mtshar gtam gyi legs bshad mkhas pa'i 'jug ngogs.* Lhasa: Bod ljongs mi dmangs dpe skrung khang.

Mortari Vergara, Paola, and Gilles Beguin.

1987 *Demeures des hommes, Sanctuaires des dieux: sources, développe-*

ment et rayonnement de l'architecture tibétaine. Rome: Università di Roma "La Sapienza."

Ngawang Gelek Demo (ed.).
1969 *The Autobiography of the First Panchen Lama Blo-bzang-chos-kyi-rgyal mtshan*. Intro. E. Gene Smith. New Delhi: Gedan Sungrab Minyam Gyunphel Series no. 12.

Paṇ chen bLo bzang ye shes.
1990 *Chos smra ba'i dge slong bLo bzang chos kyi rgyal mtshan gyi spyod tshul gsal bar ston pa nor bu'i phreng ba*. mTsho sngon: Bod ljong mi dmangs dpe skrung khang.

1981 *Chos smra ba'i dge slong bLo bzang chos kyi rgyal mtshan gyi spyod tshul gsal bar ston pa nor bu'i phreng ba*. In *Collected Works (gSung 'bum) of the Second Paṇ-chen bLo-bzang ye-shes*. From the bKra shis lhun po blocks. New Delhi: bTra sis luhn po (sic) Monastery.

Panofsky, Erwin.
1957 *Gothic Architecture and Scholasticism*. Cleveland and New York: World Publishing.

1951 *Gothic Architecture and Scholasticism*. Latrobe, PA: Archabbey Press.

Price, B. B.
1992 *Medieval Thought: An Introduction*. Oxford: Blackwell.

Ricca, Franco and Erberto Lobue.
1993 *The Great Stūpa of Gyantse: A Complete Tibetan Pantheon of the Fifteenth Century*. London: Serindia Publications.

Suzuki, D. T.
1993 *Zen and Japanese Culture*. Princeton: Princeton University Press. (Reprint of the 1959 ed.)

Vitali, Roberto.
1990 *Early Temples of Central Tibet*. London: Serindia Publications.

White, Stephen.
1990 "The Flowering of Tibetan Architecture." In *White Lotus: An Introduction to Tibetan Culture*, 139–54. Ed. C. Elchert. Ithaca: Snow Lion Publications.

Chapter 7

Neo-Confucian Scholasticism

John B. Henderson

Like the other great religious traditions discussed in this volume, that of Confucianism has a long and variegated history, ranging from classical times (fifth through third centuries B.C.) to the present day. Most of the currents and movements within this broad Confucian stream from ancient to modern times exhibit *some* of the attributes of scholasticism enumerated in the other articles in this volume. But the *most* scholastic version of Confucianism is that movement that is rather broadly and vaguely called "Neo-Confucianism," which arose and flourished in China during the Sung era (960–1279) after a long period in which "heterodox" teachings, particularly forms of Buddhism and Taoism, had been dominant. While the Neo-Confucians claimed that they were simply restoring the transmission of the Confucian Way after a prolonged hiatus, they in fact constructed new versions of Confucianism designed in part to meet the philosophical challenges posed by Buddhism and Taoism.

A particular form of Neo-Confucianism known as *Tao-hsüeh* (Learning of the Way) or the Ch'eng-Chu school, centered on the thought of the most famous Confucian philosopher of postclassical times, Chu Hsi (1130–1200), became established as the orthodoxy of both state and intellectuals in subsequent eras. Indeed, Ch'eng-Chu Confucianism was the mainstay of the all-important civil service examination system until the official abolition of that system in 1905. From the fourteenth to the early twentieth centuries, Ch'eng-Chu commentaries on and interpretations of the Confucian classics dominated the educational curriculum in schools throughout China and were "studied and mastered by millions of examination candidates for the civil service" (Elman 1994:62). Since the imperial civil service was by far the most attractive and prestigious career in late imperial China, as it was in late traditional Korea where Ch'eng-Chu orthodoxy also prevailed, the Neo-Confucian Learning of the Way was solidly situated, both institutionally and culturally.

The contemporaneity of Neo-Confucian scholasticism with Western medieval scholasticisms is striking. The paramount Neo-Confucian scholastic synthesizer Chu Hsi was a near contemporary of Thomas Aquinas (1225–1274), Maimonides (1135–1204), and al-Ghazali (1058–1111), arguably the greatest and most influential scholastic philosophers in their respective traditions. Moreover, Tsong Kha pa (1357–1419), the founder of the dGe lugs pa school of Indo-Tibetan scholastism, lived only a little later. Although these temporal correspondences may not in themselves have any great significance, they do at least suggest the possibility that scholasticism might develop as a stage or phase in the intellectual and cultural history of widely separated civilizations, a hypothesis explored as long ago as 1920 in Paul Masson-Oursel's article "La Scholastique (étude de philosophie comparée)." Masson-Oursel proposes a three-phase schema of world intellectual history in which the initial period of chaotic creativity or "sophism" is succeeded by a grand systemization and stabilization of thought achieved by scholasticism, which is superseded in turn by the advent of the critical spirit of modern science and scholarship (Masson-Oursel 1920:140 passim). Without necessarily endorsing Masson-Oursel's three-phase schema, it might be illuminating and relevant here to suggest some reasons for the rise of the second of his phases, scholasticism, before going on to examine in greater detail the attributes that distinguish Neo-Confucianism as a scholastic tradition. This will enable us to view these attributes as concomitants of historical processes that occurred concurrently, if independently, in widely separated civilizations.

First, scholasticisms both in China and in the West (including those of medieval Christianity, Islam, and Judaism) seem to require the formation and closure of a canon that not only is sacralized but also is decontextualized historically from its diverse points of origin. As such, it is regarded as an integrated and complete whole in which there can be neither inconsistencies nor superfluities. The existence and institution of such a canon inspires the enterprise of commentary, the chief literary medium of scholasticisms everywhere, designed to establish the integrity, consistency, comprehensiveness, and compactness of the classics or scriptures. Scholastic commentary does not generally take a historico-critical approach to the canon. Far from attempting to stratify texts into their various historical and authorial components, it endeavors rather to *de*stratify them, to present canonical texts as an integrated whole.[1]

The formation and historical decontextualization of a canon of scriptures may be sufficient to stimulate the rise of early or pre-scholasticisms such as existed in late antiquity and the early Middle Ages in Europe and the Han Era (202 B.C.–A.D. 220) in China. But the more mature "high scholasticisms" of twelfth- and thirteenth-century Europe, China, and the Middle East require another major input, namely a new encounter with and challenge by a superior or at least highly developed philosophical tradition. Such a tradition, such as Aristotelianism in the medieval West and Middle East, and Buddhist philosophy in Sung China, provides both the stimulus and the tools for the formation of a high scholasticism. It furnishes an impetus insofar as it challenges the religious tradition concerned to demonstrate the philosophical validity, as well as the order and comprehensiveness, of its canon. It also provides some of the tools, ranging from metaphysical and cosmological ideas to logical and dialectical procedures, that make such a demonstration possible or plausible.

However, high scholasticisms in general are profoundly ambivalent and deeply divided over how far this external philosophical tradition, be it Aristotelianism or forms of Buddhism, should be accommodated or even acknowledged in the newly constructed scholastic synthesis. In fact, it would be fair to say that this issue is perennially the most divisive and debated one in various forms of scholasticism, East and West. While Thomas Aquinas may be said to have Christianized Aristotle, both he and some of his contemporaries also were accused of having Aristotlized Christianity, as illustrated particularly in the condemnations of Aristotelian propositions at the University of Paris in 1277. And while Chu Hsi charged some of his Neo-Confucian scholastic opponents with being crypto-Buddhists or Taoists, the orthodox philosophical provenance of aspects of Chu's own philosophy was also open to question. But like the great Vedantin scholastic, Śaṅkara (788–820), Chu was loath to acknowledge the heterodox Buddhist (or Taoist) associations of some of the ideas incorporated into his scholastic synthesis of Neo-Confucianism.

This issue or conflict sometimes is presented in a Western context as one between "reason and revelation." But the problem may be more generally stated as that of a confrontation between a revered religious tradition based on a canon of scripture, and a relatively new (or newly recovered) philosophical or religious system of considerable depth and breadth. In any event, out of this confrontation emerges a final major issue in high scholasticism, the problem of where to draw the exclusionary line between orthodoxy and heresy. As noted in the article by Paul Griffiths included in this volume, scholasticism must have both a canon of sacred texts and an index of forbidden ones.

High scholasticism, at least in China and the medieval West, thus arose with the circulation and absorption of a body of philosophical sources unknown to the founders of the religious tradition concerned or to the composers of its canon. Indeed, there was a great leap forward in the quantity of philosophical sources available to the Latin West in the twelfth century, as there was slightly earlier in China with the invention of printing. But the body of new sources must not be *so* large or diverse as to overwhelm the prospective architects of a scholastic synthesis, such as Thomas Aquinas or Chu Hsi. As long as the flow of new information remains below a certain threshold, primary or high scholasticism, which attempts a rather universalistic synthesis of old and new sources, may be sustained. But when the flow of new information exceeds a certain limit, instigated in the Renaissance West by the invention of printing, the Scientific Revolution, and the Age of Discovery, and in sixteenth- and seventeenth-century China by the upsurge in the quantity of printing and the contact with Western science and religion through Jesuit missionaries, then the comprehensive syntheses that marked the apogee of primary scholasticisms are possible only by restricting the information flow, usually either through ignorance (either in the sense of "ignoring" or of "not knowing") or through the index.[2] Indeed, the index, and ecclesiastical censorship in general, may serve just as well to make a "second" or derivative scholasticism possible by artifically limiting extra-canonical sources available, as to curb "dangerous thought." Lacking either ignorance or the index, the latter-day would-be scholastic synthesizer might well wind up in the sad predicament of Voltaire's "theologian": "the difficulty of organizing in his head so many things whose nature is to be confused, and to throw a little light into so many dark clouds, often disheartened him, but as these researches were his professional duties, he devoted himself to them in spite of his disgust" (Voltaire 1983:387).

Nevertheless, various "second" and "neo" forms of scholasticism have arisen and even flourished in modern times, not just in ecclesiastical quarters but in modern ideologies as well. Even the Great Books program in American universities of the midtwentieth century may be plausibly interpreted as a form of scholasticism, as Josef Pieper has pointed out (1960:153), particularly in its attempt to present a synthesis of the Western intellectual heritage that is *well-ordered,* fairly *comprehensive, compact,* and *profound.* As the multiculturalists of our own time have pointed out, it also resembles scholasticism in its *exclusionary* dimension, although it does not explicitly condemn the excluded works as "heretical."

The above discussion has attempted to place the various attributes or aims of high scholasticisms in a comparative developmental context that might explain their appearance in various civilizations as remote from one another as China was from Europe. In other words, we see these attributes (underlined in the previous paragraph) as products or concomitants of the historical developments that gave rise to scholasticism in the first place. Now it remains to examine just how and to what extent these traits are manifested in the Neo-Confucianism that flourished in China from the Sung era. We will also point out areas in which Neo-Confucian scholasticism differs from other scholastic traditions.[3]

Scholastics were primarily commentators on a canon of scripture, the elucidation of which they regarded as their main task, even their life's work. The way in which they presented their canon, the traits they attributed to it, is thus probably a fairly reliable baseline for illuminating the main points of the scholastic world view. Moreover, there is a remarkable resemblance between high scholastics' characterizations of their canons and the characteristics of their own commentarial works on those canons. It is almost as if the scholastics were trying, through the medium of the commentaries they composed, to demonstrate those qualities which *should* have been present in the canon, and which the scholastics endeavored to prove were really there, despite some appearances to the contrary. So it is small wonder that several scholastic commentaries in various traditions, such as Chu Hsi's commentary on the canonical Four Books of Confucianism, assumed a sort of canonical aura. Far from being mere handmaidens to scripture, commentaries in various scholastic traditions could be transformed for all practical purposes into canon.

Perhaps the first priority of high scholastics, confronted with a formidable philosophical system such as Aristotelianism or Buddhist philosophy, was to demonstrate that their canon, too, was well ordered and systematic, and not just a motley collection of disparate ancient writings. The most celebrated instance of Neo-Confucians' ordering of a group of classical texts is their arrangement of the canonical Four Books into a pedagogical series that constituted a complete Confucian curriculum. In the words of Neo-Confucian scholar Fang Hsiao-ju (1357–1402), one should "begin with the *Great Learning* to rectify the foundations, follow it with the book of *Mencius* to activate the spirit, proceed to the *Analects* [of Confucius] to observe equilibrium, and bind it with the *Doctrine of the Mean* to meet the sources" (Fang 1966:6.8a).

Neo-Confucian commentators also were concerned with establishing the internal orderliness of the individual classics on the micro level of chapter and verse, and even word and phrase. As Daniel Gardner has observed of Chu Hsi's commentary on the canonical *Great Learning*, "Every effort is made by Chu to explain how one statement of the text relates to another, or one chapter to another" (Gardner 1986:44). So caught up was Chu in this rage for order that he went so far as to revise the received text of the *Great Learning* to match what he regarded as the Sage's true intentions in composing it (Gardner 1986:24, 35–36). But Chu Hsi was by no means the last Neo-Confucian commentator to revise or alter classical texts to make them conform to the more perfect order supposedly intended by their original sagely authors. Two eighteenth-century Japanese Neo-Confucian scholars, Nakai Riken and Matsui Rashu, reorganized the texts of the *Doctrine of the Mean* and the canonical "Great Commentary" of the *Changes Classic*, respectively, in order to eliminate inconsistencies and repetitions (Najita 1987:198; Shchutskii 1979:162). And K'ang Yu-wei (1858–1927) rearranged the text of the book of *Mencius*, complaining that "in the seven sections [of the standard arrangement] of the *Mencius*, the 'great meanings and subtle words' are confused and scattered" (1.1).

Like their scholastic counterparts in other cultures, Neo-Confucians devoted their energies to composing epitomes of canonical works, as well as of later-day philosophers. The most important example of the latter is the Neo-Confucian anthology composed by Chu Hsi and Lü Tsu-ch'ien (1137–1181), the *Chin-ssu-lu* (Reflections on Things at Hand). Finally, Neo-Confucian scholastics' rage for order may be illustrated even in their language, which is punctuated by parallelism and framed by formalism. In some cases, it appears that the parallelist tail is wagging the philosophical dog, as in the following statement by Chu Hsi (1973:1.36): "The essence of humanity (*jen*) is hard but its application is soft. The essence of rightness (*i*) is soft but its application is hard." In sum, Erwin Panofsky's (1957:34) statement that the scholastics made the orderliness and logic of their thought more palpably explicit than did the ancients applies just as well to Neo-Confucian as to medieval Christian scholastics. This orderliness, moreover, often took a particular form: "the scholastic machine," as Jacques Le Goff (1984:266) has observed, was "always intent on finding symmetries."

The Aristotelian and Buddhist world views that confronted medieval Christian and Neo-Confucian scholastics of the twelfth and thirteenth centuries were not only relatively systematic, but also comprehensive, at least to their adherents who believed them to contain all significant knowledge or truth. As such, they presented both a challenge and a model for Christian and Confucian scholastics, inspiring them to formulate a vision of completeness that was more in accord with their own particular religious traditions. The Neo-Confucians, in particular, saw the need to formulate such a comprehensive vision in order to avoid being relegated by their Buddhist and Taoist rivals to the limited or inferior status of specialists in statecraft or moral pedagogy who failed to grasp the big picture.

In the first place, Neo-Confucian commentators retrospectively attributed a sort of cosmological completeness to their own classical Confucian canon. The seventeenth-century Japanese scholar Ito Jinsai (1627–1705) maintained that the five Confucian classics, the *Documents*, the *Songs*, the *Changes*, the *Rites*, and the *Spring and Autumn Annals*, present "a vast panorama of heaven, earth, the ten thousand creatures, human emotions, and the changes of the world" (Yoshikawa 1983:70). Chu Hsi marveled that this relatively small corpus of classical texts covered all the subtleties of philosophy and vicissitudes of history (Quoted in Chu I-tsun 1968:296.7b–8a). According to Chu Sheng (1299–1371) (Quoted in Chu I-tsun, 1968:297.1a), the inexhaustibility of the classics derived from their sagely origins: "The Way of the sages is recorded in the classics. Since the minds of the sages are unlimited, the principles in the classics are also unlimited." Another fourteenth-century commentator, Wang Shen (Quoted in Chu I-tsun:297.4a), attributed the cosmic comprehensiveness of the classics to the sages' having patterned them on the way of nature, on the cosmos at large: "The reason why the writing in the Six Classics plumbs heaven and earth and extends over past and present without change is that it emanated from the way of nature." In sum, Neo-Confucian commentators regarded their canon as comprehensive in what Cabezón (1994:91) calls the "strong sense": it includes not only "religiously valid doctrines" but extends to "every phenomenon."

Neo-Confucian scholars also frequently ascribed comprehensiveness to the writings of the grand Neo-Confucian synthesizer Chu Hsi. They exalted Chu's synthesis of the earlier Neo-Confucian masters of the Northern Sung Era (960–1126) in the same terms reserved by Mencius to describe Confucius himself: Chu was "a complete concert" (*chi ta-ch'eng*) who harmonized and synthesized the works of his illustrious predecessors (Ch'en Ch'un:181).

As Cabezón (1994:79) has indicated, the flip side of the completeness of scripture in scholasticism is its compactness: "Most scholastics consider scripture to be both *complete* (nothing essential is left out) and *compact* (it contains nothing unessential)." Neo-Confucian scholastics, indeed, went so far as to credit Confucius himself with having expurgated inessential and inappropriate material from the original Six Classics in the course of editing them. According to Chu Hsi, Confucius "deleted [from the *Songs Classic*] what was superfluous and corrected what was disordered. As to what was good yet not fit to be taken as a model, and evil yet not fit to be taken as a warning, he cut and deleted it in order to conform with succinctness" (n.d.:1) The most famous Neo-Confucian philosopher of the Ming Era (1368–1644), Wang Yang-ming (1472–1526), credited Confucius with even grander expurgatory achievements, remarking that "when Confucius expounded the Six Classics, he feared that superfluous writing was creating a chaos in the world; so he lost no time in simplifying them to cause the [people of the] world to strive to eliminate [superfluous] writing and seek the real substance" (Wang 1971:20). Wang extended his ideas on the virtues of expurgation to the point of arguing that the notorious first emperor of the Ch'in dynasty (221–206 B.C.) should not be condemned for burning books, only for burning the wrong ones (the Confucian classics) and for harboring a selfish intention in doing so (20–21).

Confucius' alleged efforts at expurgation notwithstanding, Neo-Confucian scholastics faced allegations that repetitions and other superfluities still existed in the received versions of the classics. They dealt with such problems partly through the use of scholastic modal distinctions. Chu Hsi (1974:105), for example, explained the appearance of a repeated phrase in the *Analects* of Confucius by commenting that "the former instance speaks in terms of *action*, while this one speaks in terms of *knowledge*." However, Ch'eng I (1033–1107) interpreted the seemingly superfluous repetition of the names of four states in the canonical *Spring and Autumn Annals* as a sort of rhetorical device, meant to accentuate their crimes (Quoted in *Ch'un-ch'iu san-chuan* n.d. 48)

Finally, Neo-Confucian scholastics, like their counterparts in other scholastic cultures, were not above composing their own abridgements of those canonical and semicanonical works which seemed to suffer from superfluities that were beyond the point of local repair or rationalization. Into this category might fall Chu Hsi's *Comprehensive Explications of the Text and Commentaries of the Ceremonial Rites (I-li ching-chuan t'ung-chieh).*

From the perspective of scholastics both in Eastern and in Western civilizations, a problem in canonical texts that was even more disturbing than apparent superfluities was apparent contradictions. As Cabezón (1994:55) has pointed out, several modern students of Western scholasticism have identified the "source of scholasticism" in "the fact that it attempts systematic reconciliation of the contradictions that plague the Tradition, thereby implicitly establishing this as the essence of the scholastic method." A recent interpreter of Hellenistic hermeneutics on Homer extends this concern to characterize Western hermeneutics in general: "from its beginnings hermeneutics seems to have been bent to the task of reconciling apparent contradictions whether within the work of a single author or between authors" (Lamberton 1983:5).

To resolve such apparent contradictions, scholastics had to marshall, or devise, considerable resources of language and logic. On this point, however, scholastic traditions differ most markedly from one another, particularly according to the disparateness of the sources that the scholastics of a particular tradition recognize as authorities worthy of being reconciled. It appears that the more inclusive a scholastic tradition is, and the more disparate its recognized authorities, the larger and more important looms the task of eliminating inconsistencies and apparent contradictions. Thus, while the techniques of reconciliation, such as those pioneered by Abelard, were essential to the more ambitiously inclusive scholastic enterprise in the medieval West, they were of relatively minor importance in other traditions, such as Neo-Confucianism, that aimed to synthesize traditions that were fewer in number and less diverse in character.

Nevertheless, Neo-Confucian scholastics did find some occasion for textual reconciliation, albeit within a more limited selection of texts than those reconciled by many Western medieval scholastics. The philosopher Ch'eng I, for example, mediated between two different characterizations of human nature (*hsing*) appearing in the *Analects* of Confucius and the book of *Mencius* by saying that while Confucius was speaking of the "temperamental side of human nature," Mencius was speaking of the "basis of human nature" (Quoted in Chu 1974:119). Another method used by Neo-Confucian commentators to explain apparent divergences or contradictions in the classics bears some resemblance to the Buddhist technique of *upāya* (accommodation or skill in means). For example, both Chang Tsai (1020–1077) and Wang Yangming explain instances in the Confucian *Analects* where Confucius gave different answers to the same question by remarking that his responses were intended to meet the needs or to accord with the intellectual or spiritual attainments of particular disciples (Kasoff 1984:x; Wang 1971:100–101). However, such discrepancies within the Confucian classics were generally not of such an order as to require a highly developed skill in logic or dialectic to resolve.

While Neo-Confucian scholastics were less absorbed than were their Western counterparts with the reconciliation of apparent contradictions in authoritative texts, they were probably *more* concerned with asserting and maintaining the purity of their scholastic lineage. The Neo-Confucians of the Ch'eng-Chu school or "Learning of the Way" (*Tao-hsüeh*), in fact, identified themselves primarily by their claim to have resumed the orthodox transmission of the Way (*Tao-t'ung*) in the eleventh century, after a 1,400-year hiatus following the death of Mencius. While several prominent Confucians lived in the intervening era, none quite measured up to the high (or exclusionist) standards set by Chu Hsi and his scholastic successors. In the centuries following Chu Hsi's promulgation of the transmission of the Way, a perennial theme in Neo-Confucian discourse was the identification of those who deserved to be included in the main line of the tradition as Chu Hsi's continuators. The question of "through whom the succession ran, after Chu Hsi and his immediate disciples" became a pressing and divisive issue in Ming and Ch'ing times (1368–1911) (de Bary 1989:228). Later Neo-Confucian scholars, in fact, composed a considerable number of scholastic genealogies devoted to presenting partisan versions of the transmission of the Way.[4] Even twentieth-century neo-scholastic Confucian philosophers, such as Mou Tsung-san, have focused on this issue. As John Berthrong (1994:107, 109) has remarked, Mou's "concern for the definition of orthodoxy and the proper understanding of the 'transmission of the Way' is highly traditional. Nothing could be more Confucian than worrying about lineage and teachings."

Analogies to the Neo-Confucian transmission of the Way may be found in other traditions, as in the Catholic notion of apostolic succession. But in the history of Neo-Confucianism, this issue was perennially the main focus of debate on questions concerning the orthodoxy or heterodoxy of particular subtraditions. The most convincing version of the transmission of the Way went a long way toward validating the orthodoxy of whoever claimed and presented it. Those Confucians who could not plausibly claim affiliation with at least one of the figures in the orthodox line of transmission risked being characterized as crypto-Buddhists or Taoists. An even worse fate might await particularly obstinate or notorious opponents of the orthodox Neo-Confucian tradition of the Way: they might be fit into the parallel line of heresiarchs descending from the heterodox ancient philosophers through the Buddhists of the post-Han Era, culminating in Ch'an (=Zen).

The Neo-Confucian confrontation with the "heretical" Buddhists gave rise to a final major feature of Neo-Confucian scholasticism, the attempt to establish the philosophical profundity and respectability of their canon and tradition. On the face of it, the Four Books and Five (or Six) Classics of the Confucian canon seemed to lack the profound cosmological, metaphysical, and soteriological dimensions of some of the better-known Buddhist texts. Even the sayings of the primary Confucian sages of antiquity, as recorded in the *Analects* and *Mencius,* were seemingly sadly deficient in philosophical acumen. One scholastic solution to this difficulty was to virtually ignore those parts of the received canon that were not especially philosophical or profound and to focus attention on a few particular books, passages, and ideas in the classics that were. Indeed, the Sung Neo-Confucians went so far as to raise two previously obscure chapters of the canonical *Record of Rites* (Li-chi), namely the *Great Learning* and *Doctrine of the Mean,* to the status of being independent classics, in part because of their philosophical promise. Some Neo-Confucian commentators took a small number of selected passages from these two texts as the mainstays of their classical cogitations. Wang Yang-ming, for example, held that the first chapters of each of these two classics "taught the complete task of Confucian learning" (Chan, n.d.:271 citing *Wang Wen-ch'eng kung ch'üan-shu* 26.2a).

Along this same line, Neo-Confucian commentators extracted a limited number of scattered metaphysical terms from the classics, such as *li* (pattern or principle), *ch'i* (material force), *hsin* (heart or mind), *hsing* (human nature), and *jen* (cohumanity), and attempted to array them into some kind of philosophical order or system.[5] Indeed, so important was this project in Neo-Confucianism that various schools of Neo-Confucian thought, such as the "School of Principle" (*li-hsüeh*) and the "School of Mind" (*hsin-hsüeh*), sometimes are distinguished from each another by the particular ways in which they related such philosophical terms to one another. Some Neo-Confucian texts even give the impression that a type of enlightenment might proceed from a realization of the proper order and interrelationships of such terms. The great Korean Neo-Confucian scholar, Yi T'oegye (1501–1570), constructed elaborate diagrams showing the relationships of various Neo-Confucian philosophical terms and concepts to one another. By correctly contemplating some of these diagrams, one could achieve "a level of insight in which discordant notes fall into place and the whole may be grasped as a polyphonic unity" (Kalton 1988:108–9). But however grand was the realm of Neo-Confucian metaphysics thus constructed from scattered and diverse terms and concepts in the classics, Neo-Confucian scholars had still to confront the problem of the superficial lack of profundity in the bulk of the canon, even in the *Analects* of Confucius. Why, they asked, could the Master's discourses on profound topics such as human nature (*hsing*) and the Way of heaven (*t'ien-tao*) not be heard (*Analects* 5:12)? One possible explanation was that these ideas were too profound and subtle for the auditors of Confucius' own time to grasp (Ho, 1974:5.4b). Another, posed by Chu Hsi (1973:2.40), was that "the Sage [Confucius] taught people the broad outline. He spoke only of filiality, brotherliness, fidelity, and trust, words for daily use and constant practice." Another Neo-Confucian commentator on the *Analects*, Hsieh Liang-tso (1050–1103), averred that Confucius really did communicate his teachings on human nature, the Way of heaven, and other profound conceptions, but only subtly and indirectly, not explicitly through words (Quoted in Chu I-tsun, 1968:214.3a). However diverse these explanations of Confucius' reticence in speaking on such topics as human nature and the Way of heaven, they all support the point that Confucius was no philosophical lightweight, that he had profound things to say even if he didn't always express them directly or systematically.

As indicated at several points in the above discussion, Neo-Confucian scholasticism was by no means a carbon copy of its Western counterpart. Not only was the balance of Neo-Confucian scholastic qualities somewhat different, but Neo-Confucianism seems to lack the strong concern for technical questions of language and logic so characteristic of medieval Latin (as well as Indo-Tibetan) scholasticism. However, Neo-Confucian scholasticism shares with the Taoist scholasticism outlined by Livia Kohn in this volume a couple of traits that were not prominent in Western scholasticism: it was less divided from society as a whole as well as more politically involved. It was a more popular form of scholasticism, particularly by dint of its wide dissemination through the schools and academies of late imperial China.

Its relatively popular character as well as its firm political and institutional supports helped Neo-Confucian scholasticism to outlive the primary high scholasticism of the Western Middle Ages. Nevertheless, Neo-Confucian scholasticism increasingly was corroded by some of the same historical developments that so devastated its Western counterparts. First, as mentioned above, the explosion of printing and the input of Western science and religion that took place in sixteenth- and seventeenth-century China so increased the flow (or flood) of information that a new scholastic synthesis, one that was comprehensive and compact, systematic and consistent, was hardly humanly possible. At the same time, the new learning and science of this era showed up the deficiencies of the old scholastic synthesis by Chu Hsi. For example, Huang Tsung-hsi (1610–1695) and Chang Hui-yen (1761–1802) revealed serious flaws in Chu's understanding of astronomy and cosmology (Huang 1970:1.14;

Chang 1970:28a). Second, the rise of new movements of historico-critical scholarship in the seventeenth and eighteenth centuries undermined one of the central foundations of scholasticism, the view that canonical writings were in a sense all of a piece and could be worked into a coherent and compact system with no major inconsistencies. The historical recontextualization of the Confucian classics revealed diversity and variety in these standard texts, and even that parts of them were forgeries not composed by the sagely hands to which they were commonly attributed. Later commentators thus criticized earlier scholastic attempts to harmonize or systematize this rather unharmonious and disparate congeries of ancient writings. P'i Hsi-jui (1850–1908), for example, remarked that Cheng Hsüan's (127–200) commentaries on the three Confucian ritual classics had attempted to "reconcile the theories of the Old and New Text schools. Even in cases in which he could not harmonize them, he forcibly sought to bring them into accord" (3.54). Instead of celebrating the brilliance of scholastics' synthetic insights, critical scholars of the Ch'ing era (1644–1911) were more apt to fault them for their empirical oversights.

In this area, as in others, high scholasticism helped to sow the seeds of its own destruction: it exalted the commentary on the classics while not recognizing that this genre would develop a historico-critical mode, epitomized in the works of Ch'ing textual scholars, that undermined rather than supported scholastic approaches to the canon. While some in our day might be attracted by the promise of various neo-scholasticisms, including those of modern ideologies, to restore a higher sense of order and purpose to learning and to the world in general, such a restoration might exact a heavy price: the strict control both of historical and critical scholarship and of the parameters of learning in general to include only that which can be reasonably and comfortably integrated into a new scholastic synthesis. Scholasticism, like several other important phenomena in world intellectual history, can only thrive in its primary form within bounds governed by the quantity and rate of information flow. But this technical consideration might have little effect on romantics and ideologues who seek to establish a closed intellectual community within an open society.

Notes

I would like to thank José Cabezón and Mary Sirridge for their helpful comments and criticisms on an earlier version of this essay, and Stephen Farmer for the intellectual stimulation that made this essay possible.

1. A similiar point is made in Cabezón (1994:59).

2. The article by Robert E. Goss in this volume marks the end of medieval or "primary" scholasticism at about 1500, around the time of the invention of printing, the beginning of the Age of Discovery, and the first stirrings of the scientific revival leading to the Scientific Revolution.

3. The characteristics of scholasticism discussed in this chapter are based mainly on a sort of synthesis of those explored in Henderson (89–138) (where they are identified as "commentarial assumptions"), with those examined in the article by Cabezón included in this volume. Despite some rather superficial differences in terminology, there is a large degree of overlap between the two lists, even though Cabezón and I focus our works on different scholastic traditions (Indo-Tibetan vs. Chinese Confucian) that had little contact with one another.

4. These scholastic genealogies are examined in Wilson (1995).

5. A similar concern inspired Renaissance aestheticians who inherited from classical antiquity only "a small number of scattered notions and suggestions" on aesthetics which "had to be carefully selected, taken out of their context, rearranged, reemphasized and reinterpreted or misinterpreted before they could be utilized as building materials for aesthetic systems" (Kristeller 1980:174).

References

de Bary, Wm. Theodore.
1989 *The Message of the Mind in Neo-Confucianism*. New York: Columbia University Press.

Berthrong, John H.
1994 *All Under Heaven: Transforming Paradigms in Confucian-Christian Dialogues*. Albany: State University of New York Press.

Cabezón, José Ignacio.
1994 *Buddhism and Language: A Study of Indo-Tibetan Scholasticism*. Albany: State University of New York Press.

Chan, Wing-tsit.
n.d. *Instructions for Practical Living and Other Neo-Confucian Writings by Wang Yang-ming*. Trans. and ed. Wing-tsit Chan. New York: Columbia University Press.

Chang Hui-yen.
1970 I-t'u t'iao-pien. In *Chang Hui-yen I-hsüeh shih-shu*. Vol. 2. Taipei: Kuang-wen shu-chü.

Ch'en Ch'un.
1986 "Lectures at Yen-ling." In *Neo-Confucian Terms Explained (The "Pei-hsi tzu-i") by Ch'en Ch'un, 1159–1223).* Trans. Wing-tsit Chan. New York: Columbia University Press.

Chu Hsi.
1974 *Ssu-shu chi-chu, Hsia-Lun.* Taipei: Hsüeh-hai ch'u-pan-she.

1973 *Chu-tzu yü-lei chi-lüeh.* Compiled by Chang Po-hsing. Taipei: Shang-wu yin-shu kuan.

n.d. "Shih-ching chuan hsü." In *Ssu-shu wu-ching, Sung-Yuan jen chu.* Vol. 2. Peiching: Chung-kuo shu-tien.

Chu I-tsun.
1968 *Ching-i k'ao.* Compiled by Chu I-tsun. Taipei: Chung-hua shu-chü.

Ch'un-ch'iu san-chuan.
n.d. In *Ssu-shu wu-ching, Sung-Yuan jen chu.* Vol. 3. Peiching: Chung-kuo shu-tien.

Elman, Benjamin A.
1994 " 'Where Is King Ch'eng?': Civil Examinations and Confucian Ideology during the Early Ming." T'oung Pao 79:23–68.

Fang Hsiao-ju.
1966 "Hsüeh-pien." In *Hsün-chih-chai chi.* Taipei: Chung-hua shu-chü.

Gardner, Daniel K.
1986 *Chu Hsi and the Ta-hsüeh: Neo-Confucian Reflection on the Confucian Canon.* Cambridge: Harvard University Press.

Le Goff, Jacques.
1984. *The Birth of Purgatory.* Trans. Arthur Goldhammer. Chicago: University of Chicago Press.

Henderson, John B.
1991 *Scripture, Canon, and Commentary: A Comparison of Confucian and Western Exegesis.* Princeton: Princeton University Press.

Ho Yen.
1974 *Lun-yü Ho-shih teng chi-chieh.* Taipei: Chung-hua shu-chü.

Huang Tsung-hsi.
1970 "Ta Wan Chen-i lun *Ming-shih li-chih* shu." In *Nan-lei wen-ting, hou-chi.* Taipei: Shang-wu yin-shu-kuan.

Kalton, Michael C.
1988 *To Become a Sage: The Ten Diagrams on Sage Learning by Yi T'oegye.* Trans. and ed. Michael C. Kalton. New York: Columbia University Press.

K'ang Yu-wei.
1976 *Meng-tzu wei.* Taipei: Shang-wu yin-shu kuan.

Kasoff, Ira E.
1984 *The Thought of Chang Tsai.* Cambridge: Cambridge University Press.

Kristeller, Paul Oskar.
1980 *Renaissance Thought and the Arts: Collected Essays.* Princeton: Princeton University Press.

Lamberton, Robert.
1983 "Introduction." In *Porphyry: On the Cave of the Nymphs.* Trans. Robert Lamberton. Barrytown, N.Y.: Station Hill Press.

Masson-Oursel, P.
1920 "La Scolastique (étude de philosophie comparée). *Revue Philosophique de la France et de l'Étranger* 90:123–41.

Najita, Tetsuo.
1987 *Visions of Virtue in Tokugawa Japan: The Kaitokudo Merchant Academy of Osaka.* Chicago: University of Chicago Press.

Panofsky, Erwin.
1957 *Gothic Architecture and Scholasticism.* Cleveland: World Publishing Company, Meridian Books.

P'i Hsi-jui.
1974 *Ching-hsüeh t'ung-lun.* Taipei: Ho-Lo t'u-shu ch'u-pan she.

Pieper, Josef.
1960 *Scholasticism: Personalities and Problems of Medieval Philosophy.* Trans. R. Winston and C. Winston. New York: Pantheon Books.

Shchutskii, Iulian K.
1979 *Researches on the I Ching.* Trans. William L. MacDonald and Tsuyoshi Hasegawa with Hellmut Wilhelm. Princeton: Princeton University Press.

Voltaire.
1983. "Théologien: Theologian." In *Philosophical Dictionary.* Ed. and trans. Theodore Besterman. Harmondsworth, Eng.: Penguin Books.

Wang Yang-ming.
1971 *Ch'uan-hsi lu.* Anno. Yeh Chün-tien. Taipei: Shang-wu yin-shu kuan.

Wilson, Thomas A.
1995 *Genealogy of the Way: The Construction and Uses of the Confucian Tradition in Late Imperial China.* Stanford: Stanford University Press.

Yoshikawa Kojiro.
1983 *Jinsai Sorai Norinaga: Three Classical Philosophers of Mid-Tokugawa Japan.* Trans. Kikuchi Yuji. Tokyo: Toho Gakkai—The Institute of Eastern Culture.

Chapter **8**

Scholasticisms in Encounter: Working through a Hindu Example

Francis X. Clooney, S.J.

This chapter seeks to advance the project of a comparative scholasticism in three ways: by highlighting three interrelated religious-philosophical discourses from the Indian context which are strong candidates for the title of scholastic systems; by proposing, with those discourses as resources, further necessary distinctions regarding the origins, histories, and purposes of the various scholastic discourses under consideration; to shed new light on the comparative scholastic inquiry itself by raising some questions regarding the purpose and methods of this research. Let us begin with the necessary introductions to the Hindu material under consideration and the reasons for calling this material "scholastic." I will introduce three interconnected discourses from Hindu India:[1] Mīmāṃsā (organized around the interpretation of Vedic texts and rituals), Vedānta (organized around the Upaniṣads, in addition to the older materials), and Śrīvaiṣṇavism (organized around devotional texts in the Tamil language, in addition to those drawn from the Sanskrit heritage). We shall introduce them separately, though, as we shall see, this is not to decide in advance that they are, intellectually speaking, three separate discourses.

Three Hindu Discourses

Mīmāṃsā is India's single most influential exegetical discourse. It was developed for the sake of interpreting the ancient Vedic rituals and texts, to guarantee the right understanding which is the foundation for their right implementation. "Mīmāṃsā" means "investigation" or "inquiry" and indicates the thoughtful and incisive examination of materials already known and familiar to the inquirer, now submitted to deeper study. Mīmāṃsā gained its definitive form in the *Pūrva Mīmāṃsā Sūtras*, attributed to Jaimini (c. second century B.C.E.), and in the first extant commentary on the *Sūtras*, that of Śabara (c. second century C.E.).[2] The *Sūtras* are comprised of about 2,700 statements (*sūtras*) so brief as to require elaboration if they are to be understood; they inquire into ancient Indian rituals and the texts that accompany them—and thus into *dharma*, which is the right way of acting, ritually, according to the right ordering of the universe. *Dharma* is the sum of all right ritual relations, the activated, fully understood, and rightly connected set of all the smaller and larger activities and things which together constitute the sacrificial whole. It is the standard in relation to which all competing measures of significance—the gods, the author, human desire, the ordinary world—are judged merely supporting features. This inquiry in *dharma* proceeds by a careful delineation of the connections between ritual events and their textual sources, between texts and their places in ritual enactment; texts are inherently implicated in the world of ritual practice, and careful reading is the necessary prerequisite to coherent practice.

The Mīmāṃsakas worked with a narrow canon (*śruti*), limited rather severely to the texts connected with the orthodox Vedic rituals. In their view, the meaning(s) of texts and the purpose(s) of (ritual) actions converge; right meaning entails the realization of what one ought to do. Even abstract argumentation retains its "memory" of ritual practice and its rationale, its spatial and temporal ramifications, and truth retains its performative features. The guarding of this canon was moderated by a certain flexibility, that is, by the Mīmāṃsakas' willingness to surround it with other texts (*smṛti*) which were judged to be temporally later and authoritative only in a derivative sense. This secondary set of texts could be extended indefinitely without any changes accruing to the Vedic canon itself.[3] Mīmāṃsā's careful distinctions and connections among words and actions were articulated through a style of exegesis that proceeded by the composition and scrutiny of specific "textual loci," carefully formulated, examined, and argued "case studies" (*adhikaraṇas*). The rhetorical discourse of Mīmāṃsā is argued out in these case studies according to complex rules for correct interpretation and debate; Mīmāṃsā guides inquirers into a correct reading and, when needed, into ever more elaborate arguments in defense of that reading. In defense of this constructed and defended convergence of text and action, Mīmāṃsā conceived of the Vedic world as a sacrificially organized array of center and periphery where the only reality that ultimately matters is the event of sacrifice, *dharma*.

Later, particularly in response to critiques from outside its ritually defined world, Mīmāṃsā articulated second-order doctrines on language, the nature of the world, social structures, and religious values, some of which eventually would flourish independently of the texts and rituals they had been fashioned to support. Thus the Mīmāṃsakas argued for the authorlessness of the Veda (*apauruṣeyatva*) and the self-validation of language in order to defend the view that neither the authority nor the meaning of texts depends on the potentially unreliable authors to whom they were traditionally attributed. Despite their intellectual ramifications, such moves toward systematization remained always intrinsically performative, and the Veda was never completely abstracted from its ritual milieu.[4]

The second of our three candidates for the appellation *scholastic* is Vedānta, also known as the Uttara (Later) Mīmāṃsā. Vedānta generally refers to a body of concepts and a number of schools of thought which claim as their primary referent and authority the Sanskrit-language Upaniṣads, a group of texts from the late Vedic period (after 800 B.C.E.)—the "end" (*anta*) of the Veda.

In the Upaniṣads, a received tradition of speculation about Vedic rituals was increasingly accompanied by speculations on the nature of the world in which ritual is efficacious, on human nature, and on the nature of the "higher" or postmortem reality which renders human experience ultimately significant. Inquiries into, and discourses about, the vital breath, the self (*ātman*), and the corresponding spiritual and cosmic principle (*Brahman*) become very prominent in the Upaniṣads, though ritual speculation too continues. These Upaniṣadic explorations proceed by experiment, by question and answer, by exposition and summation; in their rough texture they replicate earlier oral debates and inquiries. The older Upaniṣads appear to be only partially homogenized collections of yet older debates and teachings and were not presented as single works by single authors, nor as complete systematizations. Consequently, Vedānta's theological appropriation of the Upaniṣads was marked from the start as a careful and constructive systematization which went beyond its texts, systematizing them.

Bādarāyaṇa's *Uttara Mīmāṃsā Sūtras* (c. fifth century C.E.) was a set of 555 *sūtras* which organize Upaniṣadic meditations and speculations into a discourse focused on the reality of *Brahman* and *ātman* and the salvific efficacy of knowing them as related or even as identical. In support of these basic truths, the *Sūtras* introduced other philosophical and religious doctrines, many borrowed directly from the Mīmāṃsā, some revised and suited to the new set of issues. Recalling and revising the views of various earlier and probably contemporary Vedānta teachers, Bādarāyaṇa systematized the Upaniṣads, identifying and regularizing their main tenets.[5]

This systematization was a conscious extension of the Mīmāṃsā paradigm. Though claiming a scope wider than Mīmāṃsā, Vedānta for the most part acted in continuity with its predecessor. If it introduced concepts and practices incompatible with Mīmāṃsā, and claimed to supersede it, even these claims were argued according to the norms of Mīmāṃsā thinking. Enlarging the canon of scripture to include the Upaniṣads (and, later the *Bhagavad Gītā* and other texts), Vedānta nevertheless reads those texts in a Mīmāṃsā fashion, extending Mīmāṃsā modes of exegesis to new materials. Consequently, Vedānta is intellectually distinctive, but nevertheless inseparable from the older Mīmāṃsā discourse. Even the Advaita (Nondualist) Vedānta, which argues that knowledge is not action and that "to know" cannot be necessarily consequent upon "to do," shares with Mīmāṃsā a concern for performance, emphasizing the need for the proper composition of a context for knowledge. Vedānta insists that liberative knowledge is acquired gradually through an engagement in texts submitted to exegesis; reading, rightly and faithfully performed, is the way to right knowledge. The final realization of *Brahman* is an achievement which is never merely available as a part of ordinary experience. The world of Vedānta remains a world that is textually and ritually described.[6]

Our third candidate for the name *scholasticism* is Śrīvaiṣṇavism, a south Indian theistic religious system focused on devotion to the God Viṣṇu and his consort Śrī. Śrīvaiṣṇava thinking combines with its Sanskrit heritage the highest possible esteem for the Tamil devotional works of the āḻvārs (sixth through ninth centuries). Among these poet saints, the most important was Śaṭakōpaṉ ("Nammāḻvār"), author of *Tiruvāymoḻi*, a classic work of Tamil literature and religion.[7] In the centuries after Śaṭakōpaṉ, his songs were recognized by the Śrīvaiṣṇavas as sacred scripture, the flawless revelation of Lord Viṣṇu. *Tiruvāymoḻi* was believed to express the truth of the Sanskrit Vedas in a perfect vernacular. Śrīvaiṣṇavism can be termed a Tamil-language Vedānta; along with its roots in Tamil culture and religion, it drew deeply on the writings of Rāmānuja, the eleventh-century Vedānta teacher who, though he may have been influenced strongly by the Tamil tradition, wrote exclusively in Sanskrit. Through its links with Vedānta, Śrīvaiṣṇavism also has links with Mīmāṃsā. In Śrīvaiṣṇavism, therefore, the great tradition of Brahmanical scholasticism, represented by Mīmāṃsā and Vedānta, takes on a devotional hue and is self-consciously extended to a new religious realm.

By the fourteenth century, five Śrīvaiṣṇava theologians—themselves part of a longer tradition of teachers who gave oral expositions of the songs—had dictated or written major commentaries on *Tiruvāymoḻi*, dealing with this "new Veda" by drawing on the Sanskrit terminology and concepts developed in Rāmānuja's Vedānta. Exploring with great reverence and in increasing detail each song's every word, image, and meaning, they treated *Tiruvāymoḻi* precisely as they would a Vedic text and commented on it accordingly, connecting its songs with the Sanskrit Vedānta tradition of philosophy and theology, re-reading the songs and the Vedānta tradition in light of one another. For the Śrīvaiṣṇava theologians, *Tiruvāymoḻi* was not simply "more" revelation; it was the sacred, superior, Tamil-language re-expression of the ancient, sacred, Sanskrit-language Vedic scriptures.[8]

Although much of the vigor and inspiration of the community was directed inward toward the spiritual development of those already in the community, in Śrīvaiṣṇavism too there was a tendency toward an integral explanation of the world in which the community existed. The sacred Tamil hymns were understood to reveal the core identity of the whole world, what mattered most in it, and what would pertain most certainly to the life of the community. As circumstances required, the Śrīvaiṣṇava system would be expanded and vigorously defended by every manner of argument, against every possible opponent.[9]

Mīmāṃsā, Vedānta, and Śrīvaiṣṇavism as Scholastic Discourses

Thus far, I have introduced the three discourses in a preliminary fashion. Let us now take up the other introductory matter to which we must attend, a working definition of scholasticism. For this, I refer to the account of scholasticism offered by José Cabezón elsewhere in this volume and in his recent *Buddhism and Language*.[10] Cabezón provides us with useful criteria in shaping a generalizable understanding of scholasticism which extends the term beyond its usual European connection and makes it usable across cultural and religious boundaries. Cabezón highlights several important features which distinguish scholasticism, of which three are the most important:[11] a strong sense of *tradition*, which includes the handing down of the texts which define the community; *proliferativity*, "the tendency to textual and analytic inclusivity rather than exclusivity"; *rationalism*, "the commitment to reasoned argument and non-contradiction." Three others fill out the list: *completeness* along with *compactness* (nothing missing, nothing extraneous); *systematicity* (the endeavor to reproduce in writing "the basic orderliness found in the world"); and *self-reflexivity* ("the tendency to objectify and to critically analyze first order practices"). Cabezón strongly emphasizes the dynamic component of scholasticism:

> Scholastic rationalism operates in large part to justify religious beliefs as expressed in doctrine. This, combined with what I have called the generally *proliferative* character of scholasticism as a movement, means that, in principle, there is for scholastics *no end to the rational process*. It is *always* possible for an opponent, real or imagined, to demand a reason, that is, to require that a particular doctrinal assertion be justified; and for the scholastic there is *never* any theoretical ground for denying the validity of such a request. To say that scholastics are rationalists is in part to say that they are *ever* willing to answer an opponent's "why"? (Cabezón 1994: 21; my emphases)

Although there will surely be modifications and exceptions to Cabezón's characterization, it is a nuanced and useful standard by which to measure whether any given (religious) tradition is scholastic or not.[12] On this basis, it is reasonable to conclude that Mīmāṃsā, Vedānta, and Śrīvaiṣṇavism are scholastic discourses. They are traditional, deeply rooted in the Sanskritic, Vedic tradition and, in the case of Śrīvaiṣṇavism, in the cultural and religious traditions of south India as well. Their concern for language is very serious indeed, as is evident in their writings about language and in the great effort they put into commentary on their respective key texts; they are well known for the complex positions they develop in the areas of epistemology, cosmology, and ontology, in support of basic religious positions and practices, in arguing very extensively against both external opponents and adversaries closer to home. Moreover, each discourse self-consciously includes rules for its own management, pointing toward a systematization of its operation. Later on, each is formalized in manuals and systematic treatises which serve to guide one through life, understanding everything that is required to make that journey a safe passage. All three aim at the inculcation of right religious values and practices, informed by a right understanding of the world. All three schools are selective, restricting the set of active participants and the expected more passive audience as well.

If we group these three discourses under the appellation *scholasticism*, along with other candidates for that title—such as medieval

Thomism in Europe and schools of Tibetan Buddhism—we not only shall have organized important discourses in a new cross-cultural framework, but at the same time we shall have provided a perspective from which to study these compared scholastic discourses.

Nevertheless, once we have agreed that these discourses are scholastic, we have reached only the *beginning* of a more elaborate inquiry into their nature as scholastic. Important further questions prompt us to nuance our study of scholasticisms in a comparative context. In the remainder of this chapter, six such questions are considered: How much of a scholasticism must be scholastic? Are Mīmāṃsā, Vedānta and Śrīvaiṣṇavism one or two or three scholasticisms? How important are the histories of scholasticisms? What kind(s) of scholasticism do Mīmāṃsā, Vedānta and Śrīvaiṣṇavism represent? What do we learn from the encounters of scholasticisms? Ought we to undertake a comparison of scholasticisms or a comparative scholasticism? Although these questions are discussed in terms of the example of Mīmāṃsā, Vedānta, and Śrīvaiṣṇavism, their implications are wider and should be applicable to scholasticisms in general.

How Much of a Scholasticism Must Be Scholastic?

First, it will be interesting to clarify just how comprehensive a claim we are making when we call a discourse "scholastic." For it is not clear that *all* the writings attributable to a school need be scholastic, even if the key, defining writings are. Thomas Aquinas is recognized as a great scholastic, but one can debate whether his hymns in praise of the Eucharist are scholastic documents; Rāmānuja wrote a great commentary on the *Uttara Mīmāṃsā Sūtras*, which will be judged scholastic by most standards, but he also wrote very emotional (and theologically dense) hymns and gave directives for the order of the daily temple schedule. Are these scholastic too? But it is also true that texts we might be inclined to mark as "nonscholastic writings of scholastic authors" will upon more refined analysis turn out to be more deeply connected with the clearly scholastic elements than we might have anticipated—at least dependent upon implied scholastic discourse. The point is not to claim that we need to read each and every work of an author or of an entire school if we are to understand it coherently and integrally, but rather that we need to specify how broad an understanding of scholasticism we are working with and how we intend to acknowledge while also limiting the possibilities instigated by a variety of genres—some of which may be local, found in relation to only one scholasticism, and yet intrinsic to its identity.

Are Mīmāṃsā, Vedānta, and Śrīvaiṣṇavism One or Two or Three Scholasticisms?

Second, when we speak of Mīmāṃsā, Vedānta, and Śrīvaiṣṇavism, it is interesting to ask whether we are dealing with *one* scholasticism which accommodates a variety of specific developments, or rather with *two*, or even with *three* scholasticisms. At issue is how far the label "scholasticism" can be stretched in this and parallel cases, and the conditions under which the methods and doctrines of obviously interconnected discourses will diverge so greatly that it is no longer possible or worthwhile to label them "scholastic."

As we have seen, Mīmāṃsā, Vedānta, and Śrīvaiṣṇavism share styles of commentary and argument, a sense of how reason, scripture, and practice go together, a sense of how reality fits together in its relevant features, and a sense of the way in which an audience must be, or can become, privileged. One can of course undertake studies which examine the extent to which styles of thought persist from text to text; but as one does so, the impression is reinforced that there are strong family resemblances which favor thinking that the three are not merely scholastic, but actually one differentiated scholasticism.

Yet, even if methodological and stylistic similarities are evident, questions of content surely still matter. If Vedānta violated the severely defined ritual canon of Mīmāṃsā by adding and esteeming Upaniṣadic materials which the Mīmāṃsakas considered inconsonant with the rest of the Veda or merely superfluous to it, under these circumstances do both cohere as a single scholasticism? Or, is it really possible to recognize the continuity of the brahmanical and renunciant traditions of Vedānta with the vernacular and popular Śrīvaiṣṇava devotionalism? Can a deeply Sanskritic Mīmāṃsā scholasticism really be stretched so far as to accommodate the canonization of a body of materials in the Tamil language? Can a Śrīvaiṣṇavism which stresses the importance of total dependence on God really form a single scholasticism with a Mīmāṃsā which is studiously, pragmatically atheistic?

Such questions also may be expressed more simply: is "scholasticism" only a question of methods and styles, or is content relevant to the definition of particular scholasticisms or "scholasticism" in general? M. De Wulf, in his weighty exposition and defense of medieval Christian scholasticism as a *philosophical* system, *Scholasticism Old and New*,[13] considers, though rather cautiously, the possibility of scholasticisms outside Europe and argues for some cohesion of content:

> Finally, what are we to think of the more abstract conception that would make scholastic philosophy a philosophy subordinated to

> any dogma whatever, and which would see in *Catholic* scholasticism a *variety* analogous to Indian, Arabian, Protestant and other scholasticisms? . . . The distinctive element in each variety is a *religious* and dogmatic element, an *extra-philosophical element*, therefore; and so we continue to characterize *a philosophy by that which is not philosophical* . . . an unscientific procedure. Furthermore, whether the ruling dogma be Brahminism or Mahommedanism, or Catholicism or Protestantism, we forget that the philosophical theories subordinated to such dogmas will nevertheless possess a meaning of their own, looked at from a properly philosophical or rational point of view. . . . Finally, where there is question of a real synthesis, it will include a multitude of solutions beyond the control of dogma, the latter having nothing to do with the questions that called forth those solutions. (de Wulf 1906: 73)

Though on a philosophical basis there may ultimately be at most one scholastic philosophical system, (cross)cultural variations notwithstanding, de Wulf's intention was not primarily to exclude other scholasticisms, but rather to make a point about where the specificity of a scholastic discourse lies. De Wulf insists that methodological features alone are insufficient to distinguish scholasticism from other schools of philosophy.[14] Although ideally one will be able to discern deep interconnections between a scholasticism's methods and its philosophical doctrines, a scholasticism is to be more strongly distinguished by its substantive philosophical positions than by its methods. So too, for de Wulf, there is nothing specifically, doctrinally Catholic—or Hindu or Buddhist—about scholasticism, whereas it is possible to identify philosophical positions which distinguish scholasticism from other philosophical systems. Otherwise, he observes, one's definition of scholasticism may become so broad that in the end too many systems with too widely diverse doctrines will be given the label "scholastic"—in a triumph of the love of methods and structures over substantive content, a triumph that is, of course, a tidy way to systematize diverse discourses.

To a certain extent, questions regarding the unity or plurality of these scholastic systems must be answered by weighing and assigning significance to factors which may or may not divide them. This must be done in detail; we must study the decisions made by Vedāntins and Śrīvaiṣṇavas themselves as they in fact defended, manipulated, and put limits upon their possible connections with each other and with Mīmāṃsā. In the end, too, one must confront the speculative question of how much weight ought to be given to the *content* of related discourses when we are deciding whether or not to group them together.

How Important Are the Histories of Scholasticisms?

Third, even if an awareness of history may not be a primary characteristic of many scholastic discourses—their strong senses of tradition notwithstanding—it is necessary for us to raise questions about their history, about the birth and vitality and death of scholasticisms. Obviously, the fact that Mīmāṃsā, Vedānta, and Śrīvaiṣṇavism are interconnected scholastic discourses does not mean that all three began together or that they invariably will continue to flourish alongside one another. Yet the fact that they are three discourses with long, interlocking histories—for much of their histories they can be thought of as contemporaries—prompts us to ask whether a scholastic family may dissipate its heritage, its scholastic character gradually diminished and rendered peripheral, reduced to being a mere facet of a discourse which is not scholastic, but which contains scholastic elements. In the end, a scholasticism may become a brilliant, finely preserved museum piece, cherished but in fact devoid of vitality. It may be that some discourses are scholastic for a period of time and then cease to be so or actually die even if they are perpetuated, taught, replicated; they actually may cease to be communities of thought and conversation, becoming unable to move beyond their established categories, remembered due to reverence and for the sake of mind training rather than for any engagement with vital contemporary issues.

One might argue, for instance, that Mīmāṃsā did not in fact adjust itself to the marginalization of the Vedic ritual discourse, neither taking that into account nor expanding its categories, and that it was not able to remedy the peripheralization of ritual and commentary by its own turn to internally bounded systematic formulations in works such as the *Mīmāṃsā Nyāya Prakāśa,* and so has survived largely as a speciality which only some scholars choose to master. If so, "Mīmāṃsā scholasticism" would live on inside Vedānta or Śrīvaiṣṇavism, but not as "Mīmāṃsā per se." Are there any scholasticisms which have not declined? Perhaps today the only scholasticism is a *comparative scholasticism,* but more on this below. Answering these questions depends on more historical study of the individual scholasticisms themselves, by criteria yet to be devised.

What Kind(s) of Scholasticism do Mīmāṃsā, Vedānta, and Śrīvaiṣṇavism Represent?

My fourth question concerns the balance of characteristics within a scholasticism. Even if numerous discourses are recognized as sharing the characteristics identified by Cabezón, it still is necessary to measure the balance of elements within each, and so to group such scholasticisms by "species." For instance, one scholasticism might be so committed to the preservation of tradition that rational argumentation primarily serves that defensive strategy; another might be committed to a complete account of the world, and for that purpose allow traditional elements of practice to recede or even disappear; a third might be so heavily soteriocentric that systematization would be sacrificed for the sake of strategies which draw the "student" into the community and its way of imagining the world; and yet another might have grown up in a hostile environment and had to develop a strong polemic strain, while another might have developed in so secure an environment as to stress unity and inclusion of the foreign and novel. Some discourses favor ever more complete understanding and aim toward assent, on terms that are universally accessible to reason. Others favor religious practice and utilize intellectual analyses for the sake of conversion of life, urging the student to join a particular community of believers. Some intend a universal audience of all reasoning persons, while others intend a small community of believers which needs primarily to be confirmed in its faith, taught to think in a way that is conducive to faith. The possible combinations are numerous.

To formalize these distinctions, I provisionally suggest that some scholasticisms can be thought of as "intellectualist," others as "performative." The former are more preponderantly focused on questions of comprehensive understanding, the latter on formation in right thinking and acting. In proposing this terminology, however, I stress that I am speaking of emphases and priorities which distinguish discourses having both intellectualist and performative elements. There can be no question of a scholastic discourse where the appeal to reasonable inquiry entirely rules out affective conversion or one where the formation of virtuous persons entirely excludes rational inquiry. The issue is rather how the balance leans in any particular scholasticism.

Mīmāṃsā, Vedānta, and Śrīvaiṣṇavism are best thought of as *performative* scholasticisms. Despite their commitments to rationality and the world-encompassing and systematic nature of their self-presentations, they are primarily concerned with the formation of proper persons within a community sharing key values where the presentation of arguments in a reasonable form is aimed not so much at gaining the assent of (all) reasoning persons, but at confirming the community in its account of itself and corresponding practices. Most of what might be said about "the world as such" is simply not relevant.

The Mīmāṃsā presentation of the Vedic sacrificial system entails a primary distinction between the *laukika* and the *vaidika*. The *laukika* is comprised of the set of the ordinary things of daily life which are originally neutral in relation to religious realities; the *vaidika* is defined not by things of a supernatural origin, but rather by a specific configuration of those *laukika* ordinary things according to textual and ritual norms, their constitution as a *vaidika* world. As things are used in the course of ritual action, they gain religious significance. The *laukika* fact of human nature is not significant in itself, though humans have relevance as potential and actual performers of rituals. Their competence—or lack thereof—is not based on human nature, except with respect to minimal functional capacities, such as the ability to understand the ritual directives and act according to them; it is primarily a matter of their ability to be positioned vis à vis the whole *vaidika* realm. We need to know what humans are going to (be able to) do, not what human nature is. The *laukika*, the ordinary, needs to be understood and explained *insofar* as it becomes ritually relevant, processed into the predictable formative process; over time the likelihood of new input becomes increasingly minimal.

The Mīmāṃsakas could not avoid the issue of human motivation: whatever uses the ordinary in general might be put to, and however it might be rethought, humans had to be willing to participate in ritual, to choose to do their part in the performance of the sacrifices. So they described functionally the motivational factors which attract humans to the demanding and tedious work of offering Vedic rites, the dynamics of human desire (*kāma*) and the search for pleasure (*prīti*). Later Mīmāṃsā eventually broke into schools based in part on whether this anthropology of desire would take center stage, as it seems to have done in the predominant Bhāṭ ṭa school, or remain a subordinate factor, as it seems to have done in the Prābhākara school. Similarly, the Mīmāṃsā debates about the status of the gods to whom sacrifices are offered—whether they are present as corporeal or verbal realities, as posited addressees or real respondents in the project of completing sacrifices—raised very basic theological questions. But in the end the Mīmāṃsakas left the issue unresolved; as long as the gods can be addressed, their status in reality does not matter. There was no impulse at work to include everything that could be said on such topics, no thrust toward a complete anthropology or theology, no impetus for Mīmāṃsakas to make explicit the positions they were working with, no concern to fill out and make explicit every further position that would follow from accepted positions. This is at best "a completeness of the practically relevant," which could leave untouched any number of incompletely considered aspects of questions already raised.[15]

Vedānta too chose to keep all theoretical and doctrinal pronouncements rooted in textual knowledge, and so to direct the student of Vedānta back into a certain kind of measured, guided practice within the community itself. Although Vedānta appears more philosophical than Mīmāṃsā and more inclined to claims about things in general, its actual articulation of theory and doctrine keeps it firmly within the confines of Mīmāṃsā's practical emphasis.

Although it is true that Vedānta was in part defined by the claims it makes about the way the world—and not just the ordinary—really is. We have seen that it makes the claim that there is an eternal self (*ātman*) within every human being, and that likewise the universe has a self or, perhaps, deeper reality (*Brahman*); these are claims about the way the world really is, claims inviting consent or objection, based on one's perceptions of human nature. But Vedānta's major trajectory is not toward the generalization of knowledge, but rather toward a selective articulation of salient points which guard knowledge of the self carefully within the *vaidika* (*aupaniṣadika*) realm, accessible to those who perform Vedānta rightly: for it is to those who know the scriptures and conform their lives to them that the self becomes manifest, and not to those who "merely" reason properly. Although it is possible, of course, to insist that this message, even if posited as available only to "the few," is complete and universal, it nevertheless falls significantly short of a completed systematization of knowledge; completeness is measured by the standard of the religiously useful.

Like the Mīmāṃsakas, the Vedāntins respected and made use of rational argumentation; and like them, they put severe restrictions on what could be achieved by argument. The primary purpose of such argumentation is the education and encouragement of the community, not the persuasion of those with opposing views.[16] The most important insights—those which would precede complete liberation—had to be learned from the scriptures alone; reason's role was to show that there was nothing in experience to contradict the scriptures. Although the Vedāntins expended considerable energy in a critique of other schools of thought, and argued (in *Uttara Mīmāṃsā Sūtras* II.2 for example) that other positions could be disproved even without an appeal to the scriptures, it is nevertheless clear that the Vedānta use of reason was deeply imbued with an Upaniṣadic perspective and did not provide a universal argumentation open to all reasoning persons; at best, one might be able to show the deficiency in the thinking of others and leave them confounded, in want of some better position and therefore in need of a turn to the *vaidika*.[17]

The Vedāntins too operated with a strong sense of the *vaidika* and a sharp sense of the difference of the *vaidika* from the *laukika*; to know one's eternal self required skilled preparation. One had to be made into the kind of person who will be able to know oneself, and the ordinary features of one's self were relevant insofar as they could serve as marks on the path of this development.

Since the Vedāntins also insisted that knowledge was not dependent on *karma,* one might see here an opening to universally accessible knowledge; nevertheless, the potential opening was confined in several ways. Even Advaita Vedānta, potentially the most radical school on this point, admitted a role for *karma,* as a preparation for the origination of knowledge; Vācaspati Miśra claimed that if one seems to have Upaniṣadic knowledge in this life without ritual preparation, this is only because the preparation had taken place in a previous life. Likewise, knowledge which is dependent on the Vedas becomes a project of knowledge, a task to be undertaken in the performance of meditation, based on the regular study of one's designated texts (i.e., *svādhyāya*), and so on (Clooney 1993, ch. 4). The Vedānta viewpoint, then, is close to the Mīmāṃsā viewpoint: reason is important, but in the end, attention to the ordinary (*loka*) has a limited, provisional role warranted by its pragmatic results.

We have seen that in comparison with the preceding discourses, the Śrīvaiṣṇava theological system is distinguished by its embrace of a yet wider canon of religious literature and, on top of that, by the insistence that *Tiruvāymoḻi,* along with accompanying works in the *Prabandham,* was the Tamil embodiment of the old Vedic canon, not merely an addition to it. On the whole, it is more explicitly open to popular devotion in its varied energies. The commitment of this community to the Tamil south Indian tradition might seem to have transgressed the boundaries of the *vaidika* universe, and to an important extent this is true. Yet this did not happen on as large a scale as one might have thought, for once the canon had been expanded, its broader pattern was quickly inscribed with all the older understandings we have been examining; in their commentaries and more systematic presentations, the Śrīvaiṣṇava ācāryas painstakingly correlated the Tamil texts with the texts of the Vedānta canon and understood them on the whole as if they were Vedic.

While the commentators praise Tamil most extravagantly, they do not attend to Tamil culture and literature—which was external to the *vaidika*—as a whole; they are very sensitive to instances of exceptional Tamil poetry, but draw back from making claims about the world in which that poetry was composed. They have little to say about the fact that long before Rāmānuja's time, Tamil was possessed of a highly refined literature composed almost entirely outside the Sanskrit realm of influence, and for the most part they do not praise this heritage in its breadth nor in terms of its own canons of interpretation; it is revealing, for instance, that the ācāryas attribute Śaṭakōpaṉ's brilliance to his extraordinary interior development rather than to any influence of earlier Tamil literature. Although we ought not to read into their texts contemporary expectations about "culture" and "literature," nevertheless they did not take the opportunity to describe a more sophisticated way of looking at a world too large to be circumscribed by the *vaidika-laukika* distinction.[18]

In summary: the Mīmāṃsā, Vedānta, and Śrīvaiṣṇava scholasticisms balanced the relationship between the rational and the religious, the natural and the religiously constructed, in such a way as to return their adherents always to issues of moral and spiritual practice with a carefully delimited world view. Though none of these three discourses abandoned reason, they subordinated it and limited its scope of inquiry by the standard of what was deemed soteriologically useful. While it is clear that these discourses explore many things, it is also clear on both the philosophical and the religious levels that there is a definite limit to inquiry, not because of an external authority terminating inquiry, but because after a certain point it is no longer required. All three excel in subtle analysis and forthright questioning, but it would be misleading to suggest that they continue to tend toward a complete explanation of the world or positively engage in acts of refinement and adjustment in the face of new eventualities.

Quite different from these "performative" scholasticisms would be the "intellectualist" scholasticisms, which would seek without ceasing to know the entirety of the intelligible world and put it all in order—even when such inquiry would have no immediate practical purpose, since the completion of knowledge itself would stand as a means to validate the truth of the tradition. In an intellectualist scholasticism the tendency would be toward a complete account of the world, the answering of all questions, the organization of all information—even if these intellectual pursuits would move forward without any immediate connection to practice. In an intellectualist scholasticism a great deal would be said about the world in general, either apart from strictly religious considerations, or with the expectation that at some point what is learned about the world ultimately will conform to, or be pertinent to, religious knowledge. While an intellectualist scholasticism would not have to be averse to some form of a *vaidika-laukika* distinction, it would, first, place both with a single frame of intelligibility and, second, be prone to revise views on the former on the basis of what is learned about the latter. Such scholasticisms would exemplify Cabezón's description of a scholasticism which sees no end to the rational process, which never refuses to take up a further question. Under the proviso that the issue is balance and that there is no question here of a scholasticism which ignores practical and spiritual concerns, one can nominate European Christian scholasticism in its varieties and later developments as intellectualist, along with its descendants in the modern West—including modern science and, perhaps, the comparative study of religions.

I conclude this section with a comment on the possibility of judgments about the strength of performative scholasticisms. On the whole, the preceding comments on the Mīmāṃsā, Vedānta, and Śrīvaiṣṇava scholasticisms must be understood as strictly descriptive, for the limitation of these systems will be judged a certain defect only from an unreflectively intellectualist standpoint. Nevertheless, one can raise further questions about the adaptability and change of discourses which do not have strong intellectualist components. Although all three discourses survive and flourish (though for Mīmāṃsā this has long been a largely intellectual survival rather than a communal one, if indeed there ever had been a community defined by Mīmāṃsaka values per se), it seems that none of the three has significantly adapted its discourse about itself in the face of change. This is so not because they deny that things ordinarily change, or because they lack the resources to cope with change (the conceptual apparatus by which to recognize the possibility of change), but rather because they have continued to view the realm of the religiously significant (the *vaidika, aupaniṣadika, śrīvaiṣṇava*) as entirely stable. This version of completeness precludes the possibility of change, since what has been explained serves as a reason for not having to make further adjustments or explanations.[19]

What Do We Learn from the Encounters of Scholasticisms?

A fifth question has to do with the history of scholasticisms in relation to one another. We will do well to inquire into the interaction of scholastic discourses (however large or small an area of research "interactions" may turn out to be) as part of our comparative project, for it will be instructive to see what happens when scholasticisms come in contact, what motivates some discourses more than others to take its others into account, and whether such encounters with "new others" (after their own styles and status as scholasticisms have been set in relation to habitual adversaries) cause shifts toward the intellectualist or performative side of the balance.[20]

Here I simply will introduce three such examples, without developing them or drawing conclusions. A first example is the encounter between the Jesuit missionary Roberto de Nobili (1577–1656) and texts of the Vedānta tradition. De Nobili devoted himself to a mastery of Sanskrit and whatever literature he had access to, and he seems to have been the first Westerner to have access to an Upaniṣad, the *Taittirīya*.

When he read it, he discovered in it intimations of two truths of the Christian tradition: the descent of the human race from a single set of parents and also the mystery of the Christian Trinitarian God. He highlighted these discoveries in order to show the value and working of reason within Indian culture: Indians could come to a recognition of truths about the world which he knew from his own background.

Of course, it is no surprise that the Vedāntins read the *Taittirīya* quite differently than did de Nobili. But the point is not simply that they did not notice any reference to a single set of original parents or to a Triune Ultimate Reality; it is rather that in their view the *Taittirīya* does not offer information of that sort on *any* topic. As a sacred text, it is not informative about deities, but is directive, guiding the reader into a way of life that leads to a knowledge, and thus on to a path of liberation which would not otherwise be available. For the Vedāntins, *Taittirīya* I locates a place in the inmost core of the human heart, from which one can begin a meditative journey toward unity with *Brahman*.[21] A vocabulary rooted in the ancient science of pronunciation is the starting point from which the meditator is led gradually toward an appropriation of his own true nature as *Brahman*. Although *Brahman* is more than a textual construct, the *Taittirīya* does not merely inform us about a reality which could be otherwise known; it tells the Vedāntin how to get through this world and beyond it, to *Brahman*.

Two scholasticisms met—incipiently, provocatively, in this very early encounter—with crossed expectations. When de Nobili read *Taittirīya* I, he was unconsciously crossing the doorstep of a scholasticism balanced quite differently than his own scholasticism. De Nobili read the *Taittirīya* with some perfectly sound scholastic expectations as to how texts are to be read, what religious texts tell us about the world, and how knowledge of the world confirms what we know religiously, but it was a different scholasticism. He met up with a scholasticism with different expectations about what kind of knowledge is religiously useful. One can tentatively recognize this as an encounter between an intellectualist scholasticism (de Nobili's) and a perfomative scholasticism (Vendānta's).[22]

My second example raises the converse possibility, how a thinker with a Mīmāṃsā or Vedānta or Śrīvaiṣṇavism affiliation might go about understanding the Christian scholastic tradition. A figure with whom one might begin is Swami Dayanand Saraswati (1824–83), a scholar and religious leader clearly learned in classical Hindu thought. In his *Light of Truth*, Dayanand rather severely critiqued the Christian Bible and the Christian theological tradition, along with just about every other tradition that he knew anything about. Although he cannot be taken as an uncontrovesial representative of Hindu orthodoxy, his learning, coupled with his insistence that he adheres to the Vedas and judges everything by Vedic principles, supports the idea that the *Light of Truth* is a kind of *vaidika* scholasticism adapting itself in its encounter with new adversaries.[23]

Should we bring our study closer to the present, a third example would be to consider the modern encounter of European thought with non-Western discourses as an encounter of scholasticisms. We might begin by looking into the flurry of writing by European thinkers a century ago about scholasticism in its European and possible non-European varieties; the work of De Wulf, referred to earlier, and that of Masson-Oursel, introduced elsewhere in this volume by Cabezón, are promising starting points.[24] Thereafter, one might turn to some of the more ambitious systematic discourses of twentieth-century theology—such as the theologians Karl Barth and Karl Rahner—and examine how they made (limited) room in their treatises for some of the great systems of Hindu and Buddhist thought.

Ought We Undertake a Comparison of Scholasticisms or a Comparative Scholasticism?

Our sixth and final question pertains to the nature of the project of comparing scholasticisms, such as is exemplified in this volume. The identification of scholasticisms as an area of study—large, integral, inquisitive, explanatory of their own and other people's realities—makes them a mirror for the inquirer and the occasion for reflection on one's own inquiry. Key questions we ask—about how scholasticisms develop, flourish, and perhaps die, how they balance performative and intellectualist ambitions, how they deal with "new others"—are questions inevitably accompanied by similar questions about the comparativist's own ambitious project. Granting that we can identify various systems as scholastic and then compare them, and that our own comparative project seeks to be complete and integral—then what is the purpose of this comparative project, and where does its completion lie?

We will do well to trace our own academic project of a comparative scholasticism to its several sources, including medieval Christian scholasticism, post-Enlightenment modernity, and the ongoing set of complex reactions to both. We need also to explain how we balance the performative and intellectualist tendencies of our project, why we organize and account for the compared material in the ways we do, and why we have undertaken this project at all. Even if this comparative study of scholasticism is primarily intellectualist, we must determine how we recognize, tabulate, and evaluate the demands that performative scholasticisms impose upon us. Their practical arrangements expect certain responses in conformity with the way the world is, and they resist merely intellectualist apprehensions. An intellectualist inquiry which intellectually reinterprets—and so defines, confines, and reduces—the clearly performative expectations of such scholastic discourses must itself be called to account for its goals. If Mīmāṃsakas, for instance, fashion every rule, make every logical distinction, and refute every opponent with the ultimate goal of showing that *vaidika* practice is the central value of human life, what are the methods by which the modern scholar manages to interpret their position, presumably without agreeing with them? Our probable lack of interest in the performance of Vedic ritual (or in Vedāntic meditation or Śrīvaiṣṇava temple worship) will manifest itself not only in our cool, disinterested observation of such practices, but also in a whole range of related attitudes which make evident the priority we give to understanding.

So we can ask: when we compare scholasticisms, is this *a comparison of scholasticisms*, carried on by scholars who are not scholastics themselves, or a *comparative scholasticism*—a true and contemporary scholasticism, perhaps the only scholasticism that might be credible today, one that flourishes in the wide reach of the comparative inquiry in today's pluralist context? The comparative project itself may be a scholastic venture; it may be an intellectualist venture which seeks to account for everything in light of what we already know, but it is more likely a performative one, filling out and organizing a picture of the world so as to defend a certain kind of attentiveness among modern scholars. To pursue this reflexive line of thinking, however, would be to embark upon an even more extended task, the comparison of models for comparative scholasticism.

Notes

1. Since it is difficult to categorize simple the range of materials covered by Mīmāṃsā, Vedānta, and Śrīvaiṣṇavism I use the word *Hindu*—though advisedly, aware of its vague and misleading connotations.

2. For Jaimini's *Pūrva Mīmāṃsā Sūtras* with Śabara's *Bhāṣya*, see Jha (1933–36).

3. The primary locus for the articulation of the orthodox notion of the canon is in *Pūrva Mīmāṃsā Sūtra* of Vaimini, sections 1.2 and 1.3. The Vedānta (Uttara Mīmāṃsā accepts the Mīmāṃsā norms while insisting on the extension of the canon to include the Upaniṣads.

4. For a more extended study of the Mīmāṃsā discourse, see Clooney (1990).

5. There are a number of Vedānta schools, distinguished on a doctrinal level most importantly over whether *ātman* is one or many, whether it is one with or different from *Brahman*, and whether it is a deeper or more superficial insight to recognize *Brahman* as a personal God. The most well-known schools are the Advaita school associated with Śaṅkara (eighth century), which holds for the ultimate, absolute nondifference of the *ātman* and *Brahman* and the provisionality of any language about a personal deity, and the Viśiṣṭādvaita school associated with Rāmānuja (eleventh century), which holds for a distinction-in-unity of *ātman* (of which there are many) and *Brahman* (which is personalized as the Lord. For the *Uttara Mīmāṃsā Sūtra* with Śaṅkara's commentary, see Gambhirananda (1983). For Rāmānuja's commentary, see Thibaut (1976).

6. For a more extended study of the Vedānta, see Clooney (1993).

7. For a translation of *Tiruvāymoḻi*, see Satyamurti Ayyangar, *Tiruvāymoḻi English Glossary* (Bombay: Ananthacharya Indological Research Institute, 1981, 2 vols.) Śaṭakōpaṉ also wrote three other works: *Tiruviruttam, Tiruvāciriyam*, and *Periyatiruvantāti*.

8. This Śrīvaiṣṇava position has been spelled out by Carman and Narayanan (1989).

9. For a more extended study of Śrīvaiṣṇava discourse, see Clooney (1996, chs. 3, 4).

10. See Cabezón intro to this volume and Cabezón (1994, ch. 1).

11. I have rearranged Cabezón's listing of the six features.

12. In effect I limit my consideration to religious discourses, though one can argue for a broader extension.

13. As the title suggests, it is a defense of the *revival* of scholasticism (at Louvain) occurring in his era.

14. The first part of his book is a detailed description of scholasticism as an integral whole of method and system which, though on various levels like other systems and methods of thought, has its own distinctive features—which both marked it in its ages) of flourishing and which can persist recognizably in new situations, such as the neo-scholastic revival of the late nineteenth and early twentieth centuries—a revival that is not archaic but quite apt, once the changed circumstances are admitted. De Wulf is much in agreement with Wiesheipl, and Śrīvaiṣṇava Vedānta would fit his expectations too: an emphasis on objectivity and accessibility; a pedagogical, analytic-synthetic process culminating in an integral system; a reverence for continuity and a strong memory of one's predecessors, while novelty is acknowledged; a system with a finality, ethical and religious; where persuasive argument is possible and urgent.

15. On the distinctively Mīmāṃsā treatment of the gods (*devatā*), see Clooney (1997).

16. See the comments of Śaṇkara and Vācaspati Miśra at the beginning of *Ut-*

tara Mīmāṃsā Sūtras II.2: apologetics are meant primarily to encourage the community of believers.

17. Even ostensibly public arguments with Buddhists and others who do not accept the scriptures remain located within a scriptural framework. See Clooney (1993:c.3).

18. The matter is actually even more complex, since the Śrīvaiṣṇava community was divided in part due to a difference of opinion as to how to balance attention to the Tamil tradition with attention to the Sanskrit tradition. The "northern" tradition of Śrīvaiṣṇavism, later identified with Kanchi and the great Vedānta Deśika, tipped its balance in favor of the Sanskrit, insofar as it argued that the new freedoms suggested by the flourishing of Tamil devotion did not in any way diminish the force of the Sanskrit, *vaidika* prescriptions. Deśika wrote large systematic and apologetic works and was accomplished in Tamil as well as in Sanskrit composition; intellectually, though his defense of the Śrīvaiṣṇava discourse ended up rooting it more and not less firmly in Sanskrit learning, albeit in a modified understanding of this learning. The "southern" tradition, identified with ācaryas of Śrīraṅgam and most famously Piḻḻai Lokācārya, favored the Tamil and in some ways adjusted Sanskrit categories to fit it. Thus, they teach that total surrender (*prapatti, śaraṇāgati*) is the true means to reaching God—or "nonmeans," since the point is that one must stand helpless before God—with the consequent judgment all are able to reach God, with or without *vaidika* training. Yet even this teaching functioned in a counterpoint to the *vaidika*, not a replacement of it: to surrender means to be without *vaidika* righteousness, to be exposed and helpless. Nothing particularly new is said about the world or about human nature; the argument is to defend salvation as exceptional—outside the *vaidika*—but not to overthrow the *vaidika*. The rhetoric in favor of total surrender and nonreliance on ritual activity points toward a goal that is still practical, rather than a broadened perspective which would move beyond the concept of the ordinary (*loka*) to a concept of 'world' as encompassing both *vaidika* and *laukika*. On the whole, it is not clear that the Śrīraṅgam ācāryas constructed any systematic Śrīvaiṣṇava thinking which, as systematic, would reach significantly beyond the Vedāntic tradition and acquire a truly Tamil foundation.

19. However much the "outside world" might change or remain the same, it was still fundamentally "that which needs transformation before it matters religiously." It is therefore a world from which potentially significant religious elements can be drawn—and this is no small conclusion to draw. But the real goal remains a selective transaction with the world, for the sake of the inculcation of the values of the community in its individual members and, on rare occasion, in outsiders who join the community. Though key resources for this project are available in all three traditions, no priority was in fact given to a presentation of communal truths in a manner open to the rational assent of anyone anywhere; except perhaps under the impetus of the social, political and economic pressures, there has been little motivation to engage "outsiders." Another way to put this is also evident, though likely to provoke controversy:

none of the three systems fostered the development of philosophy or science—discourses striving for objectivity and assent—as these would develop in the West.

20. And let us admit too that this study of their interactions must be built on a history of the individual scholasticisms themselves, from their origins to their probable or possible demise.

21. This point is complicated and is stated here rather baldly; in a longer treatment one would have to explain further how the Vedānta view of performance and the limited role of information is different from that of the Mīmāṃsa, which is more severely committed to the performative viewpoint.

22. See Clooney (1995b).

23. See Swami Dayananda Saraswati, *Light of Truth,* trans. Chiranjiva Bharadwaja (Star Press: Allahabad, 1915). Excerpts from the *Light of Truth* can be found in Griffiths (1990) a volume replete with other promising starting points. For an excellent study of Dayanand, see Llewellyn (1994).

24. See Cabezón in this volume. For an overview of the Western effort to appropriate Indian thought, see Halbfass (1988).

References

Cabezón, José Ignacio.

1994 *Buddhism and Language.* Albany: State University of New York Press.

Carman, John and Narayanan, Vasudha.

1989 *The Tamil Veda.* Chicago: University of Chicago Press.

Clooney, Francis X.

1997 "What's a God? The Quest for the Right Understanding of *devatā* in Brahmanical Ritual Theory (*mīmāṃsā*)." *International Journal of Hindu Studies* 1.1.

1996 *Seeing through Texts: Doing Theology among the Śrīvaiṣṇavas of South India.* Albany: State University of New York Press.

1995b "Religious Memory and the Pluralism of Readings: Reflections on Roberto de Nobili and the Taittirīya Upaniṣad." *Sophia* 34.1 (March–April): 204–5.

1995a "Back to the Basics: Reflections on Moral Discourse in a Contemporary Hindu Community." *Journal of Medicine and Philosophy* 20: 439–57.

1993 *Theology after Vedānta: An Experiment in Comparative Theology*. Albany: State University of New York Press.

1990 *Thinking Ritually: Rrecovering the Pūrva Mīmāṃsā of Jaimini*. Vienna: University of Vienna Press.

Gambhirananda, Swami (trans.).
1983 *Brahma-Sūtra Bhāṣya*. Calcutta: Advaita Ashrama.

Griffiths, Paul (ed.).
1990 *Christianity through Non-Christian Eyes* . Maryknoll: Orbis.

Halbfass, Wilhelm.
1988 *India and Europe: An Essay in Understanding*. Albany: State University of New York Press.

Jha, Ganganatha (trans.).
1933–36. *The Śābara Bhāṣya*. Baroda: Gaekwad's Oriental Series, volumes 66, 70, 73.

Llewellyn, John E.
1994 "From Interpretation to Reform: Dayānand's Reading of the Vedas." In *Authority, Anxiety, and Canon: Essays in Vedic Interpretation*, 235–51. Ed. Laurie Patton. Albany: State University of New York Press.

Nobili, R. de.
1972 *Roberto de Nobili on Indian Customs*. Palayamkottai: De Nobili Research Institute.

Thibaut, George.
1976 *The Vedānta-Sūtras with the commentary by Rāmānuja*. Sacred Books of the East, volume 48. New Delhi: Motilal Banarsidass.

Wulf, M. de.
1906 *Scholasticism Old and New*. Trans. P. Coffey. London: M. H. Gill and Son.

Chapter **9**

Scholasticism: The Possible Recovery of an Intellectual Practice

Paul J. Griffiths

Scholasticism was once, in ordinary spoken English, a term of praise or simple value-neutral description. Like *casuistry* and *dogma* it has become a term of abuse. It connotes a compulsive concern with uninteresting and useless matters of detail, an obsessive interest in hopelessly fine conceptual distinctions. To call someone a scholastic in this sense is close to calling her a pedant. Here the connections with casuistry are clear. But 'scholasticism' also suggests, to most native speakers of American English, a discourse based upon authority, a discourse whose axioms are unquestioned and unquestionable. And here the connections with dogma are clear. There is a complicated and interesting historical story to tell about why these words have accrued just these connotations. I shall not attempt to tell it here, but it is worth noting that for Western intellectuals it begins several centuries back, at least in the sixteenth century. By 1686, for example, when Leibniz wrote his *Discours de métaphysique*, the term *scholastic* already had become sufficiently problematic that he was obliged to apologize for it and to explain, defensively, his attempt to rehabilitate some elements of scholastic philosophy. He claims, for instance, in the eleventh section of that work:

> I know that I am advancing a grand paradox in attempting to rehabilitate to some extent the ancient philosophy, and to restore the

> almost banished substantial forms to their proper place. But perhaps I shall not be easily condemned when it is known that I have meditated long on modern philosophy; that I have given much time to experiments in physics and proofs in geometry; and that I was for a long time persuaded of the vanity of these beings [substantial forms] which finally I was obliged to embrace in spite of myself and as if by force after having myself carried out certain studies which made me recognize that we moderns do not give sufficient credit to Saint Thomas [Aquinas] and to the other great men of that time, and that there is, among the opinions of scholastic philosophers and theologians (*dans les sentimens des philosophes et theologiens scholastiques*), more solidity than one imagines, provided that one uses them appropriately and in their place.

Leibniz is right in that there is more solid merit in the substance of medieval European scholastic theory than is generally granted by contemporary academics. But there is also much merit in, and much of interest to say about, the intellectual practices that constitute scholasticism, a matter to which Leibniz pays little or no attention.

In treating this, I identify and give a formal description of scholasticism in terms of four principal variables: how scholastics typically read, how they typically compose, what their epistemological commitments are likely to be, and in what instutional contexts their practices are likely to flourish. The description given is of an ideal type, not of any specific historical phenomenon. This disclaimer does not mean that the ideal type is unrelated to any historical phenomena: many of the examples I shall use inevitably will be of just such phenomena. But I do not wish to claim that the ideal type I describe in this chapter ever has been instantiated (or ever will be) in all its details. Like all such descriptions, my identification of what scholastics do is meant as a heuristic device, a tool to use in answering certain questions. These are principally questions about the contemporary desirability and viability of scholastic practice. But they are also empirical questions as to the significance of scholastic practice for the intellectual life of tradition-based communities.

Since two of the variables (reading and composition) through which I shall identify scholasticism have to do with the relations between scholastics and their texts, I begin my description of scholasticism by offering a lexicon for the discussion of some basic and controversial theoretical problems about textuality.

Composition, Display, Storage

Texts must be composed in some fashion: this is a property constitutive of textuality. They will usually, though not always, be displayed after (or simultaneously with) their composition; more rarely they may be stored after they have been displayed; and those texts that are stored may sometimes be taken from storage and redisplayed. How may these things be done? Which technologies can be used to do them, and which are likely so to be used? These questions are important because engaging them will allow resolution of, or at least some new ways of thinking about, controverted and significant issues about the cultural and practical significance of speech, memorization, and writing. Asking the questions separately is important in another way as well: it will help to keep questions about composition and display distinct from questions about storage and redisplay. These questions often are merged or confused.

I begin, then, with the question of first display, the pivotal moment in the life of a text. This occurs when a text is first displayed in a fixed form with firm boundaries, a form in which it can enter storage. In the case of a verbal text displayed orally, the moment of display occurs when the last syllable of the text is uttered; in the case of a verbal text displayed in writing it occurs when the last graph (letter, character, word) is written.

As I use it here, the term *display* has as its contrastive term *inaccessibility*. A displayed text is one that could be (though need not actually be) consumed (read, heard, tasted, memorized) by a public. A nondisplayed text is one for which this is in principle not the case. All nondisplayed texts, then, will exist as thoughts, since only these are in principle inaccessible to a public. (I note that for God all texts are always displayed, even those that exist only as thoughts. When God is the consumer, the completion of a text's composition is also the completion of its display. But since scholastic communities are composed of human persons, this exception need not detain us.)

Given this definition, a verbal text can be displayed in only two ways. The first is by speech, understood as the creation by the human voice of semantically loaded patterns of vibration in the air; and the second is by the partial encoding of such patterns in some other form, most commonly (but not necessarily) one accessible to the eye rather than the ear. This second option usually will mean writing. Display by writing is secondary to and parasitic upon speech, because it requires that writing be understood as a secondary means of encoding or representing the primary data which are given by speech. This is true even though, in some cultural settings and some institutional locations, writing may be the only working mode of display and storage. The reason is that, both for individuals and for social groups, writing has speech among the necessary conditions for its development, while the reverse is not true. There are no instances either of individuals or of social groups in possession of writing but not of speech. This is not, of course, to say that writing, once it finds a place in the life of some individual or group, may not develop properties, semantic and other, that are neither determined by, nor in any significant way causally related to, properties of the speech-habits already possessed by that individual or group.

Given this understanding of display, the essential point of which is the in-principle public availability of a bounded text, what of composition? This always will occur either before display or simultaneously with it. For most texts, composition and display will be virtually simultaneous: the last moment of display (the moment at which the bounded text is made available) will be the same as the last moment of composition, and the processes by which a text is composed will not easily be separable from those by which that same text is displayed. Consider ordinary conversational texts. The (short) spoken text 'How do you do?' is, for most native speakers of English on most occasions of its use, effectively composed and displayed simultaneously. The same may be the case, though I think rarely, for much longer and more complex texts. Consider the performance art of an action painter, the inspired recitation of a bardic singer, or the speaking in tongues of a Pentecostal Christian. But composition (especially of long and complex texts) also may occur before the acts of speech or writing whose completion signals the moment of their display. That is to say, composition sometimes includes acts that occur prior to or alongside of productive acts and are intentionally directed toward their completion. Composition in this sense usually will include mental acts: deliberation, volition, intention, choice, and so forth. It also may include physical acts: writing a draft, scribbling phrases on paper, speaking words aloud.

Questions about display are, therefore, not necessarily the same as questions about composition. I take the former to be about the means by which a particular text is first made accessible to a public, while the latter are about the (often private) processes of thought, artifice, memorization, or draft that may have gone on before this happens. For instance, to say that some text is displayed orally is perfectly compatible with saying that it is the product of a process of conscious and lengthy artifice using nonoral methods (memorization, writing, gesture) on the part of some individual; it is compatible also with saying that it is the spontaneous result of an onrush of afflatus. The improvisations of a skilled jazz pianist usually are spontaneous in something like this way: they are prepared for in a very nonspontaneous way (the pianist listens to other pianists, practices a lot, and so forth), but the production of a musical text (a performance) may use none of these methods, even though they are among the necessary conditions for its occurrence. Similarly, the texts displayed by *rhetors* in ancient Greece, by preachers in contemporary black gospel churches, and by some politicians and lecturers often may be entirely oral in terms of their display, but have behind them much intentional work, and therefore a long process of composition that need not be exclusively or at all oral.

The third and fourth concepts that need to be explained are intimately linked: storage and redisplay. Once a text has been displayed, it may be stored in some way for later redisplay. Most texts, of course, are not stored intentionally. The vast majority of texts produced by humans are ordinary conversational ones without sufficient intrinsic interest or potential for future use to suggest that it would be proper for any individual or community to put effort into storing them. But some texts are stored, either by accident or with intention. How may this be done?

A text given its first display aurally, in speech, if it is to be reused, must be stored by an act separate from that which gave it its first display. As Augustine put it in the *De doctrina christiana* (ii.4), uttered words last no longer than the vibrations in the air in which they consist; if they are to endure longer, storage in some form is necessary. But storage need not occur only by writing. It also may occur by memorization and by various technologies of recording.

In the case of texts given their first display visually, in writing, there is a similar range of possibilities for storage and redisplay. The text may be read aloud and then memorized, written down again, or recorded electronically. But this suggests an important point about writing. Writing is unique in that it, and it alone, is a technology for composition, display, and storage all at once. A text may be composed (in part, at least) by writing (as was the case for the text you now are reading); one so composed is simultaneously and already displayed and stored, the latter for as long as the physical medium (paper, palm leaf, computer disc) upon which it is written survives. None of the other technologies mentioned have this property. Thought is a mode of composition and storage, but not of display; speech is a mode of composition and display, but not of storage; and the various electronic methods of recording are modes only of storage and (re)display, but not of composition. Writing therefore holds a unique and pivotal position, one that goes some way toward explaining the dominance it has come to have in contemporary Western culture as a tool for all three tasks (composition, display, storage).

This brief discussion should suggest that texts may be composed, displayed, stored, and redisplayed without the use of writing and without literacy understood in the narrow sense of the ability to decode marks on some enduring medium of storage. It also should suggest, by making a clear conceptual distinction among composition, storage, and display, that the use of a particular technology for one function implies nothing about the use of that same technology for others. It is important to emphasize this point because of a tendency among contemporary scholars, most of whom do their thinking in a cultural context in which writing is dominant for the composition, display, and storage of all texts, to assume that wherever writing is present at all it will assume the same kind of dominance. That it need not is obvious: it is not difficult to imagine a context in which writing is one mode of storage among others, but not the most important; or a context in which it is effectively the only mode of storage, but in which the preferred mode of display is aural; or one in which it is used for composition, but never for storage; and so forth. It also is important to notice another common assumption: that the existence and use of writing makes possible the composition of kinds of texts—texts with specifiable formal characteristics—that in principle cannot be composed orally or by thought. The correlate of this assumption is the view that "oral texts" have clear and specifiable properties that mark them off from "written texts." There is a cluster of issues here, the discussion of which has generated an enormous literature in the last thirty years. Since it is important for my argument about scholasticism to distance myself from the more dubious among the views expressed in this literature, I offer next a brief review of the current state of play in discussion about orality and literacy.

Orality and Literacy

Twentieth-century debates about orality and literacy have three axes. The first has to do with textuality itself, with the formal features of texts and what these features reveal about how they were composed, stored, and displayed. The second has to do with cognitive psychology and epistemology, with whether the presence and use of a particular technology (writing, say, or printing, or more recently electronic media) may or must have direct and specifiable effects upon the thought patterns, epistemological habits, and compositional practices of its users. And the third has to do with the effects that the presence of a particular technology of composition and storage (typically writing) may or must have upon forms of social organization. In spite of the volume of literature on all these questions, there are common threads which make it relatively easy to disentangle the issues and to isolate desirable and undesirable strategies for dealing with them.

One such thread is the tendency to tie the three issues together by making very strong claims about all of them. So, for instance, it is sometimes argued that there are formal features of texts (their length, say, or the degree of complexity of their internal organization, or the presence in them of repeated formulaic elements) that signal with a very high degree of probability how they were composed. It also sometimes is argued, as a correlate of this claim, that the presence and use of a particular compositional technology is determinative of the cognitive psychology of its users: that, for instance, users of technologies of thought rather than technologies of writing for composition and storage will, in some important respects, live in a different cognitive world than those who live in a "world on paper," as David Olson (1994) puts it. And, as a final connecting link, it might be argued that the presence of writing acts not merely as a necessary condition for the existence of certain forms of social organization (the bureaucracy of the nation-state, for example), but also as a sufficient condition.

Defenders of these strong views will place great emphasis upon the determinative force of technology: in the case of writing, if these views are defensible, almost everything of interest about a culture (the cognitive psychology of its members, the nature of the texts they compose and store, and their modes of social organization) will be more or less directly traceable to the presence or absence of this technology. The presence or absence of writing (or of whatever technology is under discussion) on these views becomes a panacea for all explanatory difficulties: technologies of composition are presented as floating free of specific cultural settings, and, upon entering a particular culture, like aliens from outer space who always turn the locals into identical gray and willing slaves no matter what they were like before the aliens got there, turning that culture into one more token of whatever type is under discussion—a writing culture, an oral culture, an electronic culture, and so on.

Such arguments are present (though perhaps never in quite the extreme form stated here) in the pivotal works from the 1960s on these topics by Marshall McLuhan, Jack Goody and Ian Watt, and Eric Havelock, as well as in later work by Walter Ong. But these strong views on the cognitive and social significance of writing and on the possibility of determining compositional technology on the basis of a work's formal features are almost certainly mistaken, or at the very least too crude. The most that can be said with any degree of plausibility is that a particular compositional technology, in certain settings, may have the kinds of effects upon cognition, compositional practice, the formal features of texts, and social organization suggested by Goody, Watt, Ong, and others.

Certainly, particular instances of such causal relations can be shown with a very high degree of plausibility—as, for example, in Elizabeth Eisenstein's study of the effects of the introduction of print technology in early modern Europe; or in the study by C. A. Read and others of the effects of alphabetic literacy (rather than ideographic literacy) upon readers of Chinese. But this is very different from claiming that the presence of such technology always will have just these effects no matter what other cultural variables are in place. Making the more limited claim should lead to studies of the effects of particular technologies in particular cultural settings and to the relations between these effects and other variables. And, as might have been expected, such studies, insofar as they have been carried out, suggest strongly that the effects of particular technologies, whether of composition or storage, are very different in different cultural settings. The monolithic views are simply not adequate to the data: they pay insufficient attention to the proper distinctions among composition, storage, and display.

Studies of culturally specific instances of the use of various technologies of composition and storage have increasingly called into question such monolithic views of the effects of literacy upon social organization and individual cognitive habits. Rosalind Thomas's work on Greece, Frits Staal's and Harry Falk's work on India, and Gregor Schoeler's on Islam all show this. Writing may, but need not, become dominant as a technology for composition and storage when it is present in a particular culture. Written texts may, but need not, become the paradigm for all texts. Writing may, but need not, be understood as a medium of representation and communication as well as an aide-memoire, as Paul Zumthor says (1987:123). Writing may, but need not, become an instrument in the bureaucratic repertoire of the capitalist nation-state. Reading (in the sense of decoding marks upon an enduring medium of storage) may but need not, upon being introduced into a specific cultural setting, or even upon becoming widespread there, become the dominant mode of ingesting texts. Whether any of these things happen will depend upon variables other than technological ones, and this is because reading and writing, like any other ways of composing and storing texts, are always social practices that involve much more than the use of a particular technology (the work collected by Jonathan Boyarin [1992] is good on this). And so, in the sketch of scholasticism that follows, I shall avoid assuming that scholastic compositional practices and storage needs must be correlated with particular technologies. There is simply no good reason to suppose this to be the case and much empirical evidence against it.

Scholastic Reading

The root-metaphor for scholastic intellectual practice is that of reading. Reading usually is understood to denote the visual consumption of ordered patterns of print on a page (or script on vellum; or scrach marks on palm leaves; or hieroglyphs on granite; or ideographs on plates of silver; or pixels of light on a liquid-crystal screen). It usually is understood, that is, to require written objects to be read, and so to entail the specific technical skill of extracting meaning from such objects. I have in mind a practice both more and less specific than this and shall call it "scholastic reading" in order to mark its differences from ordinary or generic reading. Scholastic reading has to do primarily with the establishment of certain relations between readers and the things they read, relations that are at once attitudinal, cognitive, and moral, and that therefore imply an ontology, an epistemology, and an ethic.

This kind of reading requires neither written objects nor the technical skill of extracting meaning from them, though it commonly will be connected with both and may in the end, if certain other cultural and institutional variables are in place, entail their production and use. Scholastic reading, then, though it does require texts, if texts are understood broadly as ordered systems of signs, does not require written texts. It may take as its object that which it reads, a text that exists only as an ordered pattern of sounds in the air (something spoken or musical) or a text that exists only as an ordered pattern of three-dimensional shapes (an icon or a picture) or (just conceivably) a text that exists only as an ordered pattern of tastes, smells, or tactile stimuli—as in the case of the Tathāgata Sugandhakūṭa, which are said in the *Vimalakīrtinirdeśasūtra* to be given not in words but only by means of smells (Prāsādika and Joshi 1981:505).

But scholastic reading will, in every case, imply a distinctive set of relations between reader and text. The first and most basic element in these relations is that the text read is understood as a stable and vastly rich resource, one that yields meaning, suggestions (or imperatives) for action, matter for aesthetic wonder, and much else. It is a treasure-house, an ocean, a mine: the deeper scholastic readers dig, the more ardently they fish, the more single-mindedly they seek gold, the greater will be their reward. The basic metaphors here are those of discovery, uncovering, retrieval, opening up: scholastic readers read what is there to be read, and what is there to be read always precedes, exceeds, and, in the end, supersedes its readers. According to these metaphors, there can be no final act of reading in which everything is uncovered, in which the mine of gold has yielded all its treasure or the fishpool has been emptied of fish. Reading, for scholastic readers, ends only with death, and perhaps not then: it is a continuous, ever-repeated process.

The second, almost equally important, constituent of the relations between scholastic readers and their texts is that readers are seen as intrinsically capable of reading and as morally required to read. Their capacity for retrieving the riches of the text by the act of reading is something intrinsic to them; they are essentially and necessarily readers, to the point where the phrase *homo lector* can be substituted for *homo sapiens* without loss and with considerable gain. Nonreaders, on this view, are precisely those who have renounced their humanity, renounced their defining characteristic; and it is typical of scholastic readers that for them, in George Steiner's (1989:193) phrase, the act of reading is an "unmistakable witness to the ambiguous mastery of texts over life." The text's intrinsic stability and fecundity as a resource therefore is matched by the reader's intrinsic stability and ingenuity as a discoverer. Both texts and readers are ordered: it is this that makes acts of scholastic reading possible and this that guarantees their continuation and fruitfulness.

Scholastic readers therefore treat their texts with reverence. Since the text is what it is for them, they will necessarily adopt toward it an attitude incompatible with those implied by uses of texts that treat them only as instruments for the achievement of other ends. Consider, as a contrastive case, professional academics in Europe or America at the end of the twentieth century: the attitude toward texts implied in their practice is largely instrumental. Their use of texts is presented and described almost entirely in the language and images of consumerist capitalism and is therefore dominated by talk of control (scholastic readers never control their texts; they are controlled by them), use, production, and consumption: they consume the texts of others and produce their own; they are defined and given status by the body of literature they control and upon which they are accredited to give authoritative (expert) voice for appropriate reward; they cite and mention (rather than scholastically read) and are in turn judged largely by the extent to which the texts they produce (again, the industrial metaphor, the image of mass production) are cited and mentioned.

Or, as a rather different but complementary contrastive case, consider the reading practices of the (usually male) user of pornography or the (usually female) user of romantic novels. Such readers read only to produce certain effects: sexual arousal, perhaps, in the case of the pornography user; or catharsis in the case of the romance user. When the required effects have been produced, the objects read have no more useful work to do for that consumer. They can be discarded: returned to the circulating library, sold back to the used bookstore, or given away. Analogous points could be made, mutatis mutandis, about the use of textbooks or most of the occasional writing found in magazines and newspapers: readers read such works to gain ephemeral information, to titillate rather than to cultivate, to entertain rather than to transform.

So much, in brief, for the ideal-typical relations between scholastic readers and their texts, and for the attitudes possessed by such readers to their texts. Recall that a sketch such as this neither makes nor implies any claims as to whether this ideal type, or anything like it, ever has been instanced; it serves only as a heuristic device. In order to sharpen the ideal type, and so to make it more pointedly useful for those engaged in historical or comparative studies, I would now like to contrast the root metaphor of reading used in the preceding paragraphs with another root metaphor: that of writing, using this word, as I used *reading*, in a rather different sense than the usual.

By the term *writing* I mean not necessarily a practice that involves making visible marks on some permanent medium of storage; I mean rather a practice that is quintessentially creative, a process that brings order and structure where there was none before, a process whose description involves inevitable appeal to images of making, of construction, of conceit (both in the literary and in the affective sense), of ornamentation, and of artifice. Focus on the root metaphor of writing as essential to and constitutive of human beings, makes them, as writers, the center of epistemological and metaphysical interest. The practice of writing, understood in this way, is the only creative act, the only act by means of which order and structure can be given to things. There is no order or meaning other than that inscribed by the act of writing and created by writers, and this means that writers, in writing, inscribe always and endlessly themselves, their own potential for creating order. This is a familiar, now almost a tired, trope of theory: everything, even (especially) philosophy is a kind of writing, as Richard Rorty (1982:90–109) has put it, and the proper object of all intellectual inquiry is, in the end, rhetoric.

In one important sense the postmodernist writer is about as far from the scholastic reader as it is possible to get. For the latter the world is a (textualized) field of endlessly uncoverable ordered riches; for the former, the world is an (also textualized) endlessly constructable field of play, and not just any play, but most especially the free play of signifiers that can be ordered at whim into lightly orgasmic objects of *jouissance*. Writers, according to this interpretation, are radically autonomous, subject to nothing other than the limits of their creative impulses and constrained by nothing other than the strictly limitless potential of the signifiers arrayed to serve them. To take a financial analogue: scholastic readers draw upon a very substantial savings account but have to balance the books as they go and can do so only by handling currency; postmodernist writers have to hand a credit card with a strictly infinite balance and need never touch cash. They get their pleasure solely from engaging in the process of production, and in this they are, as Fredric Jameson (1991:275–76) has claimed, most at home in the culture of late capitalism:

> One's sense, particularly when dealing with foreigners who have been enflamed by American consumerism, is that the products form a kind of hierarchy whose climax lies very precisely in the technology of reproduction itself, which now, of course, fans out well beyond the classical television set and has come in general to epitomize the new informational or computer technology of the third stage of capitalism.

This is typical of the attitude of writers to the activity of writing. It is important to have written, to be writing, and to project the process of writing into the future. The product of writing (the text) is relatively unimportant, just as the artifacts to be consumed in late capitalist cultures are unimportant in comparison to what the process of anticipating, lusting after, and consuming them signifies. Scholastic readers are, by contrast, strictly feudalist: for them, the object is of central importance and the processes of production of marginal interest.

There is some superficial similarity between scholastic reading and postmodernist writing as I have described them. Both are deeply text centered, and that this is the case goes some way toward explaining the attraction of scholastic practice for some postmodernist writers. Geoffrey Hartman (1994:343) has some perceptive comments to make about this, in the context of a discussion of Midrashic commentarial practices:

> Of course, literary commentaries and Midrashic ones have their differences. But these are not easy to define except by pseudo criteria. The very advance of contemporary theory toward Midrash makes Jewish scholars more zealous to avoid contamination. There is fear that the motive for Midrash will be mistakenly reduced from *Everything is in the text, and what the text signifies is its relevance to the actions and thoughts of the interpretive community*, to *Everything is text, and the text is a structure of imaginary relations, a tissue without issue*. I acknowledge the danger, but why be frightened by those who insist on being superficial?

According to the scholastic reader, the textualized world is intrinsically other than the human, ordered independently of it, and capable of acting upon it. But according to the postmodernist writer, as I have suggested, the nonhuman effectively dissolves into the human. Ontology becomes epistemology, and the self becomes the all-absorbing (perhaps in the end the only) topic of philosophical interest.

These contrasts may help to make clearer what I mean by saying that reading is the root metaphor of scholasticism; they also offer some suggestive possibilities in the way of classifying movements in intellectual history, categories to be used in painting, with very broad brushstrokes, the allegiance and methods of particular schools of thought and particular thinkers. Writing, as described above, is the root metaphor of postmodernity, and reading, that of the premodern scholastic, dominant in the West until the seventeenth century. Then, with Descartes, with Spinoza, with Locke, and above all with Kant, reading began gradually to be transformed into writing; and writing has been the dominant metaphor for our intellectual practices for at least the last half-century, coupled as it so often is in philosophy with what Alvin Plantinga (1990, 1992) has usefully called "creative antirealism."

More can be said about the intellectual practices that constitute the ideal type of scholastic reading. The first additional point to emphasize is the role of memory. If scholastic reading involves the kind of inexhaustibly repetitive rereading indicated here, then inevitably memorization of the text will often happen. A text can be reread or reheard only so often before it becomes stored in the memory to become recalled (reread) at will without further need for external stimuli. Scholastic readers, unlike postmodernist writers, will therefore have a large body of texts at memorial command. But although such memorial storage would occur anyway, as a by-product of the ordinary practices of scholastic reading, it typically will be actively sought and inculcated through the intentional use of mnemotechnical devices. As Paul Zumthor and Mary Carruthers have shown for Christians in medieval Europe and Paul Demiéville (245–257) for medieval Buddhists involved in the translation of Sanskrit works into Chinese, and as Jonathan Spence has entertainingly dramatized in the case of the Jesuit Matteo Ricci in China in the late sixteenth and early seventeenth centuries, large bodies of material can be stored and recalled with relative ease and rapidity by scholastic readers trained in the use of such devices. The ideal-typical community of scholastic readers will therefore harbor virtuosos of the arts of memory and will require even of its nonvirtuoso members feats of memory that are almost unbelievable to, and certainly unattainable by, most contemporary writers.

Use of the memorial arts is important for scholastic readers for more than these practical reasons, however. For such readers the ideally–read text is the memorized text, and the ideal mode of reading is by memorial recall. This is because a text whose potential for being understood and used is both inexhaustible and nonconventional, intrinsic to it and endlessly extractable from it, is worth inscribing on the tablets of the memory where neither moth nor rust can damage or destroy it, and where the only threat to its continued availability for reading and rereading is also a threat to the continued existence of its reader. Ezekiel's eating of the prophetic scroll is a representation of the kind of incorporation and internalization involved in scholastic reading: the text is ingested, incorporated, used for nourishment, and becomes the basis for action. And here again the contrast with the practices of those writers who presently dominate the academy is very striking: the memorial arts are scarcely used or recommended by them because their ideal is not retention but production, and ideally production that gives the illusion of being *ex nihilo*. Consider, as illustrative of this difference, the following view of the importance of memory, found in Hugh of St. Victor's *Didascalicon* (iii. 11), composed around 1120:

> We should, therefore, collect together brief and reliable portions (*breve aliquid et certum colligere*) of all that we study and consign them to the treasure-chest of the memory (*arcula memoriae*) so that later, when there is need, we might derive the remainder [of what we have studied] from them. We ought often to replicate these [portions], and bring them out from the stomach of the memory (*de ventre memoriae*) to be savored, so that they will not be lost by long inattention. So I ask you, reader, not to rejoice immoderately if you have been able to read much; and if you have been able to understand much not to rejoice because of the extent of your understanding, but rather because of what you have been able to retain. For otherwise there is benefit neither in much reading nor in much understanding.

The necessary condition for all other fruits of scholastic reading, according to Hugh, is placing what has been read in the treasure-chest of the memory. Only when it is there can it be ruminated over at leisure; and only then can it issue in understanding. Any other kind of reading is mere passing the time, running one's eyes over words in a daze of impatience. Hugh's claims about memorization suggest that he takes it to have a moral significance, and he is entirely right to do so. A memorized text—like a lover, a friend, a spouse, a child—has entered into the fabric of its possessor's intellectual and emotional life in a way that makes deep claims upon that life, claims that can be ignored only with effort and deliberation. Just as spouses make claims upon one another that can be ignored or removed only with pain and intentional action (in divorce), so also memorized texts are present and efficacious until uprooted. In this they differ at least in degree, and probably also in kind, from texts that have been read only as a contemporary academic reader reads. Those texts sit inert upon the shelf, usually forgotten, and if remembered at all remembered not for their flavor and fabric, but for their title and place of publication. The claims of such texts are minimal; the claims of memorized texts are maximal and properly moral.

Scholastic reading and its concomitant memorization need not, of course, always be presented in a positive light. One of the most horrifying portraits of obsessive monomaniacal madness in twentieth-century literature is that of the fictional Peter Kien in Elias Canetti's *Die Blendung* (variously translated into English as *The Tower of Babel* and *Auto-da-Fé*). Kien is the apotheosis of the scholastic reader and mnemonic artist, as the following sketch of his mnemonic capacities makes clear:

> He did indeed carry in his head a library as well provided and as reliable as his actual library . . . he could sit at his writing desk and sketch out a treatise down to the minutest detail without turning over a single page, except in his head. Naturally he would check quotations and sources later out of the books themselves; but only because he was a man of conscience. He could not remember any single occasion on which his memory had been found at fault. His very dreams were more precisely defined than those of most people. Blurred images without form or colour were unknown in any of the dreams which he had hitherto recollected. In his case night had no power to turn things topsy turvy; the noises he heard could be exactly referred to their cause of origin; conversations into which he entered were entirely reasonable; everything retained its normal meaning. It was outside his sphere to examine the probable connection between the accuracy of his memory and the lucidity of his dreams. (Canetti 1982:20)

In Canetti's novel the scholastic reader's mind is shown becoming coextensive with what he has read, becoming exclusively textualized, which means that any intrusion of a nonbookish reality—a reality that cannot be read and memorized—must end in disaster. Kien's lucid dreams and his eidetic memory for words on a page are no match for the destructive capacities of calculating stupidity. Kien ends in madness: he and his library are burned. Canetti's novel is much more (and much less) than a parable about the fate of scholastic readers; it was first published in 1935 and must be understood in part as a reflection of the European political situation at that time. But it can be read usefully as a dramatic (and unremittingly negative) presentation of scholastic reading, as a *reductio* of the ideal-typical sketch given to this point. The *Kopfbibliothek*, like all other human creations, can be demonic as well as life giving; but that this is so does not call into question my earlier claim that memorization creates a moral relation between text and reader that is unique, profound, and transformative. Stocking the *Kopfbibliothek* is the proper end of scholastic reading and the best possible basis for the composition of commentaries.

A final point is that the works in a scholastic reader's well-stocked memorial library are unlikely to be individuated in the same way as the physical objects on a library shelf. The content of a book—a physical object—is bounded both physically (by its covers) and legally (by copyright law). The content of a memorized work is not necessarily so bounded; indeed, the mnemotechnical devices used to make possible the memorization and easy retrieval of large quantities of material work against such bounding and sit more easily with fluidity. This is because text must be broken up into relatively small units in order to be stored in memory in the appropriate way, and these, together with the ordering schemata used to make their retrieval possible, are likely to be the basic units of the scholastic memorial library. Divisions among works will therefore tend to be of less importance than they are for a print-dominated culture, though there may be reasons in particular scholastic communities for paying attention to the boundaries of particular works, reasons that counteract the opposing tendencies of scholastic reading.

The entire body of text that constitutes a scholastic reader's library, as a result of scholastic reading practices, ideal-typically will be treated as a single fabric composed of interlocking parts that can be retrieved and recombined variously as occasion demands, without respect to the fact that they may have come from different works. The label often used for this state of affairs is *intratextuality*; George Lindbeck (1984:113–24), Francis Clooney (1993:77–118), and Daniel Boyarin (1990) provide some useful discussion of this idea. According to a strong version of it, every element of a given body of texts becomes part of the interpretive context within which every other element is read and understood, so that scholastic readers read, recall, and teach what is functionally a single text, even if one that is internally differentiated, composed of works that may have come from the minds of different authors at different times. The presence of this kind of intratextuality in the reading practices of ideal-typical scholastic readers has its effects upon their compositional practices, and to these I now turn.

Scholastic Composition

Scholastic reading as just sketched is connected very closely with scholastic composition: it is difficult for ideal-typical scholastics to separate the one from the other since they are related symbiotically. The very practices that constitute scholastic reading are themselves also compositional practices, as John Dagenais (1994), in his study of the *Libro du buen amor*, a fourteenth-century Spanish work on (among other things) the arts of love, has pointed out. He has coined a useful term for this intimate linkage: *lecturature*—reading that is also composition. The term serves to emphasize what has already been suggested here, that scholastic reading is typically not passive, not done with the principal goal of amassing information or sharpening writerly skills. It is done, instead, for the purpose of altering the course of the readers' cognitive, affective, and active lives by ingesting, digesting, ruminating over, and restating what is read, and the ways in which these goals are met have direct and obvious effects upon what and how scholastic readers compose.

The first such effect comes from the fact that lecturature typically involves the use of mnemotechnical devices of various kinds, since part of its active involvement with the work being read will require that work to be stored in memory in such a way that it can be retrieved easily and rapidly. This in turn often will require that the text be divided into bite-sized pieces (recall Hugh of St. Victor's words quoted earlier), and then that these pieces be ordered according to an artificial schema so that they can be retrieved almost instantly. Very long and complex works can be memorized in this way and specific parts recalled and redisplayed almost instantly; the point of such devices is precisely to prevent readers from having to suffer a sequential turning of the pages of the whole of a work engraved on their memories in order to retrieve a particular section of it. This could be a very lengthy process if the chunk of text needed occurs at the end of a long, memorized work. However, if the work is divided into gobbets (as undergraduates at Oxford still call the short sections of Greek and Latin texts they are asked to translate to demonstrate their linguistic competence—the use of such a term in such a context is almost certainly a survival from forgotten mnemotechnical practices), and the gobbets then ordered by devices that have nothing to do with the content of the work, any gobbet can be retrieved and redisplayed as rapidly as any other.

This aspect of lecturature explains (or goes a good way toward explaining) some typical scholastic compositions, compositions in genres whose existence and function is otherwise difficult to understand (and which, for precisely that reason, are largely ignored as barbaric and incomprehensible artifacts by contemporary Western scholarship).

One such is what in the West has been called the the "bouquet of flowers," *florilegium*—small but fragrant textual blooms—culled from many different works and arranged into a new work for the delectation and improvement of other readers. The blooms thus culled may be arranged topic-wise, or according to some other ordering principle, perhaps one given by the demands of the techniques of memorization; but however they are arranged, little or no attention will be paid to the integrity of the works from which they are drawn.

This kind of scholastic reading/composition survived in the West for a long time, though in attenuated form, in the habit of keeping commonplace books in which readers would note down, for delectation, digestion, and rumination, juicy morsels from their reading, and would keep and return to these feasts for subsequent ethical, religious, and aesthetic improvement. Another example is the *catena,* a kind of commentary upon Scripture that began to be produced in the Greek church in Palestine from the sixth century A.D. onwards and continued to be a popular form for almost a thousand years (on this genre see Gilles Dorival, 1984). These are commentaries on a book or books of the Bible that proceed by amassing relatively brief exegetical comments from a large number of authorities, extracting these from their original context (whether in a commentary or some other kind of work), and then "chaining" (hence *catena*) the extracts together following the section-by-section order of the biblical book under discussion.

The composition both of *florilegia* and of *catenae* makes perfect sense if those who compose such works use mnemotechnical devices as part of their normal reading practice and if those devices require that works read be stored in small pieces. In such a case, the stored pericopes will be capable of easy recall from storage independently of their location in a larger work (which is not to say that such location is forgotten by or irrelevant to scholastic readers) and therefore capable of recombination in an infinite variety of ways—hence florilegia and catenae and their like. Hence also, I suggest, the importance of commentary to scholastic readers and scholastic composers. Commentary is the archetypical and basic scholastic genre; here I can only say of it that both the ethical and the practical demands of memorization suggest that composing commentaries will be important. Ethically, as already suggested, writing a work upon the pages of the memory gives it an importance that can be given it by no other kind of reading; such importance consists in large part on the demand it makes on scholastic readers by its presence in their memories, a demand that can be met in one way by composing a commentary. Practically, the presence of the whole work in the memory, coupled with its storage in the form of gobbets, any one of which can be recalled and juxtaposed to any other, will suggest and enable the composition of commentaries that have two important formal features, both of which are typical of scholastic commentaries. The first is that the scholastic commentary will take as its first object precisely the gobbets into which the work has been divided for memorizing, which means that it will treat in the first instance small units of the work, and only secondarily larger units or the work as a whole. The second is that a comment on any one of these gobbets will presuppose knowledge of them all and may be incomprehensible without such knowledge.

Scholastic lecturature, then, most often will produce commentaries and formally similar artifacts such as florilegia and catenae. What technology is it most likely to use for its compositional purposes? It may, but need not, use writing (in the ordinary sense of making marks on some physical medium of storage) as its principal tool; it is equally likely to use some combination of mnemonic and oral technique. Although making scratch marks on paper or using a keyboard seem to most late-twentieth-century writers quite indispensable as tools of composition, especially for long or complex works, there is much evidence to suggest that this was not so (and is not so) for scholastic communities. The connection between writing (in the ordinary sense) and composition is at best a contingent one. Instances of the looseness of such a connection—and of the fact that a particular technology need not become dominant as soon as introduced, nor have the same significance in all cultural settings, *pace* Walter Ong, Jack Goody, and others—easily can be found in the premodern world. But a more contemporary example may help to drive home the extent to which composition can proceed without writing even when writing is easily available and a culturally standard technology of composition.

Charles Dickens used, at the period in his career when he was working on *Hard Times* (in the 1840s), quite frequently to compose and deliver political speeches, usually in support of reforms in the system of public education. Peter Ackroyd (1990:423), in his biography of Dickens, describes how these speeches were usually composed and delivered:

> Dickens never made or kept notes but seemed to speak spontaneously and effortlessly, all the more extraordinary since the speeches themselves are as graceful and as fluent as anything he ever wrote . . . he had an astonishing verbal memory. He did not make notes because he memorised everything he wished to say, and this for speeches that lasted some twenty or thirty minutes. Even after he had finished, he could still repeat what he had said verbatim to reporters anxious for 'clean' copy. . . . How did he achieve this? The morning before he was due to speak, he would take a long walk and in the course of that journey he would decide what topics he was going to raise. He would put these in order, and in his imagination construct a cartwheel of which he was the hub and the various subjects the spokes emanating from him to the circumference; "during the progress of the speech," he said, "he would deal with each spoke separately, elaborating them as he went round the wheel; and when all the spokes dropped out one by one, and nothing but the tire and space remained, he would know that he had accomplished his task, and that his speech was at an end." . . . One of his closest friends noticed that at public dinners he did indeed "dismiss the spoke from his mind by a quick action of the finger as if he were knocking it away.

Dickens' political speeches, for the most part, had no existence as written texts until verbatim written records of his spoken words were made by newspaper reporters present at their delivery. These speeches were composed mentally, stored mnemonically, and delivered orally, using techniques known and written about in the West at least since the *Ad Herennium*, traditionally attributed to Cicero. I mention Dickens here not because he is an ideal-typical scholastic, but rather to signal the possible endurance and use of such techniques even when they are separated from an attitude to texts that best grounds them and gives them sense. Dickens was a member of the last, or perhaps the penultimate, generation of Western intellectuals to have made much use of these techniques; they have not survived in the intellectual life of the twentieth century.

Scholastic compositional practice, I suggest, bearing this Dickensian example in mind, requires techniques both for composition and for storage. But it does not require writing (in the ordinary sense) for either, and is likely, given some of the assumptions sketched above, to lean more heavily toward the use of thought and speech as the principal tools of composition, and toward memorization as the principal tool of storage.

There are important contrasts with the technologies of composition and storage favored by contemporary Western academics. From the sixteenth to the late twentieth century our technologies of storage have been print centered and our technologies of composition have focused upon the making of marks on paper. It has become part of the ordinary mental furniture of academics and intellectuals of all kinds to think of a text as only the kind of thing that is composed on paper and in solitude, then printed, and finally stored to be reread, cited, dissected, and analyzed at will. The trope of the solitary writer is, like that of the innocent child, a cliché, but one found everywhere from high to popular culture; it is mirrored in our copyright laws and publication practices. Academic assent to all this is evident in our views as to the sanctity of authorship and its concomitant, the heinousness of plagiarism, as well as in the ways that we assess, evaluate, and reward one another. The key measures of our worth are the volume of our publication and the extent to which that publication is cited by others. Both measures are predicated upon compositional techniques that require paper and storage techniques that require print, as they also are upon a strong view as to the proper boundaries of texts and their proper relations to authors.

All this is changing at the end of the twentieth century as electronic technologies for composition and storage become increasingly dominant. I shall not venture prophecies as to the future of these technologies and their effects upon academic practice and academic views about reading, writing, and authorship, as well as upon the legalities of copyright and publication. But it is clear that their use comports very well with the intellectual life understood through the metaphor of writing as described above; and the quotation given earlier from Fredric Jameson makes the connection quite explicit. But whether print- and paper-centered technologies maintain their dominance, or whether they gradually vanish in favor of electronic technologies, one central and irreducible difference between Western academic practice and ideal-typical scholastic practice will remain. Western academics see their texts as without intrinsic value, as instruments to be consumed and discarded, or consumed and stored, just as are automobiles. The mnemonic arts are irrelevant, and the modes of reading, already discussed, that foster those arts are a positive drawback. Indeed, scholastic reading is best understood as intrinsically opposed to (perhaps even incompatible with) the dominance of technologies intended to maximize the flow of information, of consumable and discardable semantic units. There are causal connections of complex kinds between the rise of print technology from the sixteenth century onward and the decline in scholastic reading; and while the axiological and epistemological implications of the rise of computer technology in the last fifteen years are in many important respects different from those of print technology, the two technologies share a profound lack of hospitality to scholastic reading and scholastic composition. If anything, the more recent electronic technologies are less hospitable to scholastic reading than the older print technology—and much less than manuscript technology.

I do not suggest that the presence of these technologies in Western academic culture is the sole determinant of the decline of scholastic reading and composition in that culture. Just as writing by itself does not have the transformative power attributed to it by its apologists, so also print or electronic technology must be placed in a certain cultural context and combined with other variables in that context before it can become dominant. It also follows from these considerations that those who wish to preserve or recover scholastic habits in contemporary Western academia need not forswear the use of print or electronic technologies altogether. But such individuals must pay close attention to the ways in which such technologies are used. The technologies should be closely circumscribed servants rather than lively masters, and it may be that such circumscription, given the power of conformist and consumerist pressures in academia, will be difficult to maintain.

Scholastic Epistemology

Scholastic reading, as described to this point, implies an epistemology, a particular set of views as to how knowledge is to be gained, maintained, and extended. Any intellectual practice has such implications, so it is scarcely surprising that this particular practice has them. But what are they in this case?

Suppose we begin by using a distinction now standard in anglophone epistemology: the distinction between internalist and externalist epistemologies, made clear in the recent work of William Alston (1991) and Alvin Plantinga (1993a, 1993b). Epistemological theories typically are interested in distinguishing between instances of belief that are not well-grounded and that as a result have no claim to be called (or to issue in) "knowledge," on the one hand, and instances of belief that are well grounded and that therefore do have some such claim, on the other. For instance: I may believe that I can generate reliable beliefs about the course of future events by consulting the entrails of properly sacrificed goats. Most Western academics (certainly most anglophone epistemologists) would tend to say that beliefs about the course of future events generated in this way lack the property or properties that might give them claim to be called "knowledge." By contrast, I may believe that I can generate reliable beliefs about what Boris Yeltsin said in discussion with Bill Clinton last night, even though he speaks no English and I no Russian, by consulting a report of the conversation given in *The New York Times*. Many, perhaps most, anglophone epistemologists would be more likely to think that beliefs generated in this way are of a kind such that they should be considered knowledge. The debate then centers upon what account to give of the property or properties that distinguish beliefs of the first kind from beliefs of the second kind.

Internalist epistemologies typically claim that the property in question (it might be called "warrant" or "justification" or something similar) is internal to those who have the beliefs under discussion, something to which they have special access: they have had the proper experience, say, or have constructed or understood the proper argument, and to both of these facts the subject is a better witness than anyone else. Internalism in epistemology goes nicely with deontology: I may be justified (warranted) in believing that *p*, on such views, if (and perhaps only if) I have fulfilled my epistemic obligations or duties. As Plantinga (1993a:29) puts it:

> Justification, internalism, and epistemic deontology are properly seen as a closely related triumvirate: internalism flows from deontology and is unmotivated without it, and justification is at bottom and originally a deontological notion.

For the internalist, then, what counts is whether we have fulfilled our epistemic duties; and we can tell whether we have by, paradigmatically, an act of introspection, an act that will, if we are properly attentive, tell us whether, as John Locke puts it in the *Essay Concerning Human Understanding* (ch. 17, sec. 24), we are like someone who "believes or disbelieves, according as Reason directs him," or whether we are like someone who "transgresses against his own Light, and misuses those Faculties which were given him to no other end, but to search and follow the clearer Evidence."

Internalism in epistemology is, then, evidentialist, deontological, and (usually) radically individualist: one can tell whether one has fulfilled one's epistemic duties simply in virtue of one's generically human intellectual equipment.

Externalist views are quite different. They claim that what makes a particular instance of believing justified or warranted is something external to believers, some process or method of arriving at the belief in question that is not internal to them, and may not be known, understood, or controlled by them. Perhaps the most common kind of externalist epistemology is reliabilism: the view that believers are justified (warranted) in believing that *p* if and only if a particular instance of believing that *p* possesses the property of being produced by a reliable belief-forming practice or mechanism. Externalist views allow (indeed, require) a distinction between a belief's having been produced by a reliable belief-forming mechanism (sometimes called, in the trade, a "doxastic practice"), and this fact being known to a believer. One very well may have beliefs that have been so produced and that are reliable in virtue of having been so produced and yet not know this fact; or if one does know it, one need not be able to give an account of just what it is about the doxastic practice in question that makes it reliable. It may be (though it is not) the case that consulting the entrails of properly sacrificed goats is a reliable way of arriving at beliefs about the course of future events; an externalist need not require of those who perform such a practice the ability to know that it is reliable, much less why, in order for it to produce (largely) true beliefs for them. Externalist epistemologies, then, are typically nonevidentialist, antideontological (if being deontological requires not just that one has fulfilled one's epistemic duties, but that part of fulfilling them includes knowing that one has done so—as in the case of Locke), and nonindividualist (since individuals need not be—usually will not be—the final court of appeal on the question of whether and why particular beliefs are justified).

Scholastics typically will be externalist in epistemology. It should be obvious why. They will, explicitly or implicitly, hold the view that proper scholastic reading is among the belief-forming practices that usually produce true beliefs—and perhaps that it is an indispensable such practice. They will think that patterns of reasoning and the knowledge produced by them are constitutively and necessarily tradition-specific; that engaging in them is best likened to the performance of a complex skill; and that, concomitantly, the idea that some particular set of patterns of reasoning or some particular set of claims to knowledge ought to be universally comprehensible to all human persons just in virtue of some generically human intellectual equipment (a typical concomitant of internalist epistemologies) is as silly as the idea that the finer points of fugal composition ought to be so available. According to views like this, knowledge is understood as available only to those who have troubled to learn the skills necessary for access to it, and such skills can be learned only within the bounds of a set of tradition-based practices. These practices might be of many kinds; an obvious candidate would be exposure to the proper ways of reading or hearing the right texts. And this, naturally, is where scholastic practice comes in, for it is likely to be the case that scholastic readers will see their modes of reading as at least a necessary condition for the development of proper understanding. If tradition-specific reading skills are not practiced, then much knowledge (and probably the most important knowledge) simply will be unavailable. This is a typical pattern of epistemological reasoning implied by scholastic practice.

Postmodernist writers and scholastic readers are likely to have common ground here, and as a result may find themselves able to join forces against the tattered remnants of modernity, much as radical feminists and conservative Christians find themselves able to join forces against purveyors of pornography. The reason is that internalist epistemologies fit well with neither perspective. Such epistemologies require a stability and givenness to world and individual that the former cannot grant, and they require an optimism about the generic untrained intellectual capacities of human persons that is ruled out by the latter. This is one of the few signs of hope for the recovery of scholasticism in the contemporary Western academy. Internalist epistemologies are no longer dominant therein, largely because of the attacks of postmodernist critics; and once the individualism and foundationalism of internalism has been abandoned, there is at least conceptual room for the recovery of scholastic practice.

This is one of several points of convergence between scholastic reading and postmodernist writing, a fact which I am not alone in realizing. Fredric Jameson (1991), once again, makes the same point, though inchoately, in a number of ways: he acknowledges that serious religious thinkers such as John Howard Yoder (a Mennonite whom, interestingly, he wrongly characterizes as an "Amish pacifist" [391]) may properly be understood to have serious affinities with postmodernism. And he sees the surface similarities between the literary and intellectual practices of postmodernist writers and (those whom I am calling) scholastic readers:

> Commentary indeed makes up the special field of postmodern linguistic practice generally, and its originality, at least with respect to the pretensions and illusions of philosophy in the preceding period, of "bourgeois" philosophy, that with some secular pride and confidence set out to say what things really were after the long night of superstition and the sacred. Commentary, however, also—in that curious play of historical identity and difference mentioned above—now secures the kinship of the postmodern (at least in this respect) with other, hitherto more archaic, periods of thought and intellectual labor, as with the medieval copyists and scribes, or the endless exegesis of the great Oriental philosophies and sacred texts. (393)

More laconically: postmodernism is an ersatz scholasticism whose literary and intellectual practices make sense and provide nourishment only if they become religious. Recall Geoffrey Hartman's comments upon Midrashic practice, quoted earlier. The partial agreement of postmodernist writers and scholastic readers at the level of epistemology and literary practice allows, as mentioned earlier, conceptual room for the re-establishment of scholastic practice inside the contemporary academy. But the technological considerations already mentioned are at least as important as these purely theoretical ones in deciding whether it is realistic to imagine the rebirth of scholasticism; and institutional and cultural factors also will play an important part, so it is to these that I now shall now turn.

Scholastic Institutions

The institutional requirements of scholastic practice are relatively simple. Scholastic communities, I suggest, are typically stable, authoritarian, communitarian, and leisured, and such communities have obvious institutional needs if they are to come into existence and to endure. Let us begin with authority. By this I mean, minimally, the presence of some acknowledged constraints upon what and how scholastic readers should read, as well as (by entailment) upon the kinds of conclusions that properly can be drawn and taught from this reading. Authority of this kind is, of course, present in all human discursive practices—even those of modernist readers who, following a broadly Cartesian epistemology, might in unguarded moments think of themselves as freely deciding what they will read and drawing their own unfettered conclusions from this reading. But even though such authority is always present, its presence is not always acknowledged; it is part of modernist error in almost all fields of intellectual enterprise to refuse to acknowledge it, and to think, instead, of modernist intellectual practices as self-constituting and self-founding, and so as standing in no need of external authority to constrain their pursuit and outcome. Jeffrey Stout, in his *Flight from Authority* (1981), has traced this refusal of acknowledgement in ethics with great lucidity. A similar story could be told in jurisprudence, political theory, and epistemology. Scholastic readers, then, may not differ from modernist readers in the extent to which their reading is constrained by authority; but they typically will differ one from another in the extent to which such constraint is acknowledged, and, often, in the substance of the convictions underwriting the exercise of authority.

As a result, scholastic readers typically will be clear about the fact that their reading practices presuppose a select list of works worth reading, things that must be read, as well as a concomitant (and much longer) list of works not worth reading, things that ought not be read. The ideal type of such an approved list is the canon; its complement is the index (in the sense of *index librorum prohibitorum*). Scholastic readers typically will openly embrace both. Such open embracing may, but need not, go with sanctions of various kinds against those who refuse to read the canon and instead delve into what is prohibited by the index. Such sanctions, extending even to the extreme sanction of murder, have been used, for instance, from time to time by some institutions. But the use of such is not a necessary part of the open acknowledgment of the presence of constraining authority and so not intrinsic to the ideal type of scholasticism.

The constraining authority also may work itself out in various particular ways: a papal pronouncement ex cathedra is distinct, institutionally speaking, from the pronouncements of a university syllabus revision committee as to what must be read in order to gain a doctoral degree; and both are distinct from teachings given by the Dalai Lama as to whether a particular doctrine is or is not properly Buddhist, or decisions issued by a federal appeals court as to whether a particular publication is or is not obscene. So the ideal type is compatible with a wide variety of particular institutional forms; but some kind of acknowledged authority will be present in every kind of scholastic practice.

I said at the outset that the word *scholasticism* in contemporary spoken English connotes a discourse based upon authority, a discourse whose axioms are unquestioned and unquestionable. This is not, as I understand it, a necessary feature of the ideal type of scholastic reading.

Scholastics may, but need not, be committed to the view that the deliverances of their source or sources of authority are self-validating. There are many possibilities here, too many to canvass in detail. One is that the constraining authority may provide only procedural constraints rather than substantive ones. Another is that the deliverances of the constraining authority might contain within themselves, or even be partly constituted by, recursive rules of self-correction. So the tight link between the connotations of 'scholasticism' in everyday English and the use of a self-validating source of authority need to be moderated somewhat.

It also should be obvious that and how the acknowledged presence of constraining authority in scholastic practice coheres with scholastic epistemology as described in the immediately preceding section of this chapter. If, ideal-typically, scholastic practice suggests an externalist epistemology and is therefore likely to understand itself as a reliable belief-forming practice, then the acknowledged presence of an authority constraining the lineaments of that practice will simply be one more element in what constitutes this particular way of reliably forming true beliefs.

With authority, again ideal-typically, will go community and tradition. Scholastic readers do not read in isolation, either synchronically or diachronically. Their practices presuppose and engage with those who already have done what they are doing: hence tradition. And they are directed at and responsive to a community of those now doing what they also are doing: hence pedagogy. This fact explains the typical products of scholastic lecturature and florilecture as these already have been discussed: commentary is vital because it, more than any other genre, is open about its conversation with the pre-existing canon that scholastic reading presupposes; and florilegia, digests, compilations, and the like are evidence of the pedagogical engagement of scholastic readers with their present community.

Communities with a past require an institutional form; this is especially true of communities partly comprised of individuals with the leisure to engage in scholastic reading, for this practice is extremely labor intensive. It cannot be done only on weekends, and it is not a hobby. Its ideal setting, perhaps, is the monastery, for in monasteries there are communities of people for whom distractions from scholastic reading may be minimized (even if in actual monasteries they rarely are). But this means that the institutional presence of communities of scholastic readers, what George Steiner (1989:3–49) usefully has called "houses of reading," requires a social order in which there are resources free for the support of materially nonproductive people and a will to use them in that fashion. And this is the most important institutional requirement for scholastic practice: the existence of groups of leisured individuals, self-consciously communitarian and traditional, open about their constraint by authority, and committed to gaining the kind of moral relation to texts produced by repetitive reading and memorization. Literacy, in the sense of the ability to make and interpret marks on some enduring medium of storage, is unimportant by comparison.

Historically, the most obvious instances of a social order committed to providing such conditions have been medieval Europe and Tibet from the fourteenth through the early twentieth centuries. In both of these some of the most powerful institutions were the monasteries, in which at least some people were scholastic readers; and in both (perhaps more important) the ideal of being such was taken seriously enough that there was little argument about the importance of devoting resources to this purpose. But Tibet is now an "autonomous" province of the People's Republic of China and the monasteries of Europe are either gone, casualties of the Reformation, or greatly reduced, casualties of the Industrial Revolution and the rise and incipient decay of consumerist capitalism. Where then to look?

Contemporary late capitalist cultures do see fit to devote a small part of their resources to the support of institutions in which scholastic readers might flourish. These institutions are called "universities," to use the most generic term; I mean those places in which the idea that some people ought to be supported in spending most of their time reading and writing is given institutional form. This is not, of course, the only function that universities have or take themselves to have (Pierre Bourdieu usefully explores others in *Homo Academicus* [1984]). But it is a real function.

Western universities have their roots in twelfth-century Europe (Paris, Bologna, and a little later Oxford) and were given stimulus by the Renaissance and a final prod by the development of the German research universities in the nineteenth century. There are, perhaps, now a hundred or so of these institutions in the world, with the highest concentration to be found in Western Europe and North America. There is in addition a much larger number of institutions whose central reason for being is not to support people in the practice of reading and writing, but rather to train people for the performance of functions useful to late capitalist societies. These too sometimes call themselves universities, but their emphasis is different. And there are many mixed cases in which it is difficult to be sure where the central emphasis lies. All of these institutions are presently under more or less social and financial pressure to shift their emphasis away from supporting otherwise nonproductive readers and writers and toward the training of individuals with skills useful for production and consumption. But it remains unclear what the results of these pressures will be, since there are (perhaps equally strong) pressures pointing in the other direction, encouraging traditionally vocational and teaching institutions to become more like universities. I am not in the business of prediction, though, nor in that of defending the propriety of classifying any particular institution as belonging to one or another kind. All I need for my current argument is the unexceptionable descriptive claim that there are some institutions of the kind mentioned at the beginning of this paragraph.

That there are such institutions is a small sign of hope for those who might want to recover scholastic practice. It means that some of the institutional requirements for such practice can be met: there are places in which leisure and community are theoretically (and sometimes actually) available. Historically, and until the very recent past, the epistemology dominant in these institutions has made scholastic practice difficult. Modernist theories of knowledge, of the person, and of reading, are, as explained earlier, largely incompatible with scholastic reading. There have been special difficulties with the open acknowledgment of constraint by authority that is characteristic of scholasticism. But this could change. The effective demise of modernist epistemologies centered upon a putatively autonomous subject makes it no longer possible to mount a convincing and coherent theoretical argument against the desirability of scholastic practice as described here, and that this is both the case and widely acknowledged to be the case suggests that one of the major obstacles to the recovery of scholastic practice is no longer present.

Therefore, the intentional recovery of scholastic reading by those working in Western universities may now be possible. What, concretely, might this mean? First, it is important to re-emphasize that scholastic reading requires that there be a tradition of such already in place before it can occur. And there are not many actual traditions of reading available within which scholastic practice might take place, perhaps no more than half a dozen. Most of these are religious: Judaism, Buddhism, Islam, Christianity, Marxism, and perhaps others. These already have in place many of the institutional requirements mentioned in this chapter: canon, index, community, tradition, and so forth. Some of them preserve vestigial houses of reading (monasteries, yeshivas, seminaries, and the like), but most have largely abdicated that function, or no longer have the resources to maintain it effectively. Universities might well—to some extent they already do—provide a home for scholastic readers who are Jewish, Christian, Buddhist, and the like. Such readers, insofar as they can be found in universities at the moment, tend to lead a double life, cloaking their identity in the tattered garments of a *wissenschaftlich* modernity. There is, I suggest, no theoretical reason to maintain such disguises and good theoretical and ethical reasons not to do so. Scholastic readers, actual or aspiring, in any of these traditions both can and should be public about their identity as such.

The difficulties for those who come out of the closet, as it were, are likely not to be strictly theoretical but rather broadly cultural. The culture of contemporary academia is largely predicated upon an instrumentalist attitude to texts, upon a cult of individualism and novelty, and upon the uses of kinds of technology that make scholastic reading difficult or impossible. It also tends to assume without argument the validity and desirability of a particular and highly ideological version of liberalism, a liberalism that is individualistic both in religion and in politics, foundationalist and rationalist in philosophy, and rights-based and consequentialist in ethics. Specifically, this tends to mean that universities reflect the suspicion of their ambient culture about public professions of religious faith that also involve claims as to how intellectual work ought to be done, how public policy decisions ought to be made, how pedagogy ought to be practiced, and so forth. And, most of all, ideological liberalism tends to be suspicious of reference to authority as part of such claims. Insofar as such ideological liberalism attempts to maintain a foundationalist epistemology as the basis for a critique of scholastic practice it will fail; and in fact such critiques are made less and less frequently. Much more common is the attempt to rule such practice out of the public sphere by the exercise of legislative power (Michael McConnell has discussed this in two useful essays [1993a, 1993b]), or to attempt to rule it out by ornate rhetorical expressions of dislike or disgust without argument (as Richard Rorty [1994] does in responding to Stephen Carter's work).

These broadly cultural facts have a great deal of power, even if they cannot be given a coherent defense. It remains as a result unclear to what extent, if at all, Western universities—which are, historically and still to a large extent in practice, part of what Ernest Gellner (1994:9) usefully has called "that set of diverse non-governmental institutions which is strong enough to counterbalance the state and, while not preventing the state from fulfilling its role as keeper of the peace and arbitrator among major interests, can nevertheless prevent it from dominating and atomising the rest of society"—will prove capable of providing a home for scholastic readers. That they would be the better for doing so is fairly clear. Scholastic reading, pedagogy, and composition are preferable, both ethically and epistemologically, to the largely instrumentalist, consumerist, individualist, and in the end incoherent intellectual practices of the other two important players in the field: the earnest and unreconstructed modernist and the dedicated and playful postmodernist (both of whom will tend to be ideological liberals in matters of public policy). But I am not optimistic that Western universities will be able to muster the intellectual energy to acknowledge and support professed scholastics in their practice as such. And since the only other possibility—the houses of reading supported by religious institutions—seems even less likely to have the resources or the will, the outlook, on the whole, is not promising. But the future is hard to predict, and whatever may happen, either to universities or to religious houses of reading, it is at least clear what ought to happen.

References

Ackroyd, Peter.
1990. *Dickens*. New York: HarperCollins.

Alston, William P.
1991 *Perceiving God: The Epistemology of Religious Experience*. Ithaca: Cornell University Press.

1989 *Epistemic Justification*. Ithaca: Cornell University Press.

Augustine.
1836 *De doctrina christiana* (On Christian Doctrine). Cited by chapter and section. I have used the Latin text in *Sancti Aurelii Augustini Hipponensis Episcopi, Opera Omnia,* 16–152. vol. 3/1. Paris: Gaume. A recent and good English version is that by Edmund Hill, *Teaching Christianity,* Works of Saint Augustine I/11. New York: New City Press, 1996.

Bourdieu, Pierre.
1984 *Homo Academicus*. Paris: Editions de Minuit.

Boyarin, Daniel.
1990 *Intertextuality and the Reading of Midrash*. Indiana Studies in Biblical Literature. Bloomington & Indianapolis: Indiana University Press.

Boyarin, Jonathan (ed.).
1992 *The Ethnography of Reading*. Berkeley: University of California Press.

Canetti, Elias.
1982 *Auto-da-fé*. Trans. C. V. Wedgwood from *Die Blendung: Roman*. First published Munich: Hanser, 1935.

Carruthers, Mary J.
1990 *The Book of Memory: A Study of Memory in Medieval Culture*. Cambridge: Cambridge University Press.

Carter, Stephen L.
1993 *The Culture of Disbelief*. New York: Basic Books.

Clooney, Francis X.
1993 *Theology after Vedānta: An Experiment in Comparative Theology*. Albany, New York: SUNY Press.

Dagenais, John.
1994 *The Ethics of Reading in Manuscript Culture: Glossing the 'Libro de buen amor'*. Princeton: Princeton University Press.

Demiéville, Paul.
1951 "A Propos du concile de Vaisali." *T'oung Pao* 40:239–96.

Dorival, Gilles.
1984 "Des commentaires de l'Écriture aux chaines." In *Le Monde Grec ancien et la Bible*, 361–86. Ed. Claude Mondesert. Paris: Beauchesne.

Eisenstein, Elizabeth.
1979 *The Printing Press as an Agent of Change: Communications and Cultural Transformations in Early Modern Europe*. 2 vols. New York: Cambridge University Press.

Falk, Harry.
1993 *Schrift im alten Indien: Ein Forschungsbericht mit Anmerkungen*. SriptOralia vol.56. Tubingen: Narr.

Gellner, Ernest.
1994 *Conditions of Liberty: Civil Society and Its Rivals*. London: Hamish Hamilton.

Goody, Jack, and Ian Watt.
1963 "The Consequences of Literacy." *Contemporary Studies in Society and History* 5:304–45.

Hartman, Geoffrey H.
1994 "Midrash as Law and Literature." *Journal of Religion* 74:338–55.

Havelock, Eric.
1963 *Preface to Plato*. Cambridge: Cambridge University Press.

Hugh of St. Victor.
1939 *Didascalicon: De Studio Legendi*. Cited by chapter and section. In *Hugonis de Sancto Victore Didascalicon: De Studio Legendi*. Ed. Charles Henry Buttimer. Studies in Medieval and Renaissance Latin, vol. 10. Washington, D.C.: Catholic University Press. English version by Jerome Taylor, *The Didascalicon of Hugh of St. Victor*. New York: Columbia University Press, 1961.

Jameson, Fredric.
1991 *Postmodernism, or, The Cultural Logic of Late Capitalism*. Durham, North Carolina: Duke University Press.

Leibniz, G. W.
1875 *Discours de métaphysique* [Discourse on Metaphysics]. Cited by section. In *Leibniz: Die philosophischen Schriften* 4 vols. Berlin, 4:427–63. Ed. C. I. Gerhardt, English version in Roger Ariew and Daniel Garber, *G. W. Leibniz: Philosophical Essays*. Indianapolis: Hackett, 1989, 35–68.

Lindbeck, George.
1984 *The Nature of Doctrine: Religion and Theology in a Postliberal Age*. Philadelphia: Westminster Press.

Locke, John.
1975 *An Essay concerning Human Understanding*. Cited by book, chapter, and section. Edited, from the 4th ed. of 1700, by Peter H. Nidditch. Oxford: Clarendon Press.

McConnell, Michael.
1993a " 'God Is Dead and We Have Killed Him!': Freedom of Religion in the Post-Modern Age." *Brigham Young University Law Review* 163–88.

1993b "Academic Freedom in Religious Colleges and Universities." In *Freedom and Tenure in the Academy*, 303–24. Ed. William W. Van Alstyne. Durham & London: Duke University Press.

McLuhan, Marshall.
1962 *The Gutenberg Galaxy*. Toronto: University of Toronto Press.

Olson, David R.
1994 *The World on Paper: The Conceptual and Cognitive Implications of Writing and Reading*. Cambridge: Cambridge University Pres.

Ong, Walter J.
1982 *Orality and Literacy: The Technologizing of the Word*. London and New York: Routledge.

Plantinga, Alvin.
1993a *Warrant: The Current Debate*. New York: Oxford University Press.

1993b *Warrant:and Proper Function*. New York: Oxford University Press.

1992 "Augustinian Christian Philosophy." *The Monist* 291–320.

1990 *The Twin Pillars of Christian Scholarship*. Grand Rapids: Calvin College and Seminary.

Prāsādika Bhikkhu, and Lal Mani Joshi.
1981 *Vimalakīrtinirdeśasūtra: Tibetan Version, Sanskrit Restoration, and Hindi Translation*. Bibliotheca Indo-Tibetica, vol. 5. Sarnath: Central Institute of Higher Tibetan Studies.

Read, C. A., Y. Zhang, H. Nie, and B. Ding.
1986 "The Ability to Manipulate Speech Sounds Depends on Knowing Alphabetic Reading." *Cognition* 24:31–44.

Rorty, Richard.
1994 "Religion as a Conversation-Stopper." *Common Knowledge* 3/1:1–6.

1982 *Consequences of Pragmatism (Essays 1972–80)*. Minneapolis: University of Minnesota Press.

Schoeler, Gregor.
1990 "Theorien zur Frage der schriftlichen oder mundlichen Überlieferung der Wissenschaften im frühen Islam." In *Erscheinungsformen kultureller Prozesse*, 45–62. Ed. Wolfgang Raible. Tübingen: Narr.

Spence, Jonathan D.
1985 *The Memory Palace of Matteo Ricci*. London: Faber & Faber.

Staal, Frits.
1986 *The Fidelity of Oral Tradition and the Origins of Science*. Amsterdam, Oxford, New York: North Holland Publishing Company.

Steiner, George.
1989 *Real Presences*. Chicago & London: University of Chicago Press.

Stout, Jeffrey.
1981 *The Flight from Authority: Religion, Morality, and the Quest for Autonomy*. Notre Dame: University of Notre Dame Press.

Thomas, Rosalind.
1992 *Literacy and Orality in Ancient Greece*. Cambridge: Cambridge University Press.

Zumthor, Paul.
1987 *La lettre et la voix de la littérature medievale*. Paris: Éditions du Seuil.

Conclusion

José Ignacio Cabezón

In the Introduction I set forth as the principal goal of this volume the continuing cultural decontextualization[1] of the category of scholasticism. Recognizing that such a process must have a starting point, I offered my earlier reflection on the traits exemplified by the Indo-Tibetan Buddhist tradition heuristically as a point of departure. Given that much of the discussion that follows will presume this list of characteristics, let me rehearse it briefly. Scholasticism, as I conceived of it in my early research, evinces (1) a strong sense of tradition, (2) a concern with language (with scripture, and with language generally as a medium of expression), (3) proliferativity, by which I mean the tendency to include rather than to exclude (texts, categories, lists, etc.), (4) completeness (the tendency of the tradition to conceive of itself as overlooking nothing that is religiously essential) and compactness (its claim to contain nothing unessential), (5) the belief that the universe is epistemologically accessible, (6) a commitment to systematicity, which is the attempt at recapitulating in the written word the basic orderliness found in the world, (7) rationalism, a commitment to reasoned argument and the avoidance of contradiction, (8) self-reflexivity, the tendency to objectify and then to subject to critical scrutiny first-order practices such as exegesis and argumentation, yielding second-order forms of discourse such as hermeneutics and logic, respectively.

Let us now turn to the essays themselves to see how these traits have played themselves out, as it were. How do the different traditions treated in this volume exemplify, lack, amplify, suggest modifications to, or challenge us to rethink the above list of characteristics. Put another way, let us contemplate what the cross-cultural decontextualization of the category *scholasticism* has taught us, what insights have emerged as a result of a broader, comparative treatment of the topic.

Like my own earlier work, many of the essays in this volume look to medieval European (especially Christian) scholasticism as the comparative mirror against which another tradition can be reflected. If for no other reason than that it is historically the institutional precursor of the academy in which we situate ourselves, the scholasticism of the Middle Ages represents for us—at some level—the familiar. And yet, for those of us whose research is focused principally on the intellectual world views of other cultures, European scholasticism exhibits a dimension of foreignness. Such foreignness can unwittingly lead the specialist in non-Western traditions to impute a unity and wholeness to the former. It is therefore fitting that Louis Roy's essay is first, as Roy challenges the notion that Latin scholasticism was a monoculturally pristine, self-emergent whole, untainted by heterocultural influences. This of course complexifies the picture considerably for the comparativist. On the one hand, it makes our comparative mirror (medieval Latin scholasticism)—and the reflection it produces—multiple: more like that found in an amusement park fun house than that on our wall at home. On the other hand, it forces us to ask ourselves whether the traditions that we wish to reflect on that mirror are themselves pure, monolithic wholes.

Roy's essay is rich in its characterization of the matrix out of which medieval scholasticism arose, an environment that stressed the study of Scripture, that promoted a unitary vision of the world, that emphasized the importance of liturgy, and that made abundant use of diverse symbols. Using grammar and logic as "stepping stones," Latin scholasticism emerged out of that matrix driven, on the one hand, by "a logical inquisitiveness inherited from the Greeks," and on the other, by the urge to respond to a variety of foreign voices (Greek, Hebrew, and Arabic) that were made available through renewed translation efforts in the middle of the twelfth century. With the texts of foreign cultures permitted to "speak for themselves," Latin scholasticism became a truly comparative enterprise. Roy then illustrates how such a comparative synthesis was accomplished in the writings of Albert the Great.

Perhaps the principal lesson to be learned from Roy's contribution is: that it is as important to reveal the texture of heterocultural influence by focusing the comparative lens intrasystemically, within a cultural sphere where actual historical contact can be documented, as it is to reveal the structural patterns of similarity and difference by focusing that lens intersystematically, across cultural spheres in a kind of analysis where the presence or absence of actual historical contact is irrelevant.[2] Put another way, we can learn a great deal from a historical-philosophical analysis that reveals the comparative dimension within a "single" scholastic tradition, and even within the writings of a single scholastic author.

Daniel Madigan, like Louis Roy, offers us an analysis of scholasticism that is more historical than structural. Madigan analyzes the scholasticism of Islam, but as he points out, the boundaries of scholasticism in Islamic intellectual life are not always clear, given that the term has been applied to various schools and movements in Muslim history. To clarify the relationship of these various sub-traditions, he begins his essay with a useful historical overview of philosophical theology in Islam. In this regard it is interesting to note how in Islam different subtraditions will emphasize or downplay different traits (e.g., rationalism), thereby complexifying the issue of how—even within a single religious tradition—the boundaries of scholasticism are to be drawn. Like many of the other essays in this volume, moreover, Madigan's analysis also shows that even when a trait like rationalism is emphasized in a particular school, it often is evinced in a way that is different from its characterization in the above list. Hence, the use of reasoned argument by the *mutakallimûn* tends to be more constrained, more polemical, and perhaps more "performative" in tone than the use of reasoning in other scholastic traditions. But if the rationalist theology of the *mutakallimûn* evinces a more limited use of reasoning, Madigan points out that in the juridical theology of the legal *ma<u>dh</u>ahib* of Sunni Islam "we find all the characteristic features of European scholasticism already in full bloom." Like Roy, Madigan challenges us not to overlook the rich texture of intrasystemic variety that is to be found when we contemplate a category such as scholasticism, even in the case of a single religious tradition.

Whereas several of the essays in this volume describe how scholastics worked comparatively with materials from other traditions to irenic and synthetic ends,[3] Daniel Madigan's discussion of the Islamic rationalist tradition reminds us that scholastics were also polemicists. Robert Goss takes up this same theme in his essay, where he focuses on the Catholic scholasticism of the eighteenth-century Jesuit missionary to Tibet, Ippolito Desideri. Tracing the development of Catholic scholasticism through its various phases, Goss is concerned first with contextualizing and elucidating the Jesuit "second scholasticism" in which Desideri was intellectually socialized. He then demonstrates the extent to which Desideri's scholastic educational background infiltrates his Tibetan writings: in genre, style, and content. Goss believes that it was the scholastic character of Desideri's writing—

its systematicity and its commitment to rational argumentation especially—that made it both accessible to and appreciated by his Tibetan dGe lugs pa interlocutors; and, conversely, it was the scholastic character of Tibetan Buddhist philosophy—both the theory and its practice in debate—that made this system of thought both approachable and, at least as far as its methodical precision and clarity were concerned, an object of Desideri's esteem.

Although his aims were apologetic—to make Christian doctrine intelligible and acceptable to Tibetan Buddhists—Desideri realized that this could not be accomplished apart from a hermeneutical engagement of the Buddhist material. This meant understanding Buddhist doctrine not only as object of critique, but also as medium of communication, for Desideri had no means of constructing that critique apart from its formulation in terms of Buddhist doctrinal categories. If, as Goss maintains, Desideri's scholastic background aided in this hermeneutical task, is it not possible that, whatever *our* motives as academics, we too, as inheritors of the scholastic world view,[4] benefit from our own—even if only latent—scholastic structures in *our* hermeneutical engagement of this material? The question of motives aside, the problems encountered by Desideri and the solutions he found do not seem nearly so distant or foreign when we contemplate them in this light.

Most of the contributors to this volume are concerned with issues of scholastic method or ideology. Michael Swartz's contribution to this volume also is concerned with demonstrating how Rabbinic Judaism exemplifies paradigmatically scholastic traits, such as preoccupation with commentary, dialectic, and the reconciliation of inconsistency. While interested in the similarities between Rabbinic Judaism and other forms of scholasticism, however, he also is attentive to differences. Hence, Swartz, like Clooney, points out that notions such as completeness and the tendency to abstraction are not exemplified in the same way, if at all, in every tradition. He also observes that Rabbinic Judaism is more concerned with intrasystemic polemic than with a polemic that is directed outward at an external opponent. By his elucidation of this pattern of semblance and contrast, Swartz thus offers us a nuanced treatment of Rabbinic Judaism's "familial" relation to other forms of scholasticism.

But in addition to being concerned with questions of scholastic method and ideology, Swartz also wishes to draw our attention to the more sociological dimension of scholasticism: "the living context of learning in scholastic cultures," a context populated by individuals situated in institutions that are part of a broader society. Concentrating on the form, rhetoric, and transmission histories of texts from the third to the sixth centuries, Swartz attempts to reconstruct the interplay of ideas and their social context in Rabbinic Judaism. He shows, for example, how the authority of living teachers in classrooms is reinforced by their being placed in a scholastic lineage that begins with Moses, and how the depiction of scholars' interaction in texts serves as a model for the intellectual community in real life. More important, perhaps, is Swartz's consideration of the political consequences of Rabbinic scholasticism in its creation of "a class of scholarchs who has real influence over people's lives," a class of practical scholars not unlike the jurisconsults discussed by Madigan. By focusing our attention on issues of pedagogy, institutional ethos, politics, and even "scholastic magic," Swartz, like Madigan, forces us to consider the divergent ways in which scholasticism functioned socially, both internally and vis à vis the wider community. That this generally important insight should emerge out of, for example, the study of Judaism is of course no accident, for, as Swartz points out, the general scholastic tenor of Rabbinic Judaism is directed "to actions more than to thoughts."

Livia Kohn's essay on Taoism also takes up the theme of the social function of scholasticism, this time in Chinese society. She sees the rise of Taoist scholasticism in the Tang dynasty as "a direct function of the political unification and elevation of Taoism to the status of a major religious teaching," with the goal of making Taoism more accessible both to the court and to the society at large. Hence, it was a social requirement—at least in part—that propelled Taoists to strive for greater systematization of their tradition, a tendency that led to the emergence of a full-blown Taoist scholasticism. As with the Neo-Confucianism that Henderson treats in his essay, Kohn shows how Taoist scholasticism was a response to the challenge posed by Buddhism, with its relatively integrated metaphysical vision. As with the Christian appropriation of Aristotle during the Middle Ages, Taoism had an ambivalent relationship to its rival: though perceiving Buddhism as a competitor in the social sphere, Taoist scholastics were willing to borrow freely from this more highly developed system, incorporating Buddhist ideas such as Mādhyamaka logic and two-truth theory. Like other chapters in this book, Kohn's reflections thus reiterate the importance of a nuanced treatment of the interaction of scholastic traditions in history. Clearly, it is too facile to conceive of the scholastics' strong sense of tradition as leading them to an unequivocal rejection of the doctrines of competitors. When we do find Taoist texts responding polemically to a rival school, that polemic—like Desideri's against the dGe lugs pas—often is modulated by the fact that it incorporates Buddhist terminology and methods.

Kohn's contribution details how a variety of Taoist *texts* exemplify many of the scholastic attributes discussed above, but her essay is equally concerned with the *personae* of scholastics themselves. In this regard, it is interesting that she should reiterate a theme raised by other contributors (Madigan, Swartz, and Henderson), namely, the position of scholastics in the political/social sphere. Their being situated in the court meant not only that the great Taoist scholastics of the Tang dynasty had a continuing influence on Chinese political and social life, but also that they themselves were "influenced by the evolving cultural and political climate." Focusing on the life and works of three Tang figures, much of Kohn's chapter is dedicated to demonstrating how Taoist scholastic thought changed in response to the historical shifts that occurred during the Tang dynasty. It is also worth noting that, like Swartz and Clooney, Kohn illuminates the importance of ritual to scholasticism, an aspect of social life that often has been overlooked in the treatment of elitist religious traditions like those of the scholastics.

As mentioned above, my own previous work in the area of comparative scholasticism focused almost exclusively on philosophy. My chapter in this volume thus represents a departure from my previous research, addressed as it is to the relationship between scholastic ideology and architecture. Using the work of the medievalist Erwin Panofsky as a springboard, I attempt to show how the social organization, art, and especially the architecture of Tibetan Buddhist monasteries recapitulates some of the features of the scholastic world view mentioned in the list above. Panofsky believed that many of the stylistic elements of the Gothic cathedral were the direct result of scholastic influence. Although mine is a slightly weaker hypothesis, I too believe that there exists a homology between scholastic ideology and the material culture in which it flourished. We know that many of Tibet's greatest scholastic minds played a considerable role in the building, restoration, and expansion of temples and monuments. After surveying some of the (principally historical) sources that discuss the role that these scholars played as the directors of various artistic and building projects, I turn my attention to two case studies—the complex of buildings at dPal 'khor sde chen monastery in western Tibet, and the monastery of Se ra on the outskirts of Lhasa, Tibet's capital—so as to document the link between Tibet's scholastic world view and several aspects of its material and social culture.

Like Livia Kohn's contribution, John Henderson's also is focused on China, but in this case on Neo-Confucianism. His essay begins with some general remarks of a theoretical nature. What factors, he asks, are necessary for the rise of scholasticism? Although he acknowledges a closed and historically decontextualized canon as a condition for *pre*scholastic speculation, Henderson believes that the rise of "high scholasticisms" depends—frequently, if not invariably—upon an encounter between a proto-scholastic tradition and a well-developed philosophical tradition (e.g., Aristotelianism or Buddhism), where the latter challenges the former and provides it with tools of analysis (both methodological and substantive). At the same time, Henderson notes the ambivalence with which these precursorial philosophical traditions were treated by scholastics. When confronted with an increasing quantity of material to be considered, this latent ambivalence, he notes, often led to a new canon which then itself became the object of reflection of a secondary- or neo-scholasticism. When the amount of material becomes overwhelming—as was the case in sixteenth- and seventeenth-century China—scholasticism gives way to historical and critical modes of scholarship, which gradually bring about its own demise.

In Neo-Confucianism Henderson finds many of the qualities of scholasticism outlined above: a concern for order, for maintaining the completeness or comprehensiveness of world view and the compactness of the canon, the felt need to explain redundancy and to reconcile inconsistency, and especially the great preoccupation with lineage. But Henderson makes it clear that there are historical and cultural factors at play in China that make Neo-Confucian scholasticism distinct. By bringing these to the fore, his essay challenges the comparativist in several ways. (1) Even if "order" is as much a concern for Neo-Confucianists as it is for other scholastics, Henderson makes it clear that *how* order is conceptualized and made manifest in a body of religio-philosophical literature is a complex matter, thus forcing us to rethink the very notion of *order* and to offer more subtle treatments of systematicity. (2) Concern with the completeness or comprehensiveness of vision also seems to be evinced as a quality in Neo-Confucian thought, but by bringing up the issue of motives (what factors are at play in the Confucian decision to posit such a quality to their world view?), Henderson forces us to take into account the historical factors that influence this and indeed *all* aspects of scholastic ideology. (3) By showing that lineage was more of a preoccupation for Neo-Confucianists than was reconciling inconsistencies in their relatively abbreviated canon, Henderson quite explicitly raises the issue of the relative weight of these different attributes in different traditions, something that cannot be considered uniform across cultures. (4) Finally, Henderson points out that Neo-Confucianism was more enmeshed in the social and political fabric of Chinese culture than were other such movements in their respective social spheres—something that could account for the former's relative longevity.

Like John Henderson, Francis Clooney also sees the presence of many of the traits in the above list in the three Hindu traditions that are the focus of his chapter: Mīmāṃsā, Vedānta, and Śrivaiṣṇavism. But

Clooney sees this fact as only the beginning of a more elaborate inquiry that must be undertaken in treating scholasticism as a comparative category. That more nuanced treatment he focuses around six questions. He asks, for example, whether a scholastic tradition need be uniformly scholastic through and through in order to be considered a form of scholasticism, an issue also raised by Madigan. How do we reconcile the genre and stylistic diversity of scholastic literary corpuses with our attempt to ascribe an overarching trait—that it is scholastic—to that corpus as a whole? Clooney also raises a related question concerning the dividing line between scholastic discourses: are Mīmāṃsā, Vedānta, and Śrivaiṣṇavism three separate scholasticisms or three variants of a single scholastic discourse? "How much weight do we wish to give the *content* of related discourses when we are deciding whether or not to group them together?"[5] These questions are by no means trivial.

Like Roy, Clooney wants to draw attention to the increased complexity of the issues when there is historical interaction between scholastic traditions within a circumscribed cultural sphere. And like Henderson and Goss, Clooney also is interested in the dialogue that emerges in the historical encounter of culturally disparate scholastic traditions. Finally, like Henderson, he points out that in addition to attesting to the presence of traits such as the ones in the above list, it is also important to remember that the balance of these elements will vary from one tradition to the next. This leads Clooney to propose a distinction between *intellectualist* and *performative* types of scholasticism—"the former more preponderantly focused on questions of comprehensive understanding, the latter on formation in right thinking and action"—and to suggest that his three schools (perhaps like Swartz's Rabbinic Judaism) might best be thought of as belonging to the latter category. In showing how this is so, Clooney complexifies the question of what "completeness" means, forcing us again to ask ourselves not only to what extent, but also in what way, if at all, scholastic traditions exemplify this (and implicitly any other such) quality.

Clooney's essay leaves us with the tantalizing question of where our own project as comparativists falls on his intellectualist/performative spectrum, and, given that we must be located *somewhere*, what responsibilities we have in our depiction of discourses when they are differently situated than our own. How scholastic is our own enterprise as scholars? How scholastic should it be? This is the question taken up by Paul Griffiths. Griffiths begins with an interesting preamble in which he elucidates what he means by key terms (*composition, display,* and *storage*); he discusses especially how writing epitomizes these combined activities; and he deliberates on the state of affairs concerning the issues of orality and literacy. He then turns his attention to an ideal-typical scholasticism that he characterizes using a fourfold heuristic scheme focused on the questions of how scholastics read, how they compose, what their epistemological commitments are, and in what kinds of institutional settings they are likely to flourish. Griffiths' chapter is comparative, but not in the same way as the other chapters in this volume. Although he presents evidence from disparate cultures in his analysis, his primary comparative mirror is the Western academy, often in its postmodern version. Scholasticism in its ideal-typical form thus is reflected on the mirror of contemporary scholarly (mostly instrumentalist, consumerist, individualist) modes of reading, composition, and so forth, to extremely interesting and insightful ends. Although there is some overlap with my own earlier characterization of scholasticism, Griffiths' analysis—more normative in tone and less bound to a specific historical tradition—is broader, more far-reaching, and thus advances the discussion in new and interesting ways. His characterization of scholasticism raises new questions of each of the historical traditions treated by the other contributors to this volume, making it a kind of epilogical capstone to the present work.

There is, however, another reason for situating Griffiths' essay separately and last. Most of the contributors to this volume generally evince (even if only implicitly) a kind of passive admiration of—a positive attitude to—the phenomenon of scholasticism. However, Griffiths' task is proactively normative: his goal is to argue for scholasticism as a middle way between modernist and postmodernist modes of intellectual practice, one that ought to be given institutional support in contemporary society. Put another way, Griffiths's term *ideal type* as applied to the scholasticism he is constructing has, in his case, a *double entendre*. On the one hand, his scholasticism is ideal-typical in the Weberian sense of "paradigmatic"; on the other, it is an ideal type in a normative, even ethical, sense. Griffiths commends scholasticism as a type of practice that is ideal not only as a scholarly mode of discourse, but as an overall way of life even (perhaps especially) for contemporary intellectuals: a bold and well-argued claim that is likely to spur controversy.

What new insights have been gained as a result of the cross-cultural and comparative treatment of scholasticism in this volume? What directions for future research are suggested by the chapters?

If scholastic traditions are not monolithic wholes with fixed boundaries, but permeable entities that exhibit complex patterns of influence, this means that the comparative analysis of such traditions—and indeed of all traditions—must, at the very least, take this fact into account. Whether or not a particular study makes this kind of complexity explicit—and this will depend on the specific goals of the study—at the very least it is incumbent on the comparativist to be aware of the heterogeneous nature of the phenomenon he or she is studying. What is more, as several of the contributors point out, when such internal complexity *is* made explicit—when the boundaries between one tradition and another are explored, when external cultural and ideological influences are examined, or when a generalized scholasticism is constructed as an heuristic category for the purpose of cultural critique—one is engaged in an analysis of a different sort, one that, though not principally cross-cultural, is still very much comparative. Be that as it may, the first point (a methodological one) is clear: in the comparative analysis of scholasticisms, or in a comparative analysis that utilizes scholasticism as *one* of the comparanda, the notion of a scholastic tradition as a *sui generis* whole is at best a useful fiction. While perhaps serving the specific ends of the theorist in specific types of analysis, this volume speaks to the fact that we must remain open to forms of analysis that make manifest the internal complexities inherent even within a "single" scholastic tradition and that explore the diversity of scholasticisms even within a "single" cultural sphere.

Second, if scholastic traditions are related to each other not by the sharing of a collective essence as specifiable by a list of common properties, but by the more complex notion of family resemblances, then we should find that some of the "familial" traits will be present in some traditions while being absent in others, and that even when specific traits *are* exemplified, they may be exemplified in different ways or to varying degrees. By exploring whether or not a specific trait is present in a given context, and if so, how and to what extent it is emphasized, the essays in this volume continue the process of the construction of scholasticism as a category by elucidating the pattern of such resemblances between traditions, both within a single culture and across them. In addition, several of the essays remind us that discussion of the traits that characterize a tradition as scholastic cannot be divorced from a discussion of sociocultural, political, and economic factors (for example, from a discussion of the various *motives* that lie behind the claim of certain traditions concerning the completeness of their canons). It is also clear from the chapters in this volume that certain traits not preeminent in my original list should be highlighted and perhaps even added to that list as independent characteristics. These include the fact that scholastic traditions tend to be *polemical*—intratraditionally, intertraditionally, or both; that they are greatly preoccupied with *lineage* (whether historical or mythic), and with *hierarchy*; and that they are concerned with a variety of extra-intellectual practices which they see as intrinsic to the formation, maintenance, and perpetuation of their scholastic identity (*prayer, ritual,* and *liturgy* especially).

A third general insight that emerges from this volume relates to the second and points us in the direction of a preliminary typological classification of scholastic traditions. By similarly emphasizing certain traits over others, by exemplifying certain traits in similar ways, or by sharing similar motivations in their exemplification of traits, scholastic traditions will tend to form subfamilies. Several of the contributors suggest ways of construing such "types," but none as directly as Clooney, who proposes the intellectualist/performative distinction. What new types will emerge as other traditions or subtraditions are brought into the conversation? In addition, it also might be suggested that history provides us with a classificatory scheme of a different sort. This is already evident in the way that other typological schemes (pre/proto scholasticism vs. true/high scholasticism) are used in several of the essays. Clearly, future research will require the more detailed exploration of both structuralist and historical modes of typologizing the phenomenon of scholasticism.

That history cannot be taken for granted, that scholastic traditions are dynamic, is perhaps one of the most important themes in this volume, serving as a corrective to my earlier work, which is more structural (and therefore more static in its orientation). Many of the contributors are concerned with the factors that led to the rise and/or decline of specific scholastic traditions, and at least one contributor (Henderson) suggests that there might be a pattern concerning the historical evolution of scholastic traditions even across cultures. Questions of historical evolution aside, however, many of the essays stress the importance of investigating the concrete historical interaction between scholastic traditions, both within a single culture and/or religious tradition, and across cultures. How do various scholastic traditions and subtraditions influence each other through actual historical contact? How do common scholastic presuppositions ease intertradition, and even interreligious, communication? How do the lack of such common presuppositions impede it? Both in its more nomothetic and its more idiographic modes, history will continue to play an important role in the investigation of scholasticism.

Finally, if there is one single, consistent area of concern evinced by all of the essays, it is this: aside from the investigation of scholastic ideology and method—that is, aside from the exploration of the intellectual content of scholasticisms by investigating ideas in texts and their manipulation by scholastics—there is an entirely different tack that can be taken in the study of a phenomenon like scholasticism: a sociocultural one. Here the scholar is concerned with the study of scholastic institutions (their organization, their hierarchies, their relationship to the broader society), with the day-to-day process of religious education in those institutions (how teaching/learning is accomplished, and the role that memorization, formal disputation, commentary, and less "cognitive" factors such as prayer and magic play in the educational process). Equally important in this regard is the study of the political, economic, and material factors that influence and are influenced by scholasticism. Finally, under this same rubric we might situate the study of the lived lives of scholastics as individuals, their influence on the broader communities in which they are located, and in turn the pressures exerted on, and the rewards offered to, them by those communities. Not broached in this book, but falling equally under the present rubric, is the study of the relationship of scholasticism to gender. With the exception of the latter, all of these topics are broached by the various contributors, but it is equally clear that a great deal of work still needs to be done in regard to the sociocultural dimensions of scholasticism and that this field represents one of the most fertile grounds for future research.[6]

If the reader will be indulgent in allowing me to extend the horticultural analogy slightly further, only time will tell which of the areas of possible future research suggested in this volume will bear fruit. But one thing, I think, is clear: the seeds have at least been planted by the rich and provocative chapters of my fellow contributors. And so I take this opportunity of thanking all of them for making the otherwise arduous task of the editor so much less burdensome by the intellectual excitement elicited in me by their work.

Notes

1. On the role of decontextualization in the process of comparative analysis see Scharfstein (1989).

2. A similar point is made by Tracy (1990).

3. In addition to Louis Roy's essay, see also Clooney's remarks concerning de Nobili's reading of the *Taittirīya Upsaniṣad* in *his* contribution to this volume.

4. Madigan, Clooney, and Griffiths in the present volume show, albeit in different ways, the extent to which we as academics might be considered inheritors of the scholastic mindset. See also Cabezón (1994: 17–19).

5. As I have observed elsewhere (Cabezón 1994:16, 194–95), among European medievalists the attempt to define scholasticism as a general category can be divided roughly into two: those that emphasize similarity of content (de Wulf)

and those that emphasize similarity of method (Grabmann, Knowles, et al.). Both Clooney and Goss invoke de Wulf in their respective chapters in this volume, though the latter with greater trepidation. On my position concerning the comparative study of philosophical content in scholastic discourses, see Cabezón (1994:195). On a related issue concerning the dividing line between scholastic and nonscholastic movements within a single religious tradition see Cabezón (1994:197).

6. That this is already a topic of interest in the academy is demonstrated by a recent panel on comparative religious education (Buddhist/Islamic) at the meeting of the American Academy of Religion in New Orleans (1996).

References

Cabezón, José Ignacio.
1994 *Buddhism and Language: A Study of Indo-Tibetan Scholasticism*. Albany: State University of New York Press.

Scharfstein, Ben-Ami.
1989 "The Contextual Fallacy." In *Interpreting across Boundaries: New Essays in Comparative Philosophy*. Ed. Gerald James Larson and Eliot Deutsch. New Delhi: Motilal Banarsidass, reprint of the 1988 Princeton ed.

Tracy, David.
1990 "On the Origins of the Philosophy of Religion: The Need for a New Narrative of Its Founding." In *Myth and Philosophy*, 1–36. Ed. Frank Reynolds and David Tracy. Albany: State University of New York Press.

Contributors

José Ignacio Cabezón is Associate Professor of the Philosophy of Religion at the Iliff School of Theology. He received his doctorate from the University of Wisconsin, Madison, in Buddhist Studies. His most recent publications include *Buddhism and Language: A Study of Indo-Tibetan Scholasticism* (State University of New York Press, 1994) and *Tibetan Literature: Studies in Genre* (Snow Lion Publications, 1996), which he coedited with Roger R. Jackson. Currently he is working on a translation of a philosophical, polemical work on emptiness by the medieval Tibetan scholar Go ram pa and on an interdisciplinary, theoretical work on cross-cultural comparison.

Francis X. Clooney, S.J., is Professor of Comparative Theology in the Theology Department at Boston College. He received his doctorate in South Asian Languages and Civilizations from the University of Chicago. His published work includes an essay in *Myth and Philosophy* (1990), *Theology after Vedānta: An Experiment in Comparative Theology* (1993), and *Seeing through Texts: Doing Theology among the Śrīvaiṣṇavas of South India* (1996), all in this State University of New York series. He has a book forthcoming entitled *Hindu Wisdom for All God's Children* and is currently working in the area of comparative philosophical theology.

Robert E. Goss, received his doctorate in Comparative Religion and Theology from Harvard University and is currently on the faculty at

Webster University in the field of Comparative Religions. He is author of *Jesus ACTED UP: A Gay and Lesbian Manifesto* (HarperSanFrancisco, 1993), co-editor of *A Rainbow of Religious Diversity* (Monument Press, 1996) and co-editor of *Our Families, Our Values: Snapshots of Queer Kinship* (Haworth Press, 1997). In addition, he is the managing editor of the *Journal of Religion and Education.*

Paul J. Griffiths is Associate Professor of the Philosophy of Religion in The Divinity School and in the Department of South Asian Languages and Civilizations at the University of Chicago. He received his Ph. D. in Buddhist Studies from the University of Wisconsin, Madison. His major publications include *On Being Mindless: Buddhist Meditation and the Mind-Body Problem* (Open Court, 1986), *An Apology for Apologetics: A Study in the Logic of Interreligious Dialogue* (Orbis Books, 1991), and *On Being Buddha: The Classical Doctrine of Buddhahood* (State University of New York Press, 1994). He is currently working on a book entitled *Religious Reading.*

John B. Henderson is Professor of History and Religious Studies at Louisiana State University. He received his Ph.D. in History from the University of California, Berkeley. His two major publications are *The Development and Decline of Chinese Cosmology* (Columbia University Press, 1984), and *Scripture, Canon and Commentary: A Comparison of Confucian and Western Exegesis* (Princeton University Press, 1991). His most recent book, *The Grammar of Orthodoxy and Heresy: Early Christian, Islamic, Jewish and Neo-Confucian Constructions,* is forthcoming from State University of New York Press.

Livia Kohn received her doctorate from the University of Bonn. She is Associate Professor of Religious Studies at Boston University and Visiting Professor at Stanford University's Kyoto Center for Japanese Studies. Her major works include *Early Chinese Mysticism: Philosophy and Soteriology in the Taoist Tradition* (Princeton University Press, 1992), *The Taoist Experience: An Anthology* (State University of New York Press, 1993), and *Laughing at the Tao: Debates among Buddhists and Taoists in Medieval China* (Princeton University Press, 1995).

Daniel A. Madigan, S. J., is Assistant Professor of Islamic Studies and Theology of Religions in the United Faculty of Theology, Melbourne, Australia. He has a doctorate in Religion (Islam) from Columbia University, and his dissertation, on the language of "books" and "writing" in the Qur'an's description of itself, is currently being prepared for publication.

Louis Roy, O.P., is Associate Professor in the Theology Department at Boston College. He received his Ph.D. from the Faculty of Divinity at Cambridge University. His published writings include works on Maritain, Barth, and Aquinas. His most recent article, in the *Journal of Religion* (1997), is entitled "Consciousness according to Schleiermacher," and he has a book in progress on transcendent experiences in the West since Kant.

Michael D. Swartz received his Ph.D. in Near Eastern Languages and Literatures at New York University. He is currently Associate Professor of Hebrew and Religious Studies at The Ohio State University. He is author of *Mystical Prayer in Ancient Judaism: An Analysis of* Ma'aseh Merkavah (J. C. B. Mohr, 1992) and *Scholastic Magic: Ritual and Revelation in Early Jewish Mysticism* (Princeton University Press, 1996) and co-author, with Lawrence H. Schiffman, of *Hebrew and Aramaic Incantation Texts from Cairo Genizah: Selected Texts from Taylor-Schechter Box K1* (Sheffield Academic Press, 1992). He is currently working on a study of ideas of sacrifice in postbiblical Judaism.

Index

ʿAbbâsid, 41
Abelard, 24, 167
academics, Western, 221
Ackroyd, Peter, 219
adhikaraṇas, 178
Adshead, S.A.M., 66
Advaita Vedānta, 180, 190
Age of Discovery, 162
ahl al-kalâm, 36
ahl al-ḥadîth, 37
Albert the Great: Aristotelian influences on, 28, 30, 31; commentaries of, 19, 27–29; comparative work of, 26–27, 30–31; exegetical methods of, 27–28; medieval Arabic influences on, 30; and medieval Latin scholasticism, 26–31; Neo-Platonist influences on, 30; on prayer, 28; on theology, 28
al-ʿAllâf, Abû-l-Hudayl Muḥammad b. al-Hudayl, 42
Alston, William, 222
āḻvārs, 180
Ames, Roger T., 12n 2
Amoraim, 97
Aniko, 155n 3
Anselm, 24
anuttarayoga tantra, 149
apologetics: in Catholic second scholasticism, 83; description of, 83; and dGe lugs pa scholasticism, 83; as form of religious discourse, 83; in medieval Catholic scholasticism, 69–73; role of argumentation in, 84; in scholastic dialog, 83–84
architecture: and Buddhism, 147; and ideology, 141–2; tradition of, 143. *See also* Gothic architecture; Tibetan architecture
argumentation, in Hindu schools, 184
Aristotelianism, 47, 70, 161, 163
Aristotle: Albert the Great on, 29; and Christianity, 26, 241; commentaries on, 27; cross-cultural interest in, 31; dialectic in, 31n 3
al-Ashʿarî, Abû al-Hasan ʿAlî, 44-5, 48, 49
ʿAtâ, Wâṣil b., 41, 42
ātman, 179, 189, 196n 5
authority, 225-6, 227
Averroes (Ibn Rushd), 31, 35-36
Avicenna (Ibn Sîna), 35–36
Avot, 97, 98

Bādarāyana, 179–80
Baird, Robert, 7